Surtees of th

Surtees of the 95th (Rifles)

A Soldier of the 95th (Rifles) in
the Peninsular Campaign of
the Napoleonic Wars

William Surtees

LEONAUR

Surtees of the 95th (Rifles):A Soldier of the 95th (Rifles) in the Peninsular Campaign of the Napoleonic Wars

Originally published in *1833* under the
title *Twenty Five Years in the Rifle Brigade.*

Published by Leonaur Ltd

Material original to this edition and its origination in
this form copyright © 2006 Leonaur Ltd

ISBN (10 digit): 1-84677-086-6 (hardcover)
ISBN (13 digit): 978-1-84677-086-9 (hardcover)

ISBN (10 digit): 1-84677-085-8 (softcover)
ISBN (13 digit): 978-1-84677-085-2 (softcover)

http://www.leonaur.com

Publishers Notes

In the interests of authenticity, the spellings, grammar and place
names used in this book have been retained from the original edition.

The opinions of the author represent a view of events in which he was
a participant related from his own perspective;
as such the text is relevant as an historical document.

The views expressed in this book are not necessarily those of the publisher.

Contents

Introduction

These memoirs by William Surtees have been presented essentially as the author intended. The Leonaur editors have taken just two small liberties.

The author was a man much concerned with his Christian faith. Religious references appear throughout the narrative. These have been left intact with one exception which covers some pages in the original and was considered to be at odds with a military account for modern readers.

Secondly, Surtees wrote an account which spanned his entire career in the Rifles. At the First Restoration William Surtees, like Harry Smith, was posted to America to take part in the "War of 1812."

The book you are holding concerns itself with the campaigns against Napoleonic France and so concludes upon the authors return to England.

The Leonaur Editors
2006

Chapter One
I Enlist in the Pompadours

I was born on the 4th of August, 1781, in the village of Corbridge, in the county of Northumberland; of parents who may be said to have been among the middle classes, my father being a tradesman. They gave me such an education as was customary with people of their station in life; *viz.* reading, writing, and arithmetic. My mother having sprung from a pious race, was the first to implant in my mind any sense of religion; indeed, it is to the spiritual seed sown in my heart by her during my youth, that I am indebted, under God, for having been brought, many years afterwards, to consider my ways, and to turn to Him.

Nevertheless, being naturally of a sensual and wicked disposition, I, as might be expected, spent a dissolute youth, which often caused great pain and uneasiness to my good and pious mother. But I did not continue long under the paternal roof; for, having from my infancy a great predilection for a military life, I embraced almost the first opportunity that offered, after I became sufficiently grown, to enter into the militia of my native county.

I enlisted on the 15th of November, 1798, being then little more than seventeen years of age. I entered this service with the determination that, should I not like a soldier's life, I would then, after remaining a few years in it, return home; but, if I did like it, to volunteer into the line, and make that my occupation for life. It will readily be believed that this undutiful step affected deeply my excellent parents; for though my father was not then a religious man, he had a heart susceptible of the tenderest feelings; and I really believe that no parents ever felt more deeply the combined emotions of tender regret at my leaving them so young, and for such a purpose, and at the disgrace which my wayward conduct had, as they imagined, brought upon myself.

But though evil in itself, God overruled it for good to me, and, I trust, to them also. I would here remark that the life of a soldier was by no means considered in my native village, at that time, as at all creditable; and when I sometimes in my boyhood used to exhibit symptoms of a military inclination, I was often taunted with the then opprobrious expression, "Ay, thou likes the smell of poother," intimating thereby that I was likely to disgrace myself by going for a soldier.

I left my family in much grief in the beginning of 1799, and marched with several other recruits to join my regiment at Chelmsford in Essex, where we arrived in about a month, and where I began my military career. I always liked a soldier's life, consequently I did not suffer from many of those parts of it which are so unpleasant to those of a contrary disposition; and, as I took pleasure in it, I of course made more progress in acquiring a knowledge of my duty than some others who set out with me. I was early placed in the first squad, an honour which I considered no trifling one in those days,—but none of us finished our drill; for, in July of the same year, an order was issued, permitting such men as chose to extend their services, to volunteer into the line, in order to recruit the army then destined for Holland.

We had previously marched from Chelmsford to Colchester, a distance of twenty-one miles, which march was to me, I think, the severest I ever underwent; for being young, and totally unaccustomed to any thing like it, the weight of the musket, bayonet, accoutrements, and knapsack, appeared, towards the latter end of the march, to be almost intolerable; but I kept up, although excessively tired. This will show how necessary it is at all times to accustom troops, destined for service, to move in such order as they will be expected to do when they take the field—for, if unaccustomed to the carriage of the knapsack, and to frequent marches with it for exercise, they will be utterly unable to perform any movement against, or in the face of an enemy, with that celerity necessary to ensure success.

I volunteered, with several of my comrades, into the 56th regiment, or Pompadours, so called from their facings being

Madame Pompadour's favourite colour, and we set off (carried in waggons to accelerate our movements) for Canterbury, which we reached in two days and one night, having travelled without making a halt; and there we joined the skeleton of our regiment, just then returned from the West Indies, where twice, during the war, it had been nearly exterminated by disease.

In a few days after our arrival, a selection was made throughout the volunteers for fit subjects for the light company, when, fortunately, both myself and William Sutherland (who had been in the same company with me in the militia, and who, from our names and size being so nearly similar, had always stood next me in the ranks) were chosen for this, in my mind, honourable service. I felt not a little proud at my advancement, as I considered it, (and as I believe the generality of soldiers consider it,) to be made a light-bob.

The regiment had not at this time either arms, appointments, or clothing; but, being in a few days sent off to Barham Downs, where the army for Holland was assembled and encamped, we soon after were supplied with the necessary equipment, and commenced without delay to drill and get the men in readiness for embarkation. At this time the flank companies of all those regiments destined for Holland were separated from their battalions, and formed into what are termed flank battalions. That in which my company was placed consisted of eleven light companies, the command of which was given to Lieut.-Col. Sharpe, of the 9th regiment, an experienced and gallant veteran, who had commanded a similar battalion in the eastern district, under the Earl of Chatham. The grenadier battalion was composed of an equal number of grenadier companies, and belonged to the same regiments to which ours belonged.

Before our arrival on Barham Downs, the first division of the expedition, under Sir Ralph Abercromby, had sailed; and we soon after were called out to fire a *feu de joie* for their capture of the Dutch fleet, and their having effected a landing and gained a victory near the Helder. Nothing could be more brilliant than our display upon this occasion appeared to me—we were nearly 20,000 strong, I imagine, and, being formed in one extensive line, the firing of the *feu de joie*. produced a fine effect. To my non-military readers, perhaps, it will be necessary to explain what is termed a *feu de joie*. The usual mode is, when formed in line, for the fire to commence by signal with the right file of the whole, and each of those on their left take it up rapidly in succession, so that, to a looker-on, it has the appearance of a wild-fire running along the line; but on this occasion we heightened the effect, by beginning with the right of the front rank only, and when it had passed along by the front, the left-hand man of the rear rank took it up, and so it passed along by the rear to the right again. It appeared to me, at that time, certainly the finest sight I had ever witnessed. Every heart present was elated with joy, and beat high to be led on to share in those glorious achievements which we were then celebrating; but, alas I we were then ignorant that we were as unfit at that time to suffer the toils and privations of a campaign, as if we had never seen a soldier; we were all young, and inexperienced in the highest degree, and our discipline, as might be naturally expected, was far from good; for, being an army hastily collected from every regiment of militia in the kingdom, the officers of course neither had that knowledge of the characters of their men, which is so essential, nor had the latter that confidence in their officers, which only a service together for some length of time can engender, and which is absolutely necessary to secure an unreserved and active obedience to their commands.

But the period of our embarkation fast approached; previously to which, we were reviewed by his Royal Highness the Duke of York, (who was destined to command us,) accompanied by several others of the Royal Family, and by General Sir Charles Grey, my countryman. I believe they all expressed themselves highly satisfied with our appearance and movements, and hoped that we would shortly add fresh laurels to those already gained by our forerunners.

As it was expected to be a service of only a short duration, it was determined that the men should embark in what is called "light marching" or "service order," that is, with only about half the usual complement of necessaries, consequently every soldier had to leave a considerable portion of his things behind him; and, in order to deposit them safely, empty casks were procured for each company, into which every man was ordered to stow his extra things, after being properly packed and labelled with his name, &c. This rather grieved me, for I had brought with me from home as good a kit (as the soldiers term it) as any in the army. My dear mother had prepared me shirts fine enough for any officer, and abundance of them, but of those thus left I never saw one afterwards. During our stay in this camp, I never enjoyed better health or greater lightness of spirits, forgetful or heedless of the deep and lasting anguish which my late rash step must naturally inflict upon the hearts of my tender and affectionate parents; but I was no doubt stimulated to this thoughtless forgetfulness of them, by witnessing the animating scenes around me, where all was bustle and high anticipation of more glorious doings.

Chapter Two
To Holland

We marched from this camp to Deal, where we embarked in transports already prepared to receive us. As soon as we arrived we were instantly put on board, but never shall I forget the effect which the sight of the sea, and such a number of ships of various sizes and descriptions, had upon me; for before this I had never been near the sea, although I had marched from the north to the south of England. But, to add to all the strange things which then met my view, we were instantly on marching down put into a large boat that lay high upon the beach; which, when filled with troops, they run down into the sea with astonishing rapidity, turning my stomach, as we entered the water, completely topsy-turvy.

The effect of all this can better be conceived than described; we were immediately rowed off to, and put on board our transport, which happened to be a brig called the *Zephyr* of Shields. Here also every thing was quite new to me; but all was met and performed with the highest spirits, so far as sea-sickness permitted. We remained on board two or three days before the fleet was ready for sea; but at length we sailed with a favourable breeze, and in two or three days more we made the coast of Holland, and soon afterwards came to anchor within the Texel. Every thing being ready for landing, and the Hel-der being in our possession, we disembarked there on the 15th of September, 1799, having been just one week on board. We were formed on landing near the town, and waited till some others had disembarked, before we moved off. Among those regiments which landed, I remember the 35th was one. This regiment, after coming on shore, was drawn up close to us; they had not been long landed before the men began with their knives to cut off each other's hair, which then was worn in the shape of a club; this was done without any orders from their officers, and appeared to me, I confess, such a breach of discipline, as I could not have anticipated; for though on the whole it was an improvement, as later usage has shown, yet I apprehend for a body of soldiers, without any permission from higher authority, to take upon them to break through the long-established custom of the service, was such an utter renunciation of all obedience to authority, as directly to threaten with destruction the best interests of the army to which they belonged; however, at such a time it would perhaps have been attended with still worse consequences to have made an example of the offenders, although, had stricter discipline been enforced from the outset, I feel assured the army in general would have benefited by it.

Towards evening, we moved forward through the town of Helder, and proceeded on our route towards Schagen, and halted for the night on the road, and where such as could find houses, of which there were a few straggling ones in the neighbourhood, got into them. I awoke in the night, and still fancied myself on board ship; for the wind and rain were beating violently against the little hovel into which a few of us had crept, and I imagined it was the dashing of the sea against the bow of the vessel. Indeed so strong was this imagination, that when I got up, I literally could not stand steady, not having been long enough on board to acquire what is termed my "sea legs;" that is, I had not learned the art of standing steady when the vessel heeled; and, strange as it may appear to a person who has never been at sea, I believe most landsmen have the same feeling for some short time after being put on shore.

We had each man been supplied with a blanket while in camp on Barham Downs, but had no proper or uniform mode of carrying them; we had no great-coats, but made use of the blanket sometimes as a substitute in the morning, when we turned out to proceed on our march. We certainly made a strange appearance. Some had their blankets thrown around them, others had them twisted up like a horse collar, and tied over their shoulders in the manner of a plaid; while some had them stuffed into, and others tied on to the top of their knapsack;

15

in short, we appeared like anything but regular troops.

We moved forward as soon as we were formed, and early in the day reached Schagenbruck, where his Royal Highness stood to inspect us as we marched past. Near this place we fell in with some of the Russian regiments, they having landed nearly at the same time, and of which nation there were, I believe, about 20,000 troops expected to join our army. But if we appeared irregular and grotesque, I know not well how to describe them; their riflemen were shod with boots very much resembling those of our fishermen, coming up considerably higher than the knee; thus rendering them, I should imagine, incapable of celerity of movement, one of the chief requisites in a rifle corps; they also wore large cocked hats and long green coats. Their grenadiers were dressed more *apropos*, having high sugar-loaf shaped caps, mounted with a great deal of brass, and projecting forward at the top, with long coats, and gaiters reaching above the knee. Their regular infantry were nearly similar to the grenadiers, only they wore cocked hats instead of caps. The regiment which we saw on this occasion had with it, I should think, full half as many followers as soldiers, some of whom carried immensely large copper kettles; others the provisions, and others the officers' baggage; in short, these were the scullions, the cooks, and, as it were, the beasts of burden of the regiment; but this was a bad system, for it increased by one half the number of mouths to fill, and must have been attended with the worst consequences when provisions were scarce. The officers, I remember, carried what was formerly used in our service, a long sort of pole, with a head like a halberd, and called, I believe, a "spontoon." This, on passing a general at a review, the officer twists and twirls around his head, precisely as a drum-major in our service does his cane.

When we had passed his Royal Highness at the bridge, we moved forward to the town of Schagen, and took up our quarters in the church. I thought this extremely odd, as I had been accustomed to view so sacred an edifice with more reverence than to suppose they would quarter soldiers in it; but we were stowed in it as thick as we could well be, and made the best of our quarters; some taking the chancel, others the vestry, and some the body of the church; nay, some even took up their lodging in the reading-desk and pulpit. We could contrive to make out the Lord's prayer in Dutch, but could not well proceed further, although there is much similarity between that language and the English of my native county. Here, for the first time, we learnt that our brigade was what was called the reserve, and commanded by Colonel M'Donald of the 55th regiment; but on this occasion and in Egypt, the reserve was not what is generally understood by that term, for in both places it was composed of some of the best troops in the expedition, and was generally first called into action. On this occasion, the reserve consisted of the 23rd Welsh fusileers, the 55th regiment, the grenadier battalion before mentioned, and our light battalion.

We remained here till the 18th, when towards evening we were ordered under arms, having been previously supplied with provisions; and, after every preliminary was adjusted, we set forward on our march towards the city of Hoorne, situated on the Zuyder Zee. Of our destination, the men, of course, were totally ignorant, but no doubt the officers knew. It turned out that about 8000 troops had been appointed for this service, the execution of which was intrusted to that gallant old veteran, and hitherto successful general, Sir Ralph Abercromby. The intention was to make a rapid and extensive flank movement during the night, and surprise and capture the said city, while his Royal Highness was to attack the enemy in front. We moved off as it became dark, but such was the state of the roads that it became the most trying and distressing march that I believe ever troops undertook; the roads were literally knee deep in mud in most places, while every now and then they were rendered nearly impassable, both by the enemy having broken down the bridges over the innumerable canals and dikes which intersect this country, and these canals in many places having overflowed their banks.

None but those who have experienced this or something similar, can form an idea of the fatigue attending a night march in such a country, where the column is large. We marched, I think, in sections of about eight file, that is, with eight men abreast in the front rank, and the like number in the rear rank covering them. Conceive, then, your arriving at an obstacle which the darkness of the night multiplies a hundred-fold. Not more than one man will attempt to pass this obstacle at the same time, and he has to grope his way; consequently all the other fifteen men must stand still, or nearly so, till he is over, before they each move on in turn. Multiply this by the 300 sections behind, and you will have a halt for the rear of probably an hour or more; standing all this while nearly up to the knees in mire; or, what is worse, as each regiment has accomplished the task of getting over, this of course causes the others in the rear to be drawing up towards it by degrees, so that probably you are compelled to stand (or, if you choose, you may lie down in the mud) for a quarter of an hour, or more perhaps; and then move on again for the space of a few hundred yards, and then another halt; so that could you lie down to enjoy a little rest, the constant cry of "forward" resounding in your ears, just as you begin to close your eyes, renders it the most tiresome and trying situation that I know of. It is true, the head of the column does not suffer in an equal proportion with those in the rear, or a night march in an enemy's country would be a dangerous operation.

During this march, I remember, when the road was extremely deep, some one on the right of my section called out that there was an excellent path a little beyond him; when one poor fellow moved in that direction, but had not made many steps, till souse he went into a deep canal. Whether the man who called out had been actually deceived by the smooth surface of the water, which appeared in the dark like a nice level road; or whether he did it through mischief, I know not, but the poor simpleton who followed his advice paid dearly for his curiosity, being with some difficulty extricated from his uncomfortable situation. I may observe that these canals or dikes skirt both sides of every road in this part of Holland, and are even made use of as fences for the fields, there not being any hedges or walls that I remember to have seen.

About break of day we reached the city, which at once

surrendered; but just before daylight, I became so excessively weary that I could not continue in the ranks any longer; indeed men had been dropping out for some hours before, so that, I suppose, when the head of the column reached Hoorne, one half the number had fallen out; for it was beyond the powers of human nature to sustain such excessive fatigue. I, with two or three others, got behind a house that stood by the roadside, and laid ourselves down on a paved footpath which led from the back-door. Never in my life did I experience a greater luxury than this appeared to be, where something hard, and that would, keep me out of the deep and filthy mire, could be found to rest upon.

I laid me down and slept as soundly as ever I did in my life for about an hour, which quite refreshed me. We then got up and set off with all despatch to overtake the column, which we came up with and joined just as they halted after reaching the city. None of the troops entered the place, I believe; but my battalion being towards the rear of the column, was at a considerable distance from it. All now lay down to rest, and such as had houses near them occupied them; but those who had not, chose the driest parts of the canal bank or road, and all were soon buried in profound sleep, excepting those who were placed on guard.

Chapter Three
Fighting at Egmont-op-Zee

From daylight we had heard a heavy and constant cannonade towards our right and rear. His Royal Highness, with the remainder of the army, as was before intimated, had moved forward and attacked the main body of the enemy; but as I did not witness this action, I forbear to relate what I heard concerning it, further than this, that the Russians who attacked the enemy posted in the neighbourhood of Bergen, having by some mismanagement allowed themselves to be surprised after having carried that village, the whole army had been obliged to retire to their former position. In consequence of this failure, I believe, we were ordered towards evening to fall in, and (what appeared annoying in the extreme) to retrace our weary footsteps by the same dirty road by which we had advanced. Nearly the same fatigue and misery were endured as in our advance; but the column did not keep so much together as before, the men falling out by hundreds, so that the stoppages were not quite so great.

We did not return to Schagen after our retreat, but were cantoned in some villages in front of that town; and a few days afterwards we were moved to the right of Schagen, through Schagen-bruck, to a farm hamlet called Zaand Wyck.

Here we remained till the 1st of October; but I should not omit to mention, that we had, during the intervening period, several marches, all of which were made by night, and in which similar sufferings and fatigue were endured as in the march to Hoorne. This, it may probably be remembered, was one of the wettest autumns almost upon record; and in these marches we generally had the full benefit of the torrents which fell in this naturally wet country. I have actually seen the water running out at the bottom of the men's trowsers like that from the gutter which carries the rain from the roof of a house. When we had not a night march, we invariably had to be at our alarm post an hour before daybreak,—and that being about four miles distant from our quarter at this time, we never had what may be called a full night's rest.

Military men will know that the custom of being at the alarm post before daybreak is almost universal; for, that being the usual time of attack, it behoves those who are apprehensive of a visit from the enemy to be on the lookout, and to be prepared to receive them when they come— here they remain, till, as the vulgar phrase goes, "You can see a white horse a mile off," that is, till it is clear daylight, and they have ascertained that no enemy is in the neighbourhood; after which, if all be quiet, they retire to their quarters. Our accommodations at Zaand Wyck may be said to have been good, for our officers had a farmhouse to live in, and we had a good dry barn and other outhouses to lie down in; and in which I enjoyed some comfortable nights' lodgings. But on the 1st of October, in the afternoon, we were ordered to fell in, it having been previously intimated to us that we might probably have a brush with the enemy.

We were, of course, all life and glee on receiving the information, and the usual quantity of provisions having been issued, and every other preparation made in the night, we moved off by the same road by which we had usually advanced to our alarm post. This we passed, and then entered a most unpleasant country to march through; it being nearer the enemy, of course all bridges and other communications had been destroyed. As we moved on, a little after daylight we were overtaken by the 11th light dragoons, on which we were ordered to open to the right and left to let them pass us. They seemed in high spirits, and some of them cried out, as they passed us, "Go on, my lads, lather them well, and we'll come up and shave them."

Sir Walter Scott mentions this saying as made use of by some of the cavalry at Waterloo, as if it were at that time new; but I can assure him it is as old as 1799, if not much older, for I certainly heard it used on this occasion, and I know not but it may have been said long before. The cavalry inclined, after passing us, to their left, while we kept down towards the sea; and soon after,

21

on ascending a small eminence, we got a view of the village of Old Patten, where we discovered about 10,000 or 12,000 of our army drawn up near the sea-beach. We passed them, and moved forward in the direction of a high range of sand-hills, which commenced about a mile beyond the village, and which overlooked all the plain below. Here the enemy was posted, and I was told that they began as soon as we were within reach to cannonade us; but from the heads of the men in front, I could not perceive any appearance of such cannonade, nor do I believe that any of their shot reached us. A little farther on, however, we met a Russian *yager*, or rifleman, coming back and holding out his hand, which had been wounded, and from which the blood was flowing pretty copiously.

This was the first blood that I had ever seen as drawn in hostile conflict, and it certainly produced a somewhat strange effect upon me; it showed plainly that we were in the immediate vicinity of that enemy we had so often talked about, and whom we hoped to conquer; that now the time had arrived which would infallibly prove what every man, boaster or not, was made of; and that it might happen that it was my lot to fall. Having reflected (rather confusedly I own) on the passing scene before me, and offered up an occasional prayer to Him who alone can cover the head in the day of battle, we now approached the bottom of this sandy eminence, when my company was ordered to unfix bayonets, (for we had previously primed and loaded,) and dash on at double quick time till we came in contact with the enemy. No time was left for reflection now, the immediate duty we had to perform occupied all our attention fully; we soon got into a smart fire from the enemy's riflemen, which we found was the only description of troops, except a few artillery, that we had to contend with, their main bodies of heavy infantry being on the right and left of this sandy range, which in some places was about a mile in breadth, in others more or less.

After the fight had fairly commenced, we kept but little order, owing partly to the want of discipline and experience in our people, and partly to the nature of the ground, which was rugged and uneven in the extreme, being one continued range of sand-hills, with hollows more or less deep between them; and partly it may be attributed to the ardour of our young men, who pressed on perhaps too rapidly. We continued to advance, and never once made a retrograde movement, the enemy regularly retiring from height to height on our approach; but they had greatly the advantage over us in point of shooting, their balls doing much more execution than ours; indeed it cannot be wondered at, for they were all riflemen, trained to fire with precision, and armed with a weapon which seldom fails its object if truly pointed; while we were (what shall I say) totally ignorant of that most essential part of a soldier's duty. They consequently suffered little from our fire; but we could not believe this, and tried to persuade ourselves they had either buried their dead in the sand before we came up to them, or carried them off as they retreated; but experience has since taught me to know that we then must have done them little harm.

About the middle of the day, as I and a young man of the name of Thomas Bambrough (a countryman of my own, and who had volunteered with me,) were moving on in company, in passing through one of the valleys to an opposite height, we were assailed by a little volley from a group of the enemy which we discovered on a hill in front of us; one of which shots took effect in poor Bambrough's thigh just about the ham; he instantly fell, and roared out most piteously; I laid down my musket and endeavoured to hoist him on my back, in order to take him out of the fire, which they now poured in without intermission; but in this I failed, for he was so completely disabled by the wound, as to be rendered totally helpless, and it was so extremely painful that he could not bear the least movement.

I felt constrained to leave him, although I did so with reluctance, telling him that I would push on to the height we had first in view, to which I then perceived some more of our men had advanced, and would drive the enemy from their position; of course all this was not literally told him, but something to that effect was said; and I found that the moment I left him they ceased to fire on him; and, as I promised, we did drive off the enemy. Shortly after, some of our own people came up to where poor Bambrough lay, and carried him off to the rear; he was sent to an hospital, where he soon after died, they not being able, I understand, to extract the ball. Soon after this, there were some tremendous volleys of musketry heard on our left, apparently down in the plain below us. I, with one or two others, now inclined a little towards the left, in order to have a peep at the troops there, so hotly opposed to each other, in doing which, we still kept our line in front of the enemy's skirmishers.

We found it was the Russian army endeavouring to force their way towards the village of Bergen, the scene of their former disaster; but they were most distressingly retarded by the innumerable canals or ditches, by which the country was so intersected, and which were generally impassable by fording. On some occasions I could perceive, when they had found an entrance into an enclosure, and had fought their way to the farther side of it, they were obliged to retrace their steps, and get out by the same way by which they had entered, the enemy all this while pouring into them a close and destructive fire. This appeared to me to be most trying to their patience, and very disheartening; but they bore it with great steadiness.

Meantime, our own heavy troops were advancing on the right by the sea-beach, where was a plain of sand, of perhaps from 100 to 200 yards in breadth; the sand-hills between the two wings, as I said before, being swept by us, assisted by a small corps of Russian riflemen. We moved on till we got a little in advance of the Russian army, (which, from the obstacles they had to contend with, did not make very rapid progress,) and immediately over the village of Bergen, which stood on the plain, close under the sand-hills. Here, the enemy being in possession of considerable field-works, plied us pretty plenteously with shells from their howitzers, (their guns they could not elevate sufficiently to reach us,) but from which we suffered very little; for our people being much extended, and the sand being deep, the bursting of the shells was attended with very little mischief. Indeed, for a long time, I did not know what they were; for, having several times heard a loud explosion pretty near, I actually looked round to see the gun, which I imagined had fired, but could perceive nothing but a cloud of smoke rising from the spot, and the small bushes and herbs about it on fire. I thought it strange, and it was not till it was several times repeated, that we discovered what it really was, for my comrades were equally ignorant with myself.

At lengthy towards the close of the afternoon, a loud and heavy fire of musketry broke out on our right, which continued for a considerable time, and then ceased. This was our heavy infantry, who had advanced by the sea-shore, and who had now approached the village of Egmont-op-Zee, where the enemy made a most determined stand, but at last were driven back with great slaughter, and our people took possession the town. From this place the battle derives its name. A little after dark, the enemy abandoned Bergen also, so that we ceased any longer to be annoyed by their shells, which they continued to throw while they held possession of the place. But a short while before they retired, one was thrown, which pitched just close over my company, (for we had then been collected, and were formed in close order immediately above the town,) and where Colonel Sharpe and another officer were walking; it lay for a second or two hissing and burning, and might be expected every moment to explode. Their road lay close past it; the veteran however took no notice of it, but continued his walk and conversation the same as if nothing had occurred, and without going an inch out of his way. It burst with a tremendous report, but fortunately without doing either of them the least injury. I confess. I thought it rather too brave; for it appeared to me that he might have walked a little farther from it, or stopped for a moment or two without any imputation on his courage; but people do not all see things exactly alike.

Our loss in this action was but trifling, considering the extent of the operations. We had in my company only about fourteen or fifteen men killed and wounded; among the latter were my two countrymen, Bambrough, as before noticed, and Sutherland. One man of our company, I was told, in charging a fieldpiece, was struck down by the wind of the ball, and which, although it did not touch him, brought blood from his mouth, nose, and ears; he never after thoroughly recovered the effects of it. I do

25

not remember ever to have felt more fatigued than I did after this day's work. We had marched before commencing the action, I should think, twelve miles or more. We had been kept upon the run the greater part of the day, and had fought over nearly as much more ground, through loose sand, sometimes nearly up to the middle of the leg, and over ground so extremely uneven, that a few miles of leisurely walking on such, would be more than I should be able to accomplish now; and we had been nearly all the day deprived of every sort of liquid, for our canteens were soon emptied of what little they contained in the morning, and having myself fired nearly 150 rounds of ammunition, the powder of which, in biting off the ends of the cartridges, had nearly choked me. What would I not have given for a good drink?

I felt completely exhausted, and laid me down with the others with great good-will on the top of one of the sand-hills. But the night proved extremely wet, so that every one of us was very soon as completely soaked as if he had been dragged through a river; and, to crown my misfortunes, I was without a blanket. Here I must confess my folly, that others similarly situated may profit by my experience. Soon after the commencement of the action a rumour was spread along the line of skirmishers, that the Duke, seeing the very arduous duty we had to perform, had said, "Never mind, my lads, if your knapsacks are any encumbrance to you, and impede your running, throw them off, and I will take care you shall be furnished with others." No sooner did this silly report reach my ears, than I, with many others, equally simple, believed it, without taking time to consider that if even it were true, a knapsack and a blanket, (for they were together,) to be useful should be at hand when wanted. But, simpleton like, away went knapsack and blanket, and I felt greatly relieved in getting rid of such a burden, and now pushed on after the enemy with increased vigour, trying at the same time to persuade myself the report was true; although I own I occasionally had my doubts on the subject. But night came on, as I have said, and such a one as I have seldom seen for wet, and then I plainly perceived that I had played the young soldier.

An officer of ours of the name of Lacy, who had formerly been the captain of the Northumberland light company, and who volunteered with us, offered any man half a guinea for the use of a blanket for that night only, but without being able to obtain one: this will give some idea of the kind of night it was.

I had nothing for it, but just to put the cock of my musket between my knees, to keep it as dry as possible, and lay myself down as I was. I endeavoured to get as close as I could to one who had a blanket, and lay down with my head at his feet, which he had covered up very comfortably with his blanket. The rain pelted so heavily and so incessantly on my face, that I ventured after a while to pull a little corner of this man's blanket just to cover my cheek from the pitiless storm, and in this situation snatched a comfortable nap; but he awakening in the night, and finding that I had made free with the corner of his blanket, rudely pulled it from off my face, and rolled it round his feet again.

I was fain to lie still and let it pelt away, and even in this exposed situation I got some sleep, so completely were the powers of nature exhausted by fatigue. At length morning arose and showed us to ourselves, and such a group of sweeps we had seldom seen. Our clothing was literally all filth and dirt; our arms the colour of our coats with rust; and our faces as black as if we had come out of a coal-pit. In biting off the ends of the cartridges, there are generally a few grains of powder left sticking on the lips and about the mouth; these, accumulated as they must have been by the great quantity of ammunition each of us had fired, and with the profuse perspiration we were in during the heat of the day, added to the wet which fell upon us during the night, had caused the powder to run all over our faces; so that in the morning we cut the most ludicrous figure imaginable.

However we immediately set about getting our arms again in trim, for though the enemy had left us masters of the field of action, they were not far distant from us. We soon got our firelocks again in fighting order; that is, they would go off, though the brightness, on which a clean soldier piques himself, was gone past recovery at this time. I now felt rather sore from firing my piece so often; the recoil against my shoulder and breast had blackened them, and rendered them rather painful, and the middle finger of my right hand was completely blackened and swollen from the same cause.

At this time it was reported that a sad accident had occurred in our battalion; a soldier of one of our companies, in cleaning his musket, had by some awkwardness allowed it to go off, and an officer being immediately in front of where he was standing, the ball had taken effect upon him, and killed him on the spot.

After getting ourselves brushed up a little, the whole battalion was brought together, and moved to the right into the town of Egmont-op-Zee, where the guards and some other regiments had been since the evening before, after beating the enemy out of it, as I before mentioned. We remained here for that day, during which Alkmaar surrendered, and then advanced to the village of Egmont Binnen, or Egmont-op-Hoof, I am not certain which it is called, a few miles in front, and close by the sea.

I omitted to mention, that our fight of the 2nd took place over the ground from which Lord Duncan's victory derived its name, i.e. Camperdown. This headland, I fancy, we must have passed during that day's operations—But to return. We remained in Egmont Binnen till the morning of the 6th, when my battalion was ordered to fall in and march towards the outposts, a few miles in front, in order, as we understood, to relieve our grenadier battalion, which had been out since the day before.

We advanced by the seashore, but had not gone far before we saw and heard unequivocal signs that we should have something more than outpost duty to perform; the fact is, the enemy was rapidly advancing, their force in front having been greatly augmented by reinforcements; but when about two miles from the village, we met a soldier of the 11th light dragoons bringing in a French officer, whom he had taken prisoner. He belonged to the chasseurs-a-cheval, a sort of mounted light troops, who can act either as infantry or cavalry, as occasion may require. When we met them, and while they stood talking for a moment, I could not help thinking it would have made a fine subject for a painting; for the officer was most superbly dressed in dark green, with a richly embroidered pouch-belt over his shoulder, and with a deep cut across his cheek, from which the blood was streaming over an extremely handsome face; indeed he was altogether a most interesting figure, and, contrasted with the rough features and haughty bearing of the proud trooper who had taken him, produced a fine effect. The fellow gave his horse a slap over the flank with the flat of his sword, and set off with his prisoner, crying out, that there were plenty more of them to take, and that he would soon return and bring in another.

As we advanced, we could plainly perceive the enemy in front, skirmishing with our grenadiers, and we also saw that they possessed a pretty strong body of cavalry—a species of troops we had not encountered on the 2nd. We could distinctly perceive the cavalry wading into the sea as far as their horses could go, in order, as we imagined, to see past the point of a projecting sand-hill, which obstructed their view of the beach beyond it; but when they perceived that the force which was advancing against them was not great, they attacked our grenadiers with increased vivacity, and we soon after came in contact with them, for they were advancing with as great rapidity as if no force was in front to oppose them.

We soon perceived that they were nearly four times our numbers, and were obliged to adopt such a *ruse de guerre* as is frequently practised by the weaker party, but which had no effect, I am sorry to say, on this occasion,—that is, while one part of our force was skirmishing, the remainder got behind sand-hills a little in rear, and letting the men's heads just show over their tops, as if standing in columns of battalions, tried to induce the enemy to believe that each separate body which apppeared was of that force; but no, Johnny (as the soldiers sometimes call the French) was not so easily gulled, for they had previously ascertained pretty accurately the strength of our force in front of them, by the operation of the cavalry before mentioned. They therefore pressed on us with the most desperate fury, and in overwhelming numbers.

We maintained the action as well as our limited means permitted, and for a while kept tolerable order; but as the fight became hotter, and the disparity of force more apparent, I regret to say, our young troops fell into considerable disorder and confusion. This giving the enemy greater confidence, of course he availed himself of it, and attacked us with redoubled impetuosity; and, I lament to say, our dismayed and disheartened young soldiers fell from one degree of confusion to another, till at length all order seemed entirely lost amongst us; and what was at first a rather regular retreat, became at last a disorderly flight; for wherever an attempt was made to check the ardour of the enemy, the immense inequality of force they possessed soon completely overthrew the few that stood; and many were the brave fellows, both officers and men, who fell in this unequal contest, without their having the slightest chance of successfully opposing our impetuous foe.

The flight now became more like a race than any thing else, and I imagine they drove us not less than three or four miles without giving us time to breathe; but when we had reached within about a mile of the village we had left in the morning, we perceived some regiments advancing to our succour; among them was the 23rd, which advanced in line, and showed so good and steady a front as quite delighted us. We could also perceive to our left, that the Russians had become engaged with the force in front of them, and were holding it at bay; indeed by this time the action had extended considerably into the country, and some others of the British troops, I understand, were soon engaged.

On the coming up of the reinforcement, the 23rd in particular, our straggling and broken troops, which had been so wofully beaten, now united, and again advanced upon the enemy; and when the 23rd had given them a volley or two, the French gave way and retreated with as great precipitation as they had advanced. In short the tables were turned upon them, and the pursuit of them now was equally rapid with our retreat before them a short while previously; and before the action ceased, we, had driven them considerably beyond where we encountered them in the morning. Night scarcely put an end to the action, for the firing continued long after dark, each party being directed by the fire from the arms of their opponents; the unwillingness to desist on our part, I attribute to a desire of revenge for the disgrace they had inflicted on us in the morning. Towards the evening it came on exceedingly wet.

Nothing could surpass the steadiness and fine appearance of the 23rd, on entering into action; but they were all old soldiers, while our two battalions were composed altogether, I may say, of volunteers from the militia, who had as little idea of service in the field, as if newly taken from the plough. I would just remark here, that from what I have witnessed upon different occasions, I should never be inclined to put very much confidence in raw troops of whatever nation, or of what stuff so ever they may be composed, for it is certain, that without being at all deficient in point of courage, they have not that confidence in their own powers which soldiers who are inured to service possess; and if hastily or hotly set upon, while without the aid and example of others more experienced than themselves, it is many chances to one I think that they will give way. So it was on this occasion. Nothing could exceed the materials of which these two battalions were composed, had they had the advantage of a little more experience; and no troops could fight better than they did, after gaining the support and countenance of the old regiments which were sent to reinforce them.

But I confess with shame, we showed a great want of nerve in the early part of the day, although to any troops the occasion must have been one of severe trial. When the retreat had degenerated into a flight, and every one seemed intent only on making the best of his way to the rear, I, with some others who were among the hills, imagined we could get on faster if we took to the sea-beach, which, although it also was composed of deep sand, yet was level, and could not be so very fatiguing as climbing the innumerable hills over which we had to retreat. Away we accordingly set for the beach; but we had forgotten to calculate that if the beach would facilitate our retreat, it also would the enemy's advance. This we soon discovered, for we had scarcely descended from the hills when we found ourselves almost surrounded by the enemy; and it was not without the utmost exertion in our power that we were enabled to effect our escape, the balls flying thicker about us during our short stay here than they had done all the day before. My haversack was a great encumbrance to me on this occasion, for, having lost my knapsack as before related, I was obliged to stuff every thing I possessed into this inconvenient bag; which, hanging so low as to knock against my thighs, greatly impeded my progress to the rear, and had nigh got me lodged in a French prison.

A girl, who had followed a grenadier belonging to my regiment when he volunteered out of the militia, accompanied her protector during the whole of this day's operations, and shared equally with him every danger and fatigue to which he was exposed, and no argument could prevail upon her to leave him till the whole business was over, and till the battalion to which her sweetheart belonged was sent to the rear at night. I am not certain whether it was his Royal Highness's intention to have fought this day, or whether the action was brought on fortuitously; but certainly, although we began the fight under very unfavourable circumstances, and things looked rather awkward at one part of the day, no army ever got a more complete drubbing than the French did before the business terminated. I have since learnt that the action became general along the whole line towards the close of the day. Thus ended the last affair between the British and French troops during that unfortunate expedition.

The next day we fell back upon Egmont Binnen, leaving sufficiently strong outposts to occupy the ground we had taken, and this day I was fortunate enough to pick up the shell of an artilleryman's knapsack who had been killed in one of the late fights; but for necessaries I was totally destitute, and began soon after to feel the effects of my folly in throwing away my own. A little before midnight of the evening of the 7th, we were again ordered under arms with all dispatch and without noise, and had no doubt it was for the purpose of advancing as before, so as to reach the enemy's line by daylight next morning. How great then was our surprise and disappointment, when we turned our faces towards the rear, and filed out of the village by the road leading towards our old quarters! We moved on in silence till we reached Egmont-op-Zee, where the flashes from a large coal fire erected by way of lighthouse, shed a melancholy gleam over our columns as we passed beneath the hill on which it was erected. Here also by the sea lay innumerable dead bodies, both of men and horses, together with broken tumbrils and other sad emblems of the devastation which a few days previously had been made on this very ground; for here it was that the heat and principal part of the action of the 2nd took place, when the heavy columns of the opposing armies came in contact with each other. It would not be easy to describe our feelings as we moved sadly and silently along, knowing, as we now did, that we were for ever abandoning all the advantages that we had hitherto gained, after so much toil, privations, and loss as we had suffered; but it was useless to repine. Our leaders must know better than we could possibly do, what state the army was in, and what likelihood remained of effecting the object for which we came into the country; our duty therefore was to obey, without questioning the propriety of our present movement, however unpleasant it might be to our feelings.

We passed by Old Patten, near to which the action of the 2nd commenced, and finally returned to our old quarters at Zaand Wyck, which we reached some time next day, and where I found my comrade Sutherland, who had been here for some days; his wound, which was through the shoulder, not having disabled him from making his way thus far. He had some mutton already cooked, of which I partook with great relish, for I needed refreshment much; and after taking a swig out of his canteen, I laid me down and slept most soundly, rejoiced and thankful that I had so comfortable a home to return to.

We remained in this quarter only a day or two, and then our brigade was removed towards the left of the line, which, as well as I remember, rested upon Kolhorn. My battalion occupied the village of Basingohorn, to which we had retired on a former occasion; I mean on our retreat from Hoorne. This was one of the villages farthest in advance, consequently it became an outpost. A night or two passed quietly, but on the second or third night, a firing commenced from the advanced sentries all along the line. Whether the enemy had merely been making a reconnoissance, or whether they had intended to advance in force, and our discovering them altered their plan, I know not, but think the former the more probable; but be as it may, it had the effect of turning out our whole line of outposts, which, as might be expected, prepared to give them the best reception we were able. I remember on this occasion putting in two balls when we were ordered to load, as I was determined not to spare them, for I (with all my comrades I believe) felt sore at having been obliged to yield up all the advantages we had gained, to an enemy which we certainly did not consider as having fairly won them from us in action, but who were more indebted to the severity of the weather, producing such disastrous consequences on our young army, than to their prowess in the field. They retired, however, without giving us an opportunity of welcoming them in the manner we intended.

A few days after this, on the 19th October, it came to my turn to be one of the advanced sentries. About break of day, while musing of many things, of home with all its comforts, and contrasting it with my then rather uncomfortable situation, I was suddenly aroused from my reverie by the beating of drums and sounding of trumpets and music, &c, all along the French line. I could not conjecture the cause of all this, for although it is customary to sound and beat the reveille at this hour, yet never having heard the French do so before, I concluded something more than ordinary had occurred to cause them to do so on this occasion, and I need hardly inform my reader that I kept a good look-out, in order that they should not catch us napping. In a short while, however, the mystery was cleared up; for an officer of ours came round all the advanced sentries to tell us, that, as an armistice had been concluded, we were not any longer to prevent the country-people from passing and tepassing, as we had formerly had orders to do. I imagine the festive noises which I heard arose from this circumstance having taken place, for I believe the French were tired enough of the business, although they had now become in some measure the assailants; or else the cessation of hostilities allowed them to resume their wonted custom of beating the reveille in the morning.

Seeing we had failed in our attempt to wrest the country from the French, and that no hope now remained of our ever being in a condition to effect it, the prospect of returning home once more became a pleasing consideration, and I fully gave way to it. My comrades also now began to turn their thoughts homeward, and cheerfulness once more beamed on countenances which for some days past had been rather gloomy.

But by this time the dysentery had made sad ravages among our young and inexperienced soldiery, for on a day soon after this, we could in my company muster on parade only eighteen men out of one hundred, of which it was composed at the outset. This inefficiency was caused principally by disease, although we had certainly lost a fair proportion in the field. It was therefore well that our removal to a more favourable soil was about speedily to take place; and wisely had his Royal Highness acted in agreeing to evacuate a country, the climate of which had been so extremely prejudicial to his army. About this time also, I began to have my personal trials and sufferings; for now I began to feel the full effect of my folly on the 2nd inst., in throwing away my knapsack, for I had not a change of any description, and the consequence may be easily conjectured. Filth and vermin now began to add poignancy to my other sufferings, but I bore up against them all as well as I was able; and I have reason to thank God, that the strength of a good constitution enabled me to continue my duty without yielding for one day to the accumulated effects of these disagreeables.

Soon after this also, the good people of England, commiserating our uncomfortable situation, sent out presents of flannel shirts and shoes, which arrived most opportunely. I was not fortunate enough to obtain one of the former necessary articles, but my sergeant kindly put me down for a pair of shoes, of which I stood in great need, and now beg to return my best thanks to the kind friends who sent them, although at the time we expected we should have to pay for them. In a short while after this, the grenadiers and light battalions were broken up, and each company returned and joined its own proper regiment. We joined ours (the 56th) at a *weeshaus* (or poorhouse), situated on the great canal which connects this part of Holland with Alkmaer, and not far from Schagen-bruck. Here we were occupied for a few days in putting things in the best order we could, previous to our embarkation.

About the 3rd November we marched for the Helder, from whence we went on board. On our way down, one of my comrades, who was not over scrupulous in expressing his sentiments, was railing bitterly against the mismanagement (as he imagined) of the expedition, and saying, "he hoped the next time we came to that country, should we ever come again, that we would leave it under more favourable circumstances," General Manners (to whose brigade we now belonged) was riding close behind, unknown to this complainer, and overheard every word he said. When the soldier had finished, the General most good-naturedly rode up to him, and began to argue the matter with him.

"Why," says he, "although we are leaving the country, it is not from the enemy having compelled us to do so from his superior bravery or success in the field, for we have fought only five actions since landing, and in four of these we have been the conquerors; it is owing solely to the great sickness and consequent inefficiency of the army that we have been compelled to this measure."

I could not but admire the affability and kindness of the General, and was fully satisfied myself, and so were all who heard him, of, I believe, the justness of the remarks he made.

We reached the Helder the same day, where we remained doing duty till the 10th November, on which we embarked on board his Majesty's ship *Romney*, of fifty guns, commanded by Captain Lawford, (afterwards by Sir Home Popham.) She was only a small vessel of her class, and yet our whole regiment was put on board her; we indeed were not very strong, but she was crowded beyond measure, for many, nay, most of the troops had not literally lying room, each company having barely the space between two guns, which, I should think, is not more than twelve feet at the utmost, and even here the sailors, whether with or without orders I know not, slung their hammocks over us. I particularly remember this being the case, for I had the second night, by way of securing room to stretch myself, lain down between decks early in the evening, and had had some little repose, when a sailor, whose hammock was slung right over me, and while standing and making it, put his foot right on my cheek, and stood there till he had finished. I know not whether he knew that it was a human head he was treading on, but I judged it best to be as quiet as possible; preferring the pain of bearing his weight on my head, rather than, by moving or crying out, to incur the risk of his foot slipping, and peeling the skin off my face. The voyage was fortunately short, for in seven days we landed at Yarmouth, glad and rejoiced that this unpleasant and ill-fated expedition was terminated. I know not whether my reader is old enough to remember the autumn of which I have been speaking, but to me it appeared one of the wettest and most uncomfortable that I ever remember; and it was here, while exposed to its effects, that were laid, most probably, the seeds of that severe pulmonic affection from which I have since suffered so much.

Chapter Four
I Join the Rifles

We landed at Yarmouth on the 17th November, and the next day marched to Norwich, where we remained a few days, and where we found the people remarkably kind and attentive to our comforts; and, indeed, we now cut a most sorry figure, being literally nothing but rags and dirt; it was certainly a sad tax on the good landlords on whom we were billeted, to be compelled to find us lodgings, for we never left the beds unoccupied by some of the uncomfortable companions of our travels when we arose in the morning. I here began to find myself very unwell, for though I had borne up against sickness in the field, I could not now receive my food without feeling the most afflicting nausea, my stomach being completely out of order; and it was no wonder, for we had been compelled for several weeks past to drink the brackish water of the ditches of Holland, no springs (that ever I saw) being there to be found, and the little water in their wells, when we arrived in the country, being speedily exhausted. We had also been deprived of salt nearly all the time of our sojourn in that country, one of the greatest privations that I know of. Through the nursing of my kind landlady, however, I gradually regained my appetite, and with it my health, for which I have reason to be truly thankful to Him who has ever dealt so mercifully with me.

In a few days we left Norwich on our route to Chelmsford, and on our way passed through Bury St Edmunds, where my late regiment, the Northumberland militia, was quartered; they vied with each other in showing us kind attentions, but our miserable appearance put the soldiers of this regiment sadly out of love with the regular service.

We did not remain at Chelmsford long, but marched again for Horsham in Sussex, on which occasion I for the first time had a view of the metropolis, as we passed through it, by way of Whitechapel and London Bridge, &c. At Horsham we were quartered during the remainder of this winter. About the 10th or 12th of February 1800, we marched for Portsmouth, where we embarked for Ireland on the 14th. On this occasion the regiment was put on board two first-rate frigates; the *Endymion* was that on which the left wing went on board, but I do not recollect the name of the other. An agreement was entered into between the two captains, I understood, to sail for fifty guineas, they both being considered fast vessels; our destination was Cork; they were to start together, and the first there of course to be the winner.

We sailed with a favourable breeze, and got on most delightfully, having, soon after sailing, parted from our antagonist, and passing, if I recollect right, inside the Isles of Scilly, we in a few days drew near our destined port. But on the 19th, as we were pushing on with all our might, having every stitch of sail set, a squall came on so suddenly, that, before she could be stripped of her superfluous clothing, she was actually running bows under water, the sea entering the bow-ports, and making its way along between decks, like to wash every thing away before it. At this time the log was hove, and we were going at the (I believe) unparalleled rate of fifteen knots an hour. But unfortunately for our captain, the vessel was completely driven out of her course, and towards evening we entered the harbour of Kinsale, thus losing the fifty guineas, although we were no doubt the better sailer.

This was the first gale I had experienced, and I did not relish it; but when we entered the harbour, where the water was quite smooth, the sensation I felt was most delightful, after having been buffeted most violently by the sea without. The next day we landed, and were billeted in Kinsale, and here I had the first view of Irishmen and Irish manners. I need not attempt to describe them; for could I, so many have done it before me, that the subject is almost exhausted. In a day or two after landing, we marched to Cork, where the right wing had been landed, and with which we of course formed a junction.

We remained in Ireland from this time till the peace of 1802 was concluded, and were quartered successively in the towns of Cork, Kilkenny, Clonmel, Fermoy, and Kinsale; but as there was nothing which could interest a reader that occurred to me during this period, I shall pass it over in silence, save mentioning the following:—In the year 1800, it is well known the utmost distress was experienced by the poor of both countries, a scarcity, the effects of the wet harvest of 1799, having grievously afflicted all the British dominions. But in Ireland, the sufferings of the poor were great, beyond the conception of an Englishman who has not witnessed them, and many hundreds of them, I believe, actually perished of want.

But my tale relates more immediately to my own sufferings and those of my comrades; for we had then but what was termed a "black shilling a day," that is twelve pence Irish, an English or white shilling, or Hog, going in that country for thirteen pence; we had not then any beer money either, but had solely this black shilling to subsist on. Meat at this time was no less than 10d. per lb., of which each man received half a pound; bread was 5d. per lb., of which we also got half a pound. This half pound of bread, and half pound of meat, and that not of the best, was all we had to live on, and do our duty, which was not always of the easiest description. The remainder of our shilling was taken to furnish necessaries, washing, pipeclay, &c, for I do not remember that we ever laid in any sort of vegetables for the pot. Potatoes were out of the question, for they were no less than three shillings a stone of fourteen pounds.

Although we did not absolutely suffer want, the reader will perceive that we were but sparely dieted; the consequence was, innumerable robberies of potato fields, and gardens, &c, in the neighbourhood of our quarters; and many were the men that got punished for this crime, but it could not be put a stop to, for hunger is not easily borne. Indeed, on one occasion, I myself was seduced, by the persuasion of my comrades and by the cravings of hunger, into the commission of this crime. I remember well I was on what was termed the Commissariat guard, a short distance from the town of Fermoy, when my companions, thinking it a favourable opportunity for procuring something to eat, prevailed upon me to accompany them to a garden near the bridge, into which we entered, and each of us returned loaded with a fine cabbage, and which afforded us an excellent meal after our relief from guard. It is impossible to justify such an act, but the reader will be convinced, I trust, that sheer hunger alone urged me to the perpetration of this crime. Others, I have no doubt, were equally ill off, who did not resort to such disgraceful means of satisfying their hunger, but bore it with patient resignation. I believe that such was the case, and take shame to myself for yielding either to the calls of nature or the solicitations of my companions, some others of whom were not so scrupulous. Daring this distressing season I sold a watch which had formerly been my father's, and with which I felt extremely loath to part. I also received a little money from home, all, or nearly all, of which was expended in procuring food.

The hedges and fields, &c. in the vicinity, were ransacked in all directions, for the purpose of procuring bramble-berries, nettles, &c. &c.; in short, for any thing that was eatable. Such was our situation during several months, while under the command of Lieut.-Col. Skinner, who, although an excellent officer, had little idea of disposing of a soldier's pay to the best advantage; but latterly we were commanded by Major Keating, who, making the comfort of the soldiers under his command his continual study and delight, soon adopted a system which secured to us plenty in comparison of our former state. He left off the meat and bread save occasionally, and procured for us plenty of oatmeal and milk, by which means our wasted bodies began shortly after to resume quite another appearance.

We were quartered at Lap's Island, in Cork, when the news arrived of peace having been concluded; and as the bulk of the regiment had volunteered from the militia for five years, or during the war, measures were taken for discharging all those who did not re-enlist either into their own or other regiments. My mind was fully made up to return home; for although, as I said before, I never repented of having entered the regular service, yet I knew that the anxiety of my dear parents for my

41

return was so great, that I had settled it fully in my own mind to leave the army.

Another reason operated with me partly in forming this resolution—I had persuaded myself that I ought to have been promoted—for I judged myself fully capable of conducting the duties of a non-commissioned officer, and I flattered myself my conduct had been generally unexceptionable; but I was disappointed, for the great numbers in my company, who were judged both more deserving and better qualified, and withal better-looking soldiers, put it out of the question for me to look forward to promotion.

I was in this state when an officer and a party of the Rifle corps arrived at Cork, to receive such of the men of the different regiments then about to be discharged, as chose to volunteer, for this novel, and, as some thought, dangerous service. I cannot account for the impulse with which I was urged on, from the moment I had seen one of the men, to enter this corps. Something strange seemed to push me on, contrary to the full determination to return home, which had possessed me an hour before. I will not attempt to account for it, but such was the fact. I immediately, with some others of my regiment, gave in my name as a volunteer for the Rifle corps, and was in consequence in a day or two sworn into that corps, in which I have ever considered it an honour to serve, and which I have reason to thank a kind and overruling Providence I ever entered.

No news of course could be so afflictive to my dear parents, as to hear of the last rash and irretrievable step which I had taken. It had wellnigh broken their hearts, for they fully calculated on my returning home, as I had written to that effect. Judge then of their surprise and sorrow, when they learnt that I had entered, what was deemed by some, a condemned corps, and that for life—and that the West Indies would no doubt soon be my grave.

On my leaving the 56th, the officers of my company expressed their regret that I should quit the regiment, and told me, that although the mode hitherto pursued of keeping all the best-looking men in the light company had kept many from obtaining promotion, who otherwise would have been made non-commissioned officers, yet that mode was no longer to be adhered to, and that I might shortly expect to be promoted into another company, if I would consent to remain. I thanked them, and told them I had made up my mind, on which they each gave me a certificate as to character, &c, recommending me to the officers of my new corps, and which were of service to me afterwards.

The sergeant who had been sent to receive us, at once became my stanch friend, and employed me, as the party was now become pretty strong, to act as a non-commissioned officer. Every thing went on quite smoothly, and I felt happy in my new corps, and in my new employment.

We marched soon after to Waterford, and thence to Passage, and there embarked for the Isle of Wight, and without encountering any remarkable event arrived at Cowes on the 27th June, 1802; here we remained a day or two, and then marched for the regiment in Sussex. We found them at East Bourne, although Blatchington was their quarter, but they had been sent out of it on account of the assizes or election, I do not remember which.

We immediately commenced our light drill, in which I took great delight; but most of all I liked the shooting at the target. As recruits, we were first drilled at what is termed the horse, i.e. a machine to assist young riflemen in taking aim. At this I pleased my commanding-officer so much the first time I tried, that he ordered me to the front, and told me to load, and fire at the target. I did, and made a pretty good shot, hitting pretty near the bull's eye; on which he made me load again and fire, and hitting that also, he made me go on till I had fired ten rounds, all of which hit the target, and two of which had struck the bull's eye. The distance indeed was only fifty yards, but for a recruit, that is, a person unaccustomed to rifle-shooting, he called it a wonderful exhibition, and in consequence he gave me sixpence out of his pocket, and ordered me home. I thought the reward quite inadequate, so natural is it for us to overrate our own deservings.

This officer (Major Wade) was one of the best shots himself that I have almost ever seen. I have known him, and a soldier of the name of Smeaton, hold the target for each other at the distance of 150 yards, while the other fired at it, so steady and so accurate was both their shooting.

I continued to maintain my character as a good shot, which in a rifle corps is a great recommendation, and proceeded in acquiring a knowledge of my other duties with such steadiness as obtained the approbation of my officers. We soon after marched to Chatham—and while there, several non-commissioned officers being employed on the recruiting service, I was employed in doing the duty of one, having been appointed what is termed a "chosen man."

I must record the manner of my appointment. An acting-sergeant was doing the duty of pay-sergeant of our company, but he took it into his head to go all wrong, spending the money intrusted to him for the payment of the men. He of course was deprived of the situation; and on this occasion it was, that the officer commanding the company came to me one day, and said to me, "Surtees, I shall be forced to make you a chosen man." I thanked him, but could not help reflecting on the strange mode of expressing himself which he had adopted. The fact is, I believe, without thinking about the opinion I must form of the compliment he was paying me, he had been indeed forced to it, for he had no one to pay the company besides; and as I was not yet dismissed from the drill, it was an unprecedented measure. But he need not have told the whole truth on this occasion, for I should have been no worse a non-commissioned officer, had he been more complimentary; but he was a plain man, and not much given to compliment.

On our march hither, some of the men broke into the plate chest of the officers' mess, while the baggage stopped in Maidstone; one man was discovered, and tried for it, and sentenced to receive 800 lashes, all of which he took at one standing, and that without evincing much suffering; this was the most I ever saw inflicted at one time.

We marched again from Chatham in September, and on the

2nd of October arrived at Thorncliffe. While here, my parents interested Mr Beaumont, M.P. for my native county, to solicit my discharge from the Honourable Colonel Stewart, my then commanding-officer, they paying the regulated sum to the government. The colonel sent for me, and talked with me on the subject, and argued most forcibly in favour of my remaining in the regiment, saying he had intended to promote me the first vacancy; and that he had no doubt whatever of seeing me one day an officer. I own my views were not so sanguine; but his reasoning prevailed, and I consented to remain. Soon after, an opportunity offering, I was appointed corporal on the 24th of the same month.

Here again I had disappointed my beloved and tender parents, for it was not without considerable trouble and difficulty they obtained the interference of Mr Beaumont, and now I had again thrown cold water on all their endeavours to obtain my discharge. I fear I have much to answer for, as respects my conduct towards them. May God forgive me!

Chapter Five
Sergeant of the Rifles

Having given satisfaction as a corporal, I was shortly after appointed acting-sergeant; and in that capacity also, having pleased my officers, I was, on a vacancy occurring on the 19th of February following, appointed sergeant, and given the payment of a company. My head was almost turned by such rapid promotion, and I began in earnest to contemplate the possibility of my colonel's predictions being one day verified. Kind Providence watched over me, however, and kept me from being too much elated, and of committing myself as I otherwise might have done. Indeed I many times did commit things which, if strictly searched into, would have brought censure upon me, and lowered the high opinion that both myself and others entertained of me; but nothing that openly violated the law by which I was then governed (although many of God's laws I daily transgressed) was done by me.

I was at this time, although careful to secure the good opinion of my officers, little solicitous to please Him who had alone lavished all this bounty upon me. Indeed I believe I was as ungodly at this time as I ever remember to have been, and yet He caused me to prosper. Oh! how I ought to feel shame and confusion of face at the recollection of such abused goodness and mercy! May He pardon me for Christ's sake!

A short while before my appointment as sergeant, a most melancholy occurrence took place in the neighbourhood of our cantonment. A large Dutch East Indiaman, outward bound to Batavia, and full of troops, in passing down channel, mistook, I understand, the light at Dungeness for one on the French coast, and in consequence stood in towards Dymchurch wall instead of keeping out to sea. As might be expected, she was not long in striking on the wall, running with her bow quite close under the road, and in an instant, almost, went to pieces; and although numbers of people were early at the spot, and some, I believe, at the very moment she struck, they could render the unfortunate sufferers no effectual aid, although only a few yards distant from them. Out of about 800 persons on board, only seven men were saved. Many poor fellows, I understand, attempted to swim on shore, some on planks, and others without any aid; but such was the tremendous swell, and the general destruction of the ship so rapid, that only those seven before mentioned succeeded; and they not without being all more or less injured by pieces of the wreck. An admiral, I understood, was on board, and perished; several beautiful females were afterwards cast ashore among the dead, the wives or daughters, no doubt, of some on board; they were for the most part nearly naked, so that it is conjectured they had been in bed.

As might be expected, the allurement to plunder so valuable a wreck was not resisted by the natives of this part of the coast, but Colonel Stewart humanely placed strong bodies of the regiment at different points where the wreck had drifted, to secure as much of the property as he could for the Dutch government, and also to collect and bring in the numerous dead bodies which floated along the shore; all of which he had decently interred in the churchyard at Thorncliffe, and had the poor wounded survivors taken into hospital, where every care was taken of them. Indeed nothing could exceed the unremitting attention which he paid both to the dead and living on this most melancholy occasion, and for which he received, as he well merited, the thanks of the Dutch government.

About this period we had several individuals serving in the corps as soldiers, who had been officers in the army during the late war, but who, from different causes, had been reduced to the necessity of enlisting as private soldiers. The first that I remember was a person of the name of Conway Welch, who, I understood, had been an officer, and I think the Adjutant of the Surrey Rangers. He got on to the rank of Corporal, but, being excessively wild, I believe he never attained a higher rank. I do not remember what became of him.

The second was called Hughes; he was, I believe, when he enlisted, actually in the receipt of half-pay as a lieutenant of the line. He was a person of good conduct, and was soon promoted to the rank of corporal, and the colonel took him for his own private clerk, or secretary, as he was denominated; but he did not remain long in this situation, for he was shortly after called upon full pay of his rank in the army. I believe his case was a singular one.

The third unfortunate individual was of the name of Tait. He had been a captain in the Caithness Legion, but reduced when the regiment was broken up at the peace. He conducted himself extremely well for some time after he came into the regiment, and got on so far as to become pay-sergeant of a company. But in this situation, having considerable sums at his command, he became involved through his dissipation, and being unable to extricate himself from his difficulties, he adopted the fatal resolution of committing suicide, and accordingly, when quartered at Woodbridge, he one day retired to his room, loaded his rifle, and blew out his brains.

The story of the fourth individual is a scarcely less melancholy one. His name was M'Laughlan. I had known him while serving in my late regiment, as he had been an officer in the light company of the 35th regiment, and stood next in the light battalion to the company to which I belonged. He, shortly before our embarkation for Holland, got involved, through a gambling transaction I heard, and was in consequence obliged to dispose of his commission, which, it would appear from this, he had originally purchased. But interest was made in his behalf, and he was permitted to accompany his regiment to Holland in the capacity of a volunteer, and he accordingly assumed the firelock and bayonet in place of his former weapon, the sword. He was fortunate enough to obtain another commission before the return of the troops to England, but how he became deprived of that I have been unable to learn. But about the latter end of 1803, he enlisted as a private in my corps. His conduct here was far from good, and he consequently never rose higher, for he was continually in scrapes from his dissipated habits; and becoming tired of the restraint laid upon him by the strict discipline which our excellent commanding-officer enforced, he one day made an attempt to desert and join the French at Boulogne, and was picked up by one of our cruisers in endeavouring to cross the channel in an open boat. He was brought back hand-cuffed, and lodged in the guard-house one day when I happened to be sergeant commanding the guard.

As I looked on him, I could not help reflecting on the strange vicissitudes which attend some men in their passage through life. Here was a person whom I had known only a few years before while encamped on Barham Downs, a gay and handsome young officer, moving in the circle of men of gallantry and honour; and now behold him a wretched culprit, stretched on the wooden guard-bed, manacled like a felon. In contrasting his miserable situation with my own so much happier lot, what ample cause had I for gratitude to that kind and indulgent Providence, which had preserved me from those excesses, which entailed so much misery on others. He was shortly after tried by a general court-martial, and transported as a felon for life. I understand a sister of his was at Thorncliffe at the time of his trial, &c, the wife of a brevet lieutenant-colonel in the 4th regiment. What must she have felt!

It will be recollected that, in 1803, war again broke out between this country and France, as my preceding story had intimated. The army was consequently augmented again, and my corps, till now called the "Rifle Corps," was made the 95th. This year a camp was formed on Thorncliffe, under the command of that able general and excellent man Sir John Moore. This was termed by some the "Vanguard of England," for here it was that the then threatened invasion of this country by Bonaparte must most likely have taken place, it being immediately opposite to the grand camp then forming at Boulogne. Daily rencontres took place between our cruisers and his far-famed flotilla; and on one occasion, the belief that he was sending forth his invincible host was so great, that our camp was struck, the troops turned out, and received each man his sixty rounds of ammunition; the waggons and carts were all put in immediate requisition, and the inhabitants were flying in all directions. But to our disappointment, I will not say whether disagreeable or otherwise, it all ended in smoke; it happened to have been some of his flotilla making a movement along the coast, which had been set on by our cruisers and pretty roughly handled.

We remained in this camp till the 24th of November, I think, having occasionally before this period had our tents blown from over our heads by the autumnal gales. The next year a more formidable camp was formed on the same ground, the force having been augmented by a second line, composed of regiments of militia. This year also, like the last, passed over without witnessing the long-threatened invasion of Old England, although Bonaparte, in the pride of his heart and the vanity of his mind, had begun to erect a monument near Boulogne, to commemorate that glorious achievement. My regiment, on the breaking up of the camp, marched into Hythe Barracks, where we remained till the month of April, 1805.

In the spring of this year another volunteering from the militia into regiments of the line was ordered, on which occasion I was selected by my commanding-officer, Lieut.-Colonel Beckwith, to accompany Lieutenant Evans, of the regiment, down to my native county, to receive such men of the militia regiments there as chose to enter the 95th. On this occasion we were very successful, having obtained between seventy and eighty men from the different regiments in the north. It was on this occasion that I had the first opportunity, since I became a soldier, of visiting my native village, and my greatly-distressed parents and family. I need not describe the meeting that took place between us, on my first seeing them—it will be better conceived than told;—suffice it to say, joy and sorrow were strangely mingled together—joy to see me once more safe and sound—but sorrow that the line of life I had adopted should so soon, so very soon, call upon me to part from them again. In fact, I could only remain with them three days, at the end of which, I had orders to join my party at Morpeth.

With this respectable batch of volunteers we marched, and joined the regiment at Canterbury, whither it had been removed during our absence, and, on our arrival, received the thanks of our commanding-officer for our exertions. Here, and at this time, a second battalion to the 95th was formed, the sergeant-majorship of which I was in hopes of obtaining; but in this I was disappointed, for a sergeant, who was both much older than me, and had much stronger claims than I could pretend to, was selected for the situation; and although he did not turn out so well afterwards as was expected, yet these circumstances ought to have satisfied me at the time that no injustice was done me by bestowing it upon him. But such was my folly, and the over-high opinion I entertained of my own merits, that I could not quietly acquiesce in this most just arrangement; and foolishly imagining myself ill-used, the chagrin of which drove me to the adoption of one of the worst expedients possible, I immediately took to drinking and to the neglect of my proper duties, thinking, like an ass as I was, that I should thus revenge myself for my supposed ill-usage, forgetting that it was only on myself that this revenge could ultimately fall. However, the same good Providence which has mercifully and so continually watched over me, stepped in to my aid in this my most dangerous situation; for one day my captain, who had always been my friend, sent for me, and urged upon me the folly and the baseness of my present conduct, and the unhappy consequences to myself that were likely to result from persisting in a course so absurd and blame-worthy. This, with my own reasoning on the subject, brought me at length to a better disposition of mind, and induced me once more to resume my duties with cheerfulness and alacrity.

I have mentioned this circumstance, because I believe I was nearer at this time to falling into my original nothingness, than I ever have been, either before or since; and I have no doubt that many an excellent non-commissioned officer and soldier have been involved in the like error, who have not been so fortunate as I was in escaping its consequences.

From Canterbury we marched to Brabourn Lees Barracks, in the same county, where we remained till some time in October, when we were called upon to embark for Lower Germany. During our stay at Brabourn Lees, a circumstance occurred which called forth an exhibition of as great magnanimity, on the part of Colonel Beckwith, as I almost ever remember to have

51

witnessed: We had received about 200 Irish volunteers, who were wild and ungovernable in the extreme; a party of these, in strolling about one day, had fallen in with Mrs Beckwith, with her maid and child, taking a walk along the Ashford road.

Not knowing, I imagine, who the lady and her maid were, they set on and assaulted them in the most violent and outrageous manner, proceeding to such lengths as perhaps delicacy forbids to mention. It was, I believe, discovered who they were. Accordingly, the next day, the Colonel formed the battalion into a square, and proceeded to relate the circumstance to the regiment; "But," says he, "although I know who the ruffians are, I will not proceed any farther in the business, because it was my own wife that they attacked; but, had it been the wife of the meanest soldier in the regiment, I solemnly declare I would have given you every lash which a court-martial might have sentenced you." Such a trait of generous forbearance is not often met with; but by this, and similar instances of liberal feeling, he completely gained the heart of every soldier in the battalion, a thing not always attainable by very excellent commanding-officers.

Chapter Six

Expedition to Bremen

About the latter end of October, 1805, we marched to Ramsgate, and there embarked, as before noticed, for Germany. It was my lot, on this occasion, to be put on board a small and ill-shaped collier brig, called the *Jane of Shields*, but the master I have forgot. She was a most miserable sailer, making on a wind almost as much lee as head-way, and in every respect ill adapted for the transport service. We had not been many days at sea before we lost the fleet, and in our endeavours to find it again were at one time on the coast of Jutland. All this time we had been beating against a contrary wind; but while here, the wind became favourable, and we appeared to have nothing to do but to bear away for the mouth of the Elbe, which river it was our destination to enter; but unfortunately, by some mismanagement, we fell quite away to leeward of it, and got entangled between the mainland and the Island of Wangeroog, not far from the mouth of Jade River, instead of the Elbe.

While in this uncomfortable situation, it came on to blow a tremendous gale, which rendered our position not only most unpleasant, but extremely perilous, for we were embayed, and the wind blowing on a lee shore, and the vessel became almost unmanageable, her bad sailing becoming distressingly more apparent the more she was put on her mettle. In the midst of the confusion attendant on such circumstances, the master (with what intention I know not, whether to drown dull care, or to fortify him against his exposure to the watery element) went down below, and swallowed the best part of a bottle of brandy. In doing which, his corner cupboard, with all its contents, came rattling down about his ears. He would fain have had me to pledge him, but I begged to be excused. The consequence was, he became quite drunk at the time when all his abilities as a

53

seaman were likely to be called into operation; but he probably saw things clearest after having his eye wet.

My commanding-officer now became quite alarmed for the safety of the troops, seeing the master had incapacitated himself, as he conceived, for the management of the vessel; and, after a consultation among our officers, an attempt was made to deprive him of the command, and intrust it to the mate, who had in this case, in order to save as many of the troops as possible, determined on running the vessel high and dry, as he termed it, on the sandy beach, near the Jade River.

At this proposal, however, the master stormed and blasphemed like a madman, swearing there was neither soldier nor sailor on board the ship but himself. He went so far, and became so outrageous, that our commanding-officer talked of hanging him up at the yard-arm; but it being a ticklish thing to take the command of a ship from the person legally authorized to exercise it, the major did not enforce the wishes of the officers. The poor mate sat down on the companion and cried like a child, partly owing to the abuse the captain gave him, and partly, I imagine, from the hopelessness of our situation. The captain, in his refusal to yield up the command, told the major he had been several times wrecked, and had been, I know not how many times, exposed for a considerable length of time in the water; and that he was not afraid to encounter it again. This, however, was but poor consolation to landsmen, who had not been accustomed to such duckings.

A desperate case requires a desperate remedy—so our captain thought—for he instantly clapped on the vessel the square mainsail, which every moment threatened to carry away the mast, and in which case, nothing could have prevented our destruction; however, Providence so ordered it, that she bore it through the gale, and he, after putting her on the outward tack, continued to stand from the land till he imagined he had completely weathered Wangeroog; but at midnight, when he ordered to put about the ship, had it not been for the cabin-boy providentially seeing close to leeward of us the light of Wangeroog, we should instantly have been upon the rocks. This will show either what a bad sailer the vessel was, or how far the master had miscalculated the distance; for he imagined himself by this time to be quite clear of all the land, and considerably out to sea. He continued, after this providential escape, to stand on on the same tack, and just cleared the island; and in the morning, the wind having somewhat abated, and shifted a little in our favour, we were enabled, soon after, to lay our course.

We arrived in the Elbe, and landed at Cuxhaven on the 18th of November, 1805, the day on which our fleet there was celebrating the victory of Trafalgar—clouded indeed it was by the death of the hero who fell while achieving it—yet glorious to the nation to which that fleet belonged. We, immediately after landing, marched for Dorum, a village twelve or fourteen miles distant, and from thence by Osterholtz and Bremer Lhe to the city of Bremen. On our arrival there, (my battalion forming the advanced guard,) we found the gates were shut against us; a Prussian garrison was in the town, the commandant of which seemingly did not know how to act, whether to admit us as allies, or not, the policy of his government at that time being so extremely ambiguous. Colonel Beckwith, who commanded the advance, was not however easily to be deterred from executing his orders, and he hesitated not to tell them, that if they did not choose to admit us peaceably, force should be resorted to to gain an entrance. This had the desired effect, for the gate was soon after thrown open, and we were received by the authorities of the town, and by the inhabitants in general, with the warmest expressions of friendship and cordial attachment; the Prussian officers, all the while looking on, apparently not over-well pleased with the conduct of their hosts; they were soon afterwards, however, withdrawn from the territory, and we then remained sole occupiers of this part of the country.

Our army assembled in this city in considerable force, when it becoming necessary to establish outposts in advance, my battalion was sent out first to the town of Delmenhorst, and subsequently a part of it to the city of Oldenburg, and the remainder to the town of Wildishausen; to this latter place two companies were detached, under the command of Major Travers, and to which he appointed me to act as sergeant-major. We did not remain long in this situation, but were again recalled from Wildishausen to Delmenhorst, and afterwards sent to join the other companies at Oldenburg.

Here we staid some time, during which we experienced the most unbounded hospitality and kindness from the whole of the inhabitants, but more particularly from the Duke. He actually did not know how sufficiently to express his friendly disposition towards our officers in general,—his kindness also extended to the soldiers,—for when we afterwards received an order to retrograde again to Delmenhorst, he sent forward to the half-way house refreshments of every description, for both officers and men; and the night before we left this hospitable city, he gave a splendid ball in honour of the officers of our corps, to which, of course, every inhabitant of a suitable rank was invited. Nay, I heard, and have no reason to doubt the correctness of the report, that he wrote to the burgomaster of Bremen, to which city we again retired, to endeavour, if possible, to have us quartered in his immediate neighbourhood, in the best part of the town, for that not only the officers, but the soldiers of the corps, were perfect gentlemen; indeed, the conduct of the battalion at this time, under its kind and excellent commanding-officer, was such as to entitle it to the highest praise. Our retreat on this occasion, I understood, was rendered necessary, in consequence of the defeat of the allied forces at Austerlitz, and of the fatal termination by that sanguinary action of the campaign in that part of Germany.

Although I am no prophet, I predicted at this period what the result would be to the King of Prussia, whose hesitating and equivocal conduct kept him aloof from taking an active part, when his co-operation might have been of the utmost advantage to the general cause. It required no second sight to perceive, that when Bonaparte could clear his hands of his present antagonists, he would not hesitate for a moment to turn his arms against a monarch on whom he could not cordially rely, and whose dominions offered such a strong temptation to an ambitious and aspiring mind like his.

We continued to occupy Bremen till towards the beginning of February 1806, when the whole army gradually drew down towards our place of embarkation, for the purpose of evacuating the country, our stay now having been rendered useless by the unsuccessful and unfortunate turn which the allied affairs had taken. My battalion covered the retreat of the army; but as great numbers of the German Legion, which formed part of the British force in this country, were deserting and returning to their homes, we were sent away into the interior to endeavour to intercept such of them as might pass by the villages we occupied, and restore them to the army. We took some, but not many: and soon after we also retired, and went on board at Cuxhaven, and again returned to England, landing at Yarmouth on the 19th. of the same month.

During the whole of my military career, I never witnessed so cordial an attachment to the British name and character, as was manifested during this service, by the good people among whom we had been residing. Nothing was too good for us— and nothing was left undone by them to render us comfortable and happy. It is true they have their vices like other people; but barring one or two peculiar to continental nations, I believe them to be, generally speaking as moral as any people among whom it has been my lot to sojourn. But, oh! with what shame and sorrow do I look back on the part I acted at this period— how profligate and abandoned was my conduct at the very time that a kind and gracious Providence was showering its choicest blessings upon me! but, alas, I paid no regard to the remonstrances of conscience, which I endeavoured and succeeded in drowning in debauchery and intemperance.

Chapter Seven
Denmark

We landed, as I before stated, at Yarmouth, and proceeded by way of Lowestoft to Woodbridge, in Suffolk, in the barracks of which my battalion was quartered. Here also was the 23rd regiment, that which I had seen act so nobly in Holland: and as it was determined by its commanding-officer to give the regiment some idea of light movements, I was selected for the purpose of instructing their non-commissioned officers. But I did not long continue to instruct them, for in the May following, an offer was made me by Colonel Beckwith of the situation of sergeant-major in the Cornwall Miners, a regiment of militia, with the prospect, he told me, of shortly becoming adjutant. This, however, after due consideration, I declined accepting — preferring to remain in a regiment and service which I liked so well, and in which I hoped one day to rise to something higher than my present situation. I believe my conduct on this occasion was approved, for not long after, it was intimated to me, that the offer I had refused, had been made to the quartermaster-sergeant of our second battalion, and that he had, after some hesitation, accepted it, thus leaving his situation open for me. Accordingly, I departed for the purpose of joining that battalion, and entering on my new duties.

I joined it at Feversham, in Kent. My means increasing, the sinfulness of my course of life was increased in proportion. It is true, I generally performed my various military duties to the satisfaction of my superiors; but could not at all times please my present commanding-officer, against whose wish and inclination I had been appointed to my present situation; he naturally wishing to have a person of his own selection. Soon after this, an expedition being ordered for South America, of which three companies of my present battalion were to form a part, I waited on him, and requested him to permit me to accompany them in the capacity of acting quarter-master. He said no; but if I chose to resign my present situation, and go as a sergeant, he would permit me. This I of course declined, as it would have been paying a bad compliment indeed to my benefactor, Colonel Beckwith, thus to give up for nothing what he had been at pains to procure for me.

This, and some other little things which occurred about the same time, proved to me that I was no favourite with my new lieutenant-colonel, and that it behoved me to be very guarded in my conduct. We were, after this, removed to Brabourn Lees again, and remained there, without any occurrence arising, till we were summoned to take part in the expedition fitting out for Denmark.

We accordingly repaired to Deal, where we embarked on the 26th of July, 1807, and shortly after sailed for our destination. We arrived in the Sound about the 10th of August, where the whole fleet was assembled; one of the largest I had yet seen. On the 16th, every thing having been previously got ready, we landed at the village of Vedbeck, in the island of Zealand, about ten or twelve miles below Copenhagen. It was a most beautiful and glorious sight to witness the debarkation of the first division, or advanced guard, to which my battalion belonged. The most perfect arrangements had been made by Sir Home Popham, who superintended the landing of the troops; and nothing could exceed the beauty and regularity in which the different divisions of boats approached the shore, covered by some small brigs and bombs, which had orders to clear the beach by grape shot, of any enemy that might appear. Some light artillery also landed with us, prepared for immediate action, for it was not known but the Danes might attempt to oppose our landing, they having rejected every overture on the part of our commanders for the delivery of their fleet.

After landing, mine and the first battalion of my regiment were sent forward in the direction of Copenhagen; and on this occasion, I for the first time saw the illustrious General, who has since made the world, resound with his exploits. He commanded us, who formed the advance, and directed our two battalions during the operations of the day. But we met with no force of the enemy, save a small patrol of cavalry, which passed in front of us, and then retired towards the city; this showed that they were observing our movements. We halted for the night at a village called, I think, Lingbye, on the great road from Copenhagen towards Elsineur. We rested on our arms all night, and early in the morning moved forward on the Copenhagen road, and about midday took up cantonments within a long gun-shot of the city, and began to invest the place. All was quiet till about three o'clock in the afternoon, when a general cry of turn out, set the whole of our people in motion. A considerable body of the enemy were advancing from the town, and by this time had attacked the advanced picquets on our left, towards the sea-shore; but instant succour being sent, they maintained their ground.

The force opposed to the enemy was but small, consisting of two companies of the 4th regiment, four of the 23rd, and four of my battalion, with two light fieldpieces; in all not more than 1000 men, while the Danes were near 3000. Nevertheless, the moment the armies came in contact, they instantly gave way, leaving a considerable number of killed and wounded behind them, and retreated into the town.

On this occasion, I attached myself to my commanding-officer, who, with the surgeon, and some others of the staff, advanced with one of the guns on the great road, having some of our companies on each flank. He gave me his glass to take care of, with which I soon after busied myself in watching the motions of the enemy. I discovered at a short distance to our left and front, a considerable body of troops, dressed in long red coats, which I knew could not be British, for that description of dress had long been laid aside by us; I accordingly began, pointing them out as an excellent mark for the artillery, which was then with us; but I had scarcely spoken, when an officer present, cried out, after looking, did I wish the artillery to fire on our own people? The colonel also made some severe and reproachful remarks, telling me, if I would fight, to go and take a rifle. I said nothing; but he had scarcely finished his harangue, when a round shot came directly from this body of supposed British troops, which nigh carried away one of the legs of the first officer who spoke.

The enemy were soon repulsed, and the troops retired again to their former cantonments. After their troops retreated, a body of their gun-boats advanced against some of our small craft which happened to be rather close in shore, but their attack occasioned little injury, the distance being considerable.

The next morning the enemy opened a heavy and rather destructive fire of artillery upon our outposts, by which we lost an officer of artillery and several men; their fire was chiefly directed against what was called the wind-mill battery, which was our farthest advance at this time.

On the 19th, my battalion was moved farther to the right, and nearer the town; there was constant firing between the advanced posts of the two armies, and this continued for several days, during which the investment of the city was proceeding with, and batteries, &c. marked out for the purpose of bombarding it. All kinds of ordnance stores were at the same time disembarked, and sent off to the army with the utmost dispatch. In short, nothing could exceed the vigour with which the siege was now prosecuted, after the final rejection of pacific overtures by the Danish general.

On the 24th, we were ordered under arms at two o'clock in the morning, and immediately advanced, driving in the enemy's outposts, with the view of carrying our works nearer the town. In this movement we experienced considerable opposition and suffered some loss, from their guns on the town walls, and from musketry from the windows.

We this day established two strong and well advanced batteries, and at night set fire to a wind-mill in their possession, which obstructed our view of some of their works. During the whole of the 25th, there was a constant fire both of artillery and fire-arms, by which one of the light battalions of the German Legion suffered rather severely. My battalion relieved them at the outposts a little before dark, and was fortunate enough not to lose a man, where they had lost considerable numbers.

On the 26th, a corps or division of the army was assembled,

and placed under the immediate orders of Sir Arthur Wellesley. It consisted of the following regiments, *viz*. 43rd, 52nd, 92nd, 95th, and 6th Battalion King's German Legion, with six squadrons of German cavalry, and some artillery, and was destined to advance against a body of the enemy composed principally of militia, which had been for some time past collecting in the neighbourhood of Kioge.

At three o'clock p.m., we started from the neighbourhood of Copenhagen, the troops making their way through the country to the left of the great road to Roskild. I had charge of the baggage, which was carried on light German waggons, the bodies of which are formed chiefly of wicker-work, and are so light and easy of draught that the natives travel in them in the same manner nearly of our coaches—they going sometimes at a considerable rate.

I found it impracticable to continue in the same direction the troops had gone, for they presently left all traces of a road, and struck right across the country—and as I knew I should be expected to have the baggage with them that night if possible, I determined to run all hazards, and proceed along the great high-road in hopes of afterwards being enabled to find them out—accordingly I moved forward, and presently passed the outposts of the German cavalry stationed in the direction of Roskild; the men, I doubt not, wondering at my temerity in pushing on with a few baggage waggons, where they were all on the alert with swords drawn, and with carbines and pistols loaded. I own it was a hazardous undertaking, for a very small party of the enemy would easily have captured both me and my baggage; but I knew my commanding-officer to be such a person as to pay little attention to excuses of any kind when he wished a thing to be done, and withal he loved his comforts, and would not have been easily pacified had he been deprived of them. Fortunately, after advancing for some miles beyond the outposts of our army before mentioned, I fell in with a road branching off towards the left, apparently in the very direction the troops had taken.

Till I reached this point, I had advanced with considerable caution, and slowly; determined, if any enemy should appear in front, to endeavour to effect a retreat. But now, having left the great road, and taken that which I judged would bring me to the neighbourhood of those I was seeking, I accordingly ordered all my guards to mount, and set off at a brisk trot, keeping a good look-out to my right flank, for fear of surprise, and fortunately fell in with the division at the very moment it was entering the road by which I had come. I received great credit for my generalship, and was complimented by the officers of my corps, they being the only people in the division, I believe, who had the comfort of their baggage that night. The name of the village where we halted is Caughstrup.

The next day we continued to advance in the direction of Kioge, and in the afternoon we reached a village which I forget the name of, and where evident traces appeared of the enemy having shortly left it; indeed, we found two or three stragglers in the village, who were of course made prisoners. We halted outside the village for the night.

A short while before we reached this village, I saw a body of troops dressed in red, marching on our right flank, at right angles to the road by which we were advancing, and which I instantly concluded must be a part of the enemy's force, as we had no troops in that direction. But remembering the rebuke I received on the 17th for interfering with concerns that did not belong to me, I shut my mouth in silence, and did not, I believe, mention the matter. It is evident it was a part of the enemy's force, for the General's information led him to take that very same direction the next day; and that being towards Roskild, we set out and reached that city in the afternoon, but found the enemy had again given us the slip, and doubled back to nearly the same place from whence we had started.

The next morning about three o'clock we left Roskild, and took the road for Kioge, near which it was now ascertained the enemy had come to a resolution to make a stand. I forgot to mention that previous to this our force had been divided and formed into two brigades; the 52nd, 92nd, our 1st battalion, and some cavalry and artillery, remaining under the command of Sir Arthur; while the 43rd, the 6th German Legion, and our five companies, with the remainder of the cavalry, were put under the command of Baron Linsengen, one of the generals of the German Legion. Sir Arthur's people had not been with us for a day or two back, but where I do not exactly know. But this morning it was arranged that his brigade was to march directly upon Kioge and attack it in front, while we fetched a circuit behind, and came upon a part of their force stationed in a forest or wood behind the town—and thus cut off their retreat. But the poor creatures were unable to stand above a round or two, and almost immediately broke and fled in all directions.

As we approached the wood we were destined to attack, the appearance was certainly rather formidable; for from the immense cloud of dust they raised in performing their movements, we calculated on meeting with a considerable body of troops; and indeed, just as we approached the wood, our cavalry laid hold of an officer of their horse, dressed partly in uniform and partly as a civilian. From him we obtained information that they had in the field 12,000 men; 5000 of which were armed with pikes, 1000 cavalry, and the remainder consisted of artillery and infantry. He must, I think, have overrated their numbers, or surely they might have made some sort of a stand against 5500 men, the strength of our division.

On Sir Arthur attacking them in the town of Kioge, they stood, as before said, only for a round or two, and fled, many of them coming in contact afterwards with our brigade; but from the extent of (and intricate roads through) the wood, very few of them were made prisoners; till towards evening, when a company of my battalion, with some of the German cavalry, overtook a considerable body in the village of Herfolge, apparently the rearguard of the enemy. In this village they made a stand, getting into the churchyard, which afforded an excellent position, it being considerably higher than any other part of the village. Here also they soon began to waver, and after a few shots from our people, they all laid down their arms and became prisoners of war. Their numbers were 1550 men, with 56 officers, and Major-General Oxholm, the second in command of this part of the Danish army. A considerable quantity of artillery, small arms, baggage, and provisions, &c, with two stands of colours, fell into the hands of the captors on this occasion. These poor creatures were instantly sent off as prisoners, and put on board our ships at Copenhagen; many of them apparently quite glad that they had done with fighting. Great numbers of them had nothing better by way of shoeing than wooden clogs—a very inconvenient kind I should imagine for a rapid retreat.

The loss of the British during this day's operations was, as might be expected, quite trifling. I had this day followed the ill-natured advice of my commanding-officer on a former occasion, and had taken a rifle, but had little opportunity of using it, not having fired more than eight or ten shots. My battalion halted in the village of Herfolge for the night, and the next morning moved forward towards the town of Kingsted, that being the direction in which the broken fragments of the Danish army had retired.

Our two battalions had been employed all the day of the 29th, after the first onset, in scouring the woods from Kioge to Herfolge. We continued this service on the 30th also, and took numbers of poor creatures who had been engaged in yesterday's operations, but who had not yet been able totally to divest themselves of their military habiliments, although apparently anxious to do so. We reached Kingsted on the 31st, and finding that the only regular part of the late army had retired into one of the islands in the Great Belt, and that the militia portion had totally disbanded itself, we halted here till the fall of Copenhagen, which took place on the 7th of September. But to prevent surprise from any lurking parties of the enemy, which might still have kept together, and to deprive them of the means of injuring us, strong detachments were sent out to scour the country, and to bring in all the military arms they could discover. A party of this description, consisting of 100 cavalry, and 100 of my battalion mounted on light waggons, traversed the country for a considerable distance, and returned after having discovered and taken possession of ten pieces of ordnance of small calibre, and forty rifles belonging to the Kallundburg rifle company, with several muskets. They also gained correct information respecting the regular troops that had been lately opposed to us, and found they had retired into the islands of Falstar and Meon.

On the capitulation of Copenhagen, terms of amity and peace were entered into between the Danish forces in the island of Zealand and the British; but these did not extend to the islands before mentioned, nor to the other parts of his Danish Majesty's dominions; consequently, we still remained at war with such of his forces as were not included in the capitulation; and he might at any time have collected an army, had he been able, and attacked us without any infringement of those terms. It behoved our generals, therefore, to watch against any attempt of this nature; and accordingly strong outposts were established all along the Belt, composed principally of the men of our two battalions. The 1st battalion occupied Kallundburg, Slagelse, Korsoer, and Skielskiore; whilst the following towns and ports were occupied by my battalion, viz. Mestyed, Lundbye, Wordingburg and Prestoe; thus forming a complete chain of posts around the west and south coasts of the island. We remained so posted till the 15th of October, by which time the greater part of the naval stores taken in the dockyard having been taken on board, and the period fast approaching for our evacuation of the country, we began to retire towards Copenhagen, which we reached on the 17th, and immediately embarked on board the Princess Caroline, a Danish seventy-four which had been surrendered with the others of that fleet, and which are mentioned below.★

We remained in the roads till the 20th, when the fleet dropped

---

★ List of Ships and Vessels captured at Copenhagen. 7th September. 1807.

	Guns.		Guns.
Christian the Seventh....	98	Three Crowns.....	74
Neptune.......	84	Shield.......	74
Walderaer......	84	Crown Princess Maria.....	74
Princess Sophia Fredrica..	84	Denmark.......	74
Justice.......	74	Norway.......	74
Heir Apparent Frederick...	74	Princess Caroline....	74
Crown Prince Frederick...	74	Conqueror......	64
Frien........	74	Norge.......	74
Oden.......	74	Dalmakin......	64
Pule........	44	Elbe........	20
Wory Wife......	44	Eydeman......	20

down towards the Sound; and on the 21st the whole passed the Castle of Elsineur, with a favourable and pleasant breeze, the British ensign waving proudly from the lofty masts of their late gallant fleet; it must have been an extremely galling sight for them (the Danes) to witness, and I dare say they did not pray for many benedictions on our heads; I pitied them from the bottom of my heart. On taking leave of this country, I could not help remarking on the great similarity between its inhabitants and the Germans about Bremen—kind-hearted, hospitable, and inoffensive in the highest degree; and although suffering at that time so severely from the policy of our country, they were high in our praises as individuals and as a nation. I have great cause to speak well of those innocent and worthy people, for I have seldom experienced more kindness and attention than was shown me by them whenever circumstances rendered such kindness and attention suitable, particularly at Nestyde, where I met a young man who had formerly been in the West Indies, where he had learnt to speak a little English, (for of Danish I could not understand a word.) He introduced me to one worthy man, who had been an officer, and fought in the famous action of Kioge above narrated. Poor fellow, he felt heartily ashamed of the sorry attempt they had made to act the part of an army, and I daresay would gladly have blotted from his memory for ever the recollection of the ridiculous part they had acted. I was not aware of this circumstance at first, and when it was brought

	Guns.		Guns.
Liberty.......	44	Gluckstadt......	20
Iris........	44	Sarp........	18
Rotar.......	44	Glowman......	18
Denry.......	44	Nid Elvin......	18
Mayed.	36	Dolphin......	18
Triton........	28	Marcur.......	18
Fredrington......	28	Cousier.......	14
Kline Belt......	28	Flying Fish......	14
St Thomas......	22		—
Tylto........	24	Total. 40	

Together with eleven gun boats. with two guns each in the bow and fourteen do. with one gun in the bow and one astern.

upon the tapis in the course of conversation, (my young friend being interpreter,) I unluckily said, that "any man armed with a bludgeon only, could easily beat three such soldiers."

I felt quite ashamed of myself afterwards, when I discovered that he, poor man, had made one in that memorable action; but he took it all in good part, apparently conscious of the justness of my remark. Indeed, I was partly led on to use such expressions by the young fellow condemning so bitterly their conduct, and which I afterwards would have given something to have unsaid. He, however, bore no resentment, and kindly took me home and introduced me to his wife, and requested me to salute her with a kiss. I hesitated, thinking that I could not have understood him right, and feeling awkward in such a situation; but my young friend assured me it was the custom there to do so, on which I of course complied. They are, in my opinion, an extremely moral race of people, no vices that I know of being practised by them, save occasionally a little drunkenness by some few individuals. I heartily wish them well.

We sailed, as I said before, on the 21st of October, and had fine weather till we arrived in Yarmouth Roads. We passed one Sunday on our voyage home, at a certain hour of which our pious naval commander (Lord Gambier) made signal for the whole fleet to lay to, and have divine service, that is, in such ships as there were chaplains on board of. This caused the irreligious and profligate part of our people on board the *Princess Caroline* to blaspheme and storm at a terrible rate, for being so long detained when the wind was so fair.

It happened, when we arrived in the Roads at Yarmouth, or near there, I think it was on the Galloper Sand, that a tremendous gale began to blow, which baffled all exertions to withstand it. We cast out the anchors, but without effect, for we ran away with them both, and in the endeavour to vere out cable, or rather by the rapidity with which it was dragged out of the ship by the force of the wind, our bits caught fire, which with considerable difficulty were got extinguished after great exertions. During the gale, I understand a sailor was blown off the foreyard; and nearly at the same moment a woman, one of our corporals' wives, fell down the hatches into the hold, and broke her back, of which, indeed, she afterwards recovered, but never after regained her upright posture.

Those scoffing gentlemen before mentioned, attributed the whole of our misfortunes to the delay occasioned by the divine service before adverted to, and were not sparing of invective against the individual who caused its performance, forgetful, it would seem, that He, whom that commander invoked on that day, holds the winds in His hand, and can at pleasure let them loose upon an ungodly fleet, whether for correction or judgment, at what time, and in what manner, best pleases him. I doubt not the excellent commander alluded to has been a blessing to many. May he long continue to ornament the exalted station he fills! We weighed again after the storm abated, and proceeded round to the Downs, and the next day, the 16th of November, landed at Deal, and from thence marched to our old quarters at Hythe Barracks.

Chapter Eight
To the Peninsula

Some little time after our return from the Baltic, I obtained a short leave of absence, for the purpose of visiting my parents, and the other members of my family; and, during my stay in my native village, contracted a marriage with a young woman whom I had known from my boyhood, she having been one of my earliest schoolfellows. I cannot say that I enjoyed in the marriage state that happiness which I expected from it, partly owing to the frequent and long separations which my calling rendered unavoidable, and partly from other causes which have no connexion with my narrative. I believe, during the eight years which my wife lived after our union, I spent more than six of these in absence from her.

At the expiration of my leave, we set off to join the regiment, which still remained at Hythe, where we remained till the beginning of September following, when my battalion having again been ordered for foreign service in the; expedition fitting out for Corunna, it became indispensable that my poor wife should return to Northumberland, and remain under the protection of her parents, till my return, should it please God to spare me. This, no doubt, was a severe trial to us both, but particularly to her, who had such a journey to undertake, alone and unprotected, and she at the time far advanced in pregnancy; but, however distressing, it must be undertaken, and I unfortunately could not be spared from the regiment, for our orders were to proceed immediately to Ramsgate, for embarkation.

We parted, after I had accompanied her as far as I was able, and seeing her safely stowed in the coach. It may be supposed that a new-married pair, under such circumstances, would part with heavy and afflicted hearts.

My battalion embarked at Ramsgate on the 10th of September. On this occasion, I was very fortunate in getting on board an excellent transport, called the *Nautilus*, of Shields, commanded by Captain Watson (my wife's maiden name), and the steward, a native of the Hermitage, a place within four miles of my home. Of course, we were mutually glad to meet each other, and often talked over old Northumbrian stories, which recalled delightful recollections of our younger years. The fleet in which we sailed rendezvoused at Falmouth, whence we took our departure, and arrived at Corunna on the 26th of October.

On our passage, when we made Cape Ortegal, a pilot-boat came off, in which were the first Spaniards I remember to have seen; certainly, they did not prepossess me greatly in favour of their countrymen, but they are now so well known in England, that a description of those I here saw, would be only to repeat what has been so often and so much better told by others. We landed at Corunna, as before said, on the 26th, and a day or two after, proceeded up the country, halting for the first night at Betanzos. Our force consisted of cavalry, infantry, and artillery, in all, about 10,000 men, and was commanded by General Sir David Baird, and intended to co-operate, or form a junction, with that under Sir John Moore, then in Portugal, and who was then advancing into Spain.

My battalion, and some companies of the first battalion of my regiment, formed the advanced guard, a situation which I consider the most enviable of any in the army—-for here all is untried, and, as it were, unbroken ground; every thing is fresh, and although attended sometimes with a little more danger of being cut off while separated from the main body, yet possessing so many countervailing advantages, that I hesitate not to say it is the most desirable post of any in an army.

At Betanzos, we began to experience the great defective-ness of our commissariat department, at this period of our history; for the gentleman sent forward to provide our two battalions with food, was so utterly unacquainted with his business, that he was actually afraid to make an attempt to issue provisions. Although bread had been baked by order of the Spanish authorities, he not understanding, as he said, the Spanish weights and measures, durst not issue any thing without his own, which were behind; but it was evident the troops could not remain without provisions. We were here, as in most of the towns we afterwards passed through, lodged in convents, the officers generally either being quartered on the inhabitants of the town, or lodged by the monks in their cells. On these occasions the men occupied only the corridors, into which straw was generally put by the authorities of the place, the men lying as close as pigs in a sty, which indeed was necessary to keep each other warm; but these lodgings were not to be complained of, as clean straw, and shelter overhead in that country, are no contemptible quarters.

We moved forward by fair and easy stages, by way of Lugo, Villa Franca, Cacabelos, and Astorga; this latter place we reached on the 19th November, but during the march, we had experienced considerable difficulty in obtaining supplies both of provisions and the means of transport. This is a considerable town, containing probably about 5000 inhabitants. Both it and Lugo are surrounded by old Moorish walls, which may formerly have been considered strong, but which, according to the present mode of warfare, would offer but a feeble resistance to a besieging army. It contains a number of convents, both in the town and suburbs, and, of course, a proportionate number of idle monks, &c. Here, as in many towns in Spain, they have a curious mode of keeping out of their houses unwelcome visiters; for the doors being all made remarkably strong, and kept constantly shut, you cannot enter till the inmates have first reconnoitred you through an aperture above the door, made for the purpose; and it is not till they are satisfied who you are, and with your business, that they will open the door, which they generally do by a cord communicating with the latch from their peep-hole above. Here we were pretty plentifully supplied with provisions, and rested for some days, my battalion having been pushed forward to a village called Zalada, about a league in front of the town. After having been refreshed by a few days' rest, my battalion was again pushed forward, and occupied the town of Labeneza, about four leagues in front of Astorga, while the main body of the army assembled in and around that town; but we had not remained more than a few days in Labeneza, before a report arrived of

72

the enemy being in our front, and advancing in force; and we were consequently recalled to Zalada, in order to form a junction with our main body. Not long after this, about the latter end of November, orders were received from Sir John Moore, for our division to retreat and fall back upon Corunna. This measure, I understand, was rendered necessary, in consequence of the Spanish armies having been completely beaten and dispersed, so that nothing remained to oppose an overwhelming French force, which it was ascertained had entered Spain, but the few British troops comprising the armies under Sir John Moore, and ours.

We accordingly set to the right-about, and fell back as far as Cacabelos, the main body occupying Villa Franca and its neighbourhood. This movement was not by any means liked by any of us; for, independent of its being so uncongenial to the spirit of Britons to turn their backs upon an enemy, we felt disappointed at what we saw and heard of the celebrated Spanish patriots. We had been given to understand that the whole nation was up in arms against the French, and that we should have been received, on entering their country, as liberators, and treated as brethren, but in both these points we were miserably disappointed; for, instead of a hearty welcome on our arrival, we could with great difficulty obtain leave to land, and still more to obtain the necessary supplies of carriages and provisions to enable us to come forward; and with regard to the patriotism of the people, whatever might have been their good-will to act in defence of their beloved country and Ferdinand, they appeared as little likely as any people I had ever seen, to effect any thing against such an enemy as the French. In fact, those of them who formed their armies, at least of those straggling parties we so often met, could be called nothing better than mere rabble—no organization, no subordination, but every one evidently pursued that plan which seemed right in his own eyes.

While we remained at Cacabelos, (a place famous for good wine,) many were the schemes adopted by some of our bibbers, to obtain a sufficient quantum of this excellent beverage. I understand they occasionally borrowed each other's clothes; that is, a 43rd man would borrow a rifleman's green jacket, and vice versa, and

73

go and steal, or in some other illegal mode obtain, a camp-kettle full or two; and when the owner came to point out the person who had robbed him, of course he could not be found.

We had not remained above a day or two in our new quarters, before an express arrived from Sir John Moore, with orders for us to advance again immediately; and which, notwithstanding we had little or no prospect of assistance and co-operation from the Patriots, was cheerfully complied with. We retraced our former steps, passing through Astorga and Labeneza, and reached Benevente on the 15th December.

Our cavalry, consisting of the 7th, 10th, and 15th hussars, under Lord Paget, had by this time come up from Corunna, and had been pushed forward to join Sir John Moore's force; they fell in with a party of the French cavalry at the town of Rueda, not far from Tordesillas, and of which they either killed, or took prisoners, nearly the whole; in fact, through the whole of this service, nothing could exceed the gallantry and intrepid conduct of our cavalry under his lordship. At this town, as well as at Astorga and Villa Franca, depots of provisions began to be formed soon after our arrival.

On the 17th December, we again advanced from Benevente, in order to form a junction with Sir John Moore's army, and passing through Valderas, Majorga, and Sahagun, we reached the convent of Trianon, about a league in front of the latter place. On the 20th, here the two forces were united, and a fresh distribution into brigades took place. Ours, under Brigadier-General Crawford, was termed the Light Brigade, and consisted of the 1st battalion 43rd, 2nd battalion 52nd, and the 3rd battalion of my regiment.

The whole army was assembled in this neighbourhood, and consisted of about 26,000 men, the whole now under the command of Sir John Moore. Previous to our arrival at Sahagun, Lord Paget, with a part of the 10th and 15th hussars, discovered that a considerable body of the enemy's cavalry occupied that town. He therefore detached the 10th by a circuitous road, while he with the 15th approached it by the more direct one. They were, however, discovered by the French before reaching

74

the town, which gave the enemy time to turn out and form to receive the attack. His lordship, when a favourable opportunity offered, charged the French, who were greatly superior in numbers, and completely overthrew them, taking two colonels, eleven other officers, and about 150 men.

On the evening of the 23rd, the whole army was put in motion, with an intention, it was said, of attacking Marshal Soult, who, with a corps of about 16 or 18,000 men, was posted behind the River Carrion, his head-quarters being at Saldanha. The Spanish General Romana, was to take a part in this movement; his small and sadly inefficient force had approached the left of our army, or rather we had drawn towards his position, and he was, I believe, perfectly willing to lend all the assistance in his power, in the contemplated attack; but our General, I fancy, did not calculate upon any material help, from a force so greatly out of order as his was said to be. Soon after dark, the troops fell in; and as it was understood an attack was going to be made on the enemy, every pulse beat high, in expectation of soon congratulating each other on a victory- All was life and animation; and the necessary preparations, by the light of our blazing fires, for such an event as a battle, after the many long and harassing marches we had had, gave an interesting appearance to the scene.

When all was ready, the troops moved forward. It was a cold and bitter night, and there were some small brooks on the road. An officer of my battalion, who was not very well, when he came to one of those, instead of marching straight through, as it appears had been ordered, went a little way round by the bridge, although not off the road. A certain general officer, who happened to be there at the time, observed it, and getting into a great rage at the officer leaving his section, made him turn back, and march through and through repeatedly, by way of punishment. Such a mode of treating an officer, certainly appeared rather harsh; but this general piqued himself on his being able to make his brigade better marchers than any other troops in the army; and in this he certainly succeeded, although it was not without frequent exhibitions, such as the above. Our people had not gone far, however, till they were countermanded, and returned back to our convent. I rather think the main body of the army had not moved out of their cantonments; but ours being the advanced brigade, it was necessary we should move before the others.

It appears Sir John Moore, just before he intended to set out, had received information, not only of Soult having been greatly reinforced, but that several strong corps of the French army were marching directly upon us, by which, should he delay only a few days, we should be completely surrounded, and cut off from a retreat. This was most distressing information, for never was an army more eager to come in contact with the enemy than ours was at this moment, and never was there a fairer prospect of success, had things remained as they were; but now, instead of honour and glory being acquired, by showing the French what British troops could do in the field, it was evident nothing remained but to commence a retrograde movement, the worst and most unpleasant, in a British soldier's view, of any other.

Winter had now completely set in; the face of the country being covered with deep snow, the weather was unusually severe. Our prospect, therefore, was by no means a pleasant one. To commence a retreat in front of a greatly superior force, and with the probability that other French armies might be before us, and intercept our retreat upon the sea, which was distant from us nearly 250 miles, with the country in our rear being already exhausted of every thing that could contribute to our support, and with such excessively bad weather to perform the retreat in, rendered it, I may say, as unpleasant a situation as troops could well be placed in. Added to which, our commissariat was by no means so efficient in those days as they have latterly become; and our troops in general being young, and unaccustomed to privation, it was but too obvious, that should the retreat continue long, many would be the disasters attending it. On Christmas day, our brigade, as the rear of the infantry, commenced its uncomfortable retreat, and continued marching till late at night, when we reached a convent near Majorga. The next day, although we started early, we only reached the village of St Miguel about midnight.

Here I had considerable difficulty with the baggage. I had

had charge of it all day, my guard being composed of officers' servants, &c, who, the moment they got into the village, set off to their masters, and left me alone with the mules, the troops having, by the time I got in, all lain down to sleep. Several of the muleteers had been pressed into the service against their wills, and of course would have made their escape whenever an opportunity offered. I was therefore compelled to drive them all into the churchyard, and watch them myself, till luckily, after waiting in this situation a considerable time, without daring to go to sleep after the fatigues of such a day, some men happened to wander in that direction in search of meat, by whom I sent to our quartermaster to request he would send a guard, which he did soon after, and I had the happiness to be allowed to throw myself down and take some rest.

This day Lord Paget had another brush with the French cavalry, who, being apprized of our retreat, had advanced to Majorga. He attacked them with that gallantry which shone so conspicuously in the cavalry during the whole of this service, and completely overthrew them, killing and wounding many, and taking a number prisoners; in this affair the 18th Hussars were engaged, and behaved nobly. The next day we reached Castro Gonzales, and Castro Pipa. At the latter village, my battalion halted for the night and the next day. These two villages command the passage over the river Eslar, they being about equidistant from the bridge, and something more than a mile apart on high ground over the river, which runs about a league in front of Benevente. Here we were obliged to remain during the time mentioned, in order that the heavy divisions of the army might get sufficiently forward before we moved. I had still the charge of the baggage, and not knowing where my battalion was to be quartered for the night, I had crossed the Eslar to the Benevente side, till I learnt long after dark that Castro Pipa was its quarters.

I consequently turned back and recrossed the river, and just as I reached the end of the bridge, I heard a shot immediately in my front. The 43rd regiment guarded the bridge. It turned out to be a patrol of the enemy's cavalry who had come close to the top of the slope leading down to the bridge, and where a double sentry of the 43rd was posted. By some accident these two men were not loaded; the French dragoons were consequently permitted to come close up to them without their being able to give any alarm. One of them, however, run his bayonet into one of the Frenchmen's horses, and retreated, but the other was not only cut down with the sabre, but had a pistol fired at him, which was the report I had just heard. I saw the wounded man, who was severely hurt, but whether he survived or not I know not.

When I reached Castro Pipa, my commanding-officer would scarcely credit the report I gave him, conceiving it impossible the French could be such near neighbours. I was a good deal chagrined at his suspecting my veracity, but he had never been what I may call a friendly commanding-officer to me, as the story of the rifle at Copenhagen will prove; indeed, as I had been put into the situation I held contrary to his wish, it was hardly to be expected that he would show himself very friendly. During the night, however, our quarters were beat up, not indeed by the enemy, but by our brigadier, who was not sparing of his censure for our want of alertness in turning out. Indeed, we neither had so good a look-out as we ought to have kept, nor did we get under arms with that promptitude which was desirable, and from the cause before assigned; that is, that our commandant did not believe the enemy was so near.

I own I was not sorry that the General paid us such a visit, as it not only put us more upon our guard, a thing so indispensably necessary in the presence of an enemy, but it gave me some satisfaction for the dishonour put upon me by disbelieving my information.

The enemy did not disturb us during the remainder of the night, and next morning the brigade was assembled on the height above, and in front of the bridge; considerable bodies of the enemy's cavalry appearing in the plain before us. Some skirmishing between our people and the enemy took place, but nothing of any importance occurred. Our brigade was left in this position to cover the working party who were preparing to blow up the bridge, at which they worked all day; during the night our people were withdrawn from the farther side, and the explosion soon after took place, but the destruction of the bridge was by no means so effectual as was wished and expected. When we turned out in the morning to move towards the bridge, I (still having charge of my battalion's baggage) discovered that a vast quantity of excellent biscuit was stored up in an empty house in the village, which, no doubt, had been baked for the purpose of supplying the magazine at Benedetti; and as our people had been but very indifferently supplied with bread since we commenced the retreat, I determined to load a bullock-cart with it, and try to get it to a place of safety, where I hoped to be able to issue it to them.

I accordingly took a cart and two bullocks, there being plenty in the village, and apparently without owners, for the inhabitants had mostly either abandoned the place on the appearance of the French, or had hid themselves, I loaded the cart, but still I wanted a person to drive it; and although I used both promises and threats, I could not prevail upon any person to go with me. I therefore mounted the cart myself, and using my sword by way of a goad, I entered the river at a place which looked like a ford, and had the good fortune to reach the other side in safety. I mention this to show that so much importance need not have been attached to the destruction of the bridge, as both here, and near Castro Gonzales, the river was perfectly fordable, for pear the latter place the French cavalry forded it on the following morning.

I now made my way to Benedetti, where I remained during the day of the 28th; and at night, as before hinted, the troops which had been guarding the bridge arrived, leaving cavalry piquets on the plain between the town and the river. The next morning our people left Benevente, and as I was a little behind them with the baggage, on my reaching a height in rear of the town, I observed in the plain in front a considerable body of the enemy's cavalry, who had, as before stated, crossed the river near Castro Gonzales, and were advancing towards the town, opposed, though feebly at first, by the few of our cavalry left there on piquet; but the cavalry regiments which were in town quickly turning out to their support, they were at length completely able to oppose, and finally overthrow them.

During the time I remained here, I saw our brave dragoons make three most gallant and successful charges against superior numbers of the enemy, completely breaking and dispersing the different bodies against which the charges were made. The enemy appeared to be drawn up in different lines, the front one of which was that always charged; and I observed, that as our people advanced upon them, they were always received with a fire either from the carbines or pistols of the enemy, but this never appeared in the least to check the ardour of the charge, for in a minute or two after I observed the French troops retired in confusion, and formed behind the other lines. At length they were completely driven back to the ford by which they had crossed; and in a charge now made upon them, General le Febvre, with about seventy men, fell into our people's hands.

These troops were a part of Bonaparte's Imperial Guard, and the flower of his army, being fine-looking men, dressed in dark-green long coats, with high bear-skin caps, and mustaches, which gave them a formidable appearance. It was said that Bonaparte was looking on at this affair, and witnessed the defeat of his hitherto invincible Old Guard; it is certain that he slept the night before at Villalpando, a place only four leagues distant from the field.

I now set off and overtook the baggage and the bullock cart, not having had an opportunity of issuing the biscuit; but before I had proceeded above a few miles, the bullocks knocked up, and notwithstanding every exertion I found it impossible to get them any farther. Thus was I reluctantly compelled to abandon a cart-load of excellent biscuit, after having had so much trouble with it, at the time when I knew it was greatly needed by my hungry fellow soldiers, and to whom it would have been a most welcome offering. On this day's march, a most lamentable number of stragglers were overtaken by us, we being in rear of all the infantry; they had either fallen out from excessive fatigue, or from having (as in too many instances) drunk too much; indeed, the destruction of the magazine of provisions at the place we had left, enabled too many of them to obtain by one means or other considerable quantities of spirits, and which, of course, rendered them incapable of marching. This was a long and wearisome day's journey of nearly thirty miles; we did not reach Labeneza till late at night, where a considerable quantity of ammunition was obliged to be destroyed, the animals failing which drew it.

The next day we reached our old quarters at Zalada, a league in front of Astorga, where we halted for the night, the remainder of the brigade going into the town. It was to this village, it may be remembered, that we were sent on our first advance, and subsequently after our first retreat from Labeneza; but besides these movements from the village and back again, during the time we remained in it, we almost every morning had orders to pack up and move a short distance out of the place. This was done no doubt to accustom us to a ready turning out, as till this period our baggage had been transported on bullock-carts; but now we had mules, and it was necessary to accustom those whose duty it was, to load the mules with dispatch. But on every occasion of this kind, the inhabitants always imagined we were actually going to leave them, and the moment we were clean gone, as they thought, they set to work and rung the church bell with all their might. This was either to testify their regret at losing our company, or to evince their gratitude to Heaven for having got rid of such a band of heretics, by which their most pure and holy dwellings had been defiled; it was laughable to see the long faces they put on when we, so contrary to their hopes and expectations, always returned to our wretched and uncomfortable quarters.

During the whole of the time we remained in this village, I, as a staff-sergeant, could find no better lodgings than a dirty open shed; the reader will therefore judge how ill the privates must have been off. Our fellows began about this time to pick up little bits of Spanish, and would often exercise their ability to converse in the native tongue, by telling the inhabitants that we were certainly going to *"marcha manana"* that is, to march to-morrow, so that it became quite a by-word, which annoyed our hosts not a little. If I mistake not, the Padre of this village was a great knave, and did not scruple to help himself to such things as he had a mind for, belonging to our officers, whenever

81

a fit opportunity presented itself. The next day, the 31st, we moved into Astorga, where we halted for an hour or two, till the destruction of the magazine there was completed, although nothing but rum remained; and here I witnessed such a brutal and swinish eagerness for drink as was quite disgusting. The rum casks were ordered to be staved, and to let the contents run out on the street, that they might not fall into the hands of the enemy: thus the rum which had cost so much trouble in bringing up all the way from Corunna was about to be lost for ever; a thing most heart-rending to the numerous soldiers looking on, who loved it so dearly. However, they were determined not to lose all, for when the heads of the casks were knocked in, and their contents permitted to run in streams down the gutters, some of those brutes deliberately took off their greasy caps, and laving up the m and the mud together, drank, or rather ate, the swinish mixture. What noble soldiers would our country produce, were not that detestable vice of drunkenness so common among us; but to it how many have I seen deliberately sacrifice their own and country's honour, nay their very life itself, rather than forego the beastly gratification!

All this morning we had been told to keep a sharp lookout on the Leon side of Astorga, for the enemy was every moment expected to make his appearance from that quarter; however, we were not disturbed during the short time we remained. We here fell in with a considerable body of Romana's army, apparently all confusion, and destitute of every thing. We understood that they were not to be marched in the same line we were taking, but that it had been concerted between the two generals that our route should be kept free; however, here, and for several days afterwards, we suffered greatly from their contiguity.

We continued our march, from Astorga the same day, and reached at night the village of Foncevadon, about twenty miles distant. Here we pigged in as well as we were able, there being only five or six houses; but as we had a few tents with us, we managed not amiss. Till now our brigade had formed the rear of the infantry, there being some cavalry in rear of us; but it was now determined that ours and the Light German Brigade under

Brigadier-general Charles Alten, should strike off from the great road, and take the route for Orense and Vigo. This was done, I understand, with a view to secure a passage across the Minho at the former place, should Sir John, with the main army, be compelled to retreat in that direction, and probably with the view also of drawing off a part of the enemy's overwhelming force from the pursuit of that body, and to induce them to follow us into the mountains. Notwithstanding this, they continued to pursue Sir John on the great road, whilst they left us free altogether.

I beg to notice here, that both Mr Gifford and Mr Moore (Sir John's brother), have fallen into a trifling error respecting the period of our separation from the main body, they both making us be detached before our arrival at Astorga, whereas it was not till we had passed a day's march beyond it that we were sent off. The thing is of no consequence, only it is as well to be correct.

The next day, the 1st of January 1809, we marched by a most difficult road through the mountains, to Ponferrada, situated about a league to the left of the great road to Co-runna, on which the main army was retreating. When we got in, our commissary immediately made a requisition to the Alcalde of the town, to provide bread for the two brigades, as we began to be in most fearful want. He promised to set the bakers to work immediately, and in a few hours, he said, the bread would be ready. We called on him repeatedly, without obtaining any, he still alleging it was not yet quite ready, and putting us off from time to time, till midnight, when the patience of our commissary being fairly worn out, he yielded to the anger so naturally inspired by such shuffling conduct, and used some strong language to the Alcalde. Whereupon, we discovered at once that he had been only amusing us with promises he did not intend to fulfil; and told the commissary that he did not fear any of his threats, for that, as Romana's army had now also entered the town, he had no doubt they would protect him, and revenge any insult offered to him. The commissary had indeed talked about hanging him for his double-dealing, and leaving the troops utterly starving; but if he could have got any bread ready, it is most natural to suppose he would prefer letting his own countrymen have it;

this, however, as might be expected, had a most pernicious effect upon our suffering soldiers, for when provisions could not be procured in the regular and ordinary mode, it is evident they would take them wherever they were to be found —for hunger is not easily borne, accompanied by incessant fatigue.

In the morning, when we turned out to continue our march towards Orense, we heard a heavy firing towards our right and front, and this proved to be an attack made by the enemy's light troops upon our first battalion, who, with some cavalry, had been left in Cacabelos as a rearguard. Our first battalion gained great credit for their conduct on this occasion. The force of the enemy greatly exceeded ours, yet our people drove them back with great loss, killing General Colbert, who commanded the advance. This was done by a noted pickle of the name of Tom Plunkett, who, fearless of all danger to himself, got sufficiently nigh to make sure of his mark, and shot him, which, with the fire of the others, caused great havoc in the enemy's ranks, and set them flying to the rear much faster than they advanced. Our situation was thus, in a manner, in rear of the enemy's advance guard, yet they did not turn in our direction. Cacabelos was distant from us only about a league.

Our road this day lay over high and almost inaccessible mountains, deeply covered with snow. On the top of one of these, as our General was passing the column, a cry was passed from the rear to open out to allow him to pass, the road being very narrow. One of our men, as the General came near, happened to say, loud enough for him to hear, that "he had more need to give us some bread," or words to that effect, which so exasperated the General, that he instantly halted the whole brigade, ordered the man to be tried by a drum-head court-martial, and flogged him on the spot. It was a severe, but perhaps necessary discipline, in order to check in the bud the seeds of murmuring and insubordination, although I own it appeared harsh.

Our march was a long and toilsome one indeed, and did not terminate till about ten at night, when we reached St Domingo-Flores, where nothing could be procured but a very small quantity of black bread, the village being quite small. Tired with the journey, we felt rather inclined to sleep than eat; and, wet and dirty as we were, we laid ourselves down till dawn, when we commenced another such day's march, and reached at night the village of La Rua. During these two days, want and fatigue had compelled many to fall out, some of whom, no doubt, perished in the snow on the bleak mountains, over which our road, or rather path, had lain; others fell into the hands of the enemy, and some few rejoined us after having obtained some little refreshment from the natives.

It would but be a repetition of the privations and fatigues we underwent, to notice all that befell us on our way thence to Orense, which place we reached on the 7th of January, having previously pushed on, by double forced marches, a few hundred men, to take possession of the bridge over the Minho at this place. Here we remained a day, and obtained provisions, then much needed by us all, for the men had been literally starving for several days past. We had time and opportunity here also to strip and change our linen, that is, those who had a change; the others washed the shirt they took off, sitting without one till it was dry. Indeed, by this time we were in a most miserable plight; our shoes, of course, were nearly all worn out, and many travelling barefoot; and our clothes, as might be expected, were ragged and filthy in the extreme; indeed they could not be otherwise, for I suppose none of us had put any thing off since we commenced the retreat. This day's rest, however, refreshed us greatly, and enabled us to perform the remainder of our toilsome journey with more comfort; indeed, since we had secured the passage of the Minho, and thus prevented the enemy from getting in before us, our minds were more at ease, for strong apprehensions were entertained that the French would have detached a corps from their main body to seize this pass, and thus cut off our retreat to Vigo. A part of Romana's army entered Orense before we left it, worse, if possible, in point of appearance than ourselves; but they, in their best days, are more like an armed mob than regularly organized soldiers.

It is a pity that Romana did not adopt the plan pointed out to him by Sir John Moore, either to retire into the Asturias with his army unbroken, or hang upon the flanks of the enemy as he passed through the mountains; and which he could have done with ease and safety, for these fellows could live where regular troops would starve, and there was no doubt but the peasantry would have assisted their countrymen with all their means. This would have in some measure retarded the too rapid progress of the French, and probably been the means of saving to our country one of its bravest and most skilful generals.

Some of our men who had been compelled to stop behind from fatigue and starvation, rejoined us here, having generally been assisted by the peasantry, who gave them food, and helped them forward.

On the 9th, in the morning, we left Orense, crossing the Minho to the north side of that river, and continued our march to the town of Ribadavia, situated at the junction of the rivers Avia and Minho, both of which, from the melting of the snow, and the immense quantities of rain that had fallen, were greatly swollen. So much so, that when I approached the town with the baggage, (the troops having gone on before,) and which I did not reach till near midnight, I found the road completely overflowed with water; and being without a guide, I could not of course in the night be certain where the road lay, the whole bank of the river being completely under water. We were in consequence obliged to climb the mountains to our left, and proceed in the best manner we were able with the loaded mules; but so precipitous were they in one place, that a load of ammunition slid off the mule's back, and the casks rolled rapidly down the hill towards the river. I durst not venture to leave them, although my chance of finding them in such a situation appeared small indeed; however, we halted the remainder of the mules, while a few of us set off down the steep in the direction we had seen them go, and after a long and anxious groping in every hollow of the rocky mountain, succeeded in recovering them; but the powder in them, and indeed nearly all the ammunition we had, was rendered completely useless, from the constant heavy rain that had fallen. I am almost astonished that no accident happened to either man or beast in this perilous journey, for our feet literally "stumbled upon the dark mountains," without either guide or path, and where the ground was most uneven and dangerous. We however at length reached our destination, wet and weary enough, and, just as we entered the town, were informed that the corridor of one of the convents where two of our companies were sleeping, had just fallen to the ground with a tremendous crash, and that several men had had their limbs broken by the fall; I do not remember that any were killed. It being so late, I could not procure any kind of quarter, so I was fain to sit down by the side of a fire kindled in the yard of this convent for the remainder of the night.

We next morning resumed our journey, and in three days more from this place we reached Vigo. On this last day's march we had a pretty high eminence to ascend at some distance from the town, from which the view of the town, the shipping, and the sea, broke all at once upon us. It was a most delightful prospect, and it was highly amusing to observe the joy which seemed to animate the woe-worn countenances of our ragged and dirty soldiers. Fellows without a shoe or a stocking, and who before were shuffling along with sore and lacerated feet like so many lame ducks, now made an attempt to dance for joy; laughter and mirth, and the joke, now succeeded to the gloomy silence with which they had in general prosecuted their wearisome journey for several days past, as the friendly element before them promised shortly to put a period to long and toilsome wanderings. Indeed, although I am a bad sailor, and suffer always severely when at sea, I do not remember ever to have witnessed a sight which inspired me with greater pleasure than the shipping and the sea did on this occasion.

The fleet of transports for the army under Sir John Moore, was just clearing the bay as we came in sight, but we observed that a sufficient number remained at Vigo to transport us to our native land, a place we sorely longed for, as we had often contrasted the happiness and security and comfort of our friends at home, with the poverty and misery we had lately witnessed in the country we were leaving; and this no doubt increased our anxiety for the change. We marched into Vigo, and were soon after put on board the vessels destined to receive us. It was my fortune to be sent on board the *Alfred*, with two of our companies; a great number of men were still behind, for even the few last days' marches had deprived us of many who till then had braved the toils and privations of the journey, but who now had fairly sunk under exhaustion. The Commodore, therefore, remained as long in the bay as it was safe, sending the stragglers as they arrived on board the different ships; but within a few days after our arrival, the enemy entered the town, which of course precluded all hope of more escaping. We consequently weighed and stood out towards the outer bay, where we again came to anchor.

A Russian ship-of-war was in a small harbour in this bay, which it was intended to board and cut out. As we were then, I believe, on rather bad terms with that nation, never did I witness such alacrity and delight as our tars on board the Alfred manifested when buckling on their cutlasses for the occasion, and I feel certain that if confidence in themselves would tend to insure the victory, no men had a better chance of succeeding; but from some cause or other with which I am unacquainted, the enterprise was abandoned.

On the 21st January we weighed and stood out to sea; but a gale coming on we were obliged to come to anchor again under the shelter of the Isle of Bagona. We did hot get to sea till the 24th, but on the 25th we spoke a frigate going out to Lisbon with General Dyatt on board, who informed us of the fatal business at Corunna. Indeed the people on board this ship had, from vague reports, greatly magnified our loss on that occasion, telling us that the whole army had been nearly cut to pieces, and that very few indeed had been able to effect their escape. We each, of course, mourned for his particular friends, not doubting but they had fallen among the rest. I think it was the same night on which we saw this ship, a fatal accident had very nigh taken place. Our captain was the Commodore, and the captain of the *Hindostan* store-ship had charge of the rear of the fleet; his place was consequently always behind all the other vessels. Some time after dark, however, our lookout people gave notice of a large vessel on our starboard quarter. We shortened sail and let her come up pretty close to us, and made the private signal, but no answer was returned. At length, when near enough, we hailed her, but still no answer. An order was now given to stand to quarters and prepare for action, not doubting she was an enemy which had got among the fleet. The guns were accordingly run out, the matches lit, and every thing prepared for action. She appeared a large ship, but of what force they could not guess. Again she was hailed, and again she disregarded it. Our first lieutenant was now fully convinced she was an enemy, and pleaded hard with the captain to give the word fire, but the captain said he would hail her once more, and if she did not answer he would fire. Providentially they heard us this time, and answered it was the *Hindostan*. What they had been about I know not, for we were quite near each other; and had she received our broadside) as was the intention had she not then answered, it is most probable she would have gone down; at all events the consequences must have been awful, for she had the whole of the 43rd regiment on board, besides her own crew. Our captain certainly censured him in no very mild terms for leaving his station in the rear, and getting to the very head of the fleet. She was a very lofty ship, and carried forty-four guns I believe, and had not less than 1000 men on board, many of whom must have suffered had we fired upon her.

A few days after this we encountered a most tremendous gale, and came in sight of the English coast, somewhere near the Lizard or the Start; but our master not knowing exactly where he was, we stood off again towards the French coast.

The next day the gale was if possible more severe, and the ship rolled so much that they were afraid her guns would break loose from their lashings, in consequence of which large spikes were driven in behind the wheels of each gun-carriage to prevent such an accident. In this situation, I know not whether I did not almost wish myself on the snowy mountains of Galicia again, rather than where I was, so miserable a sailor am I, and so much do I suffer from sea-sickness.

The fleet was by this time completely scattered, every one making the best shift he could for himself; some got into Plymouth, some reached Portsmouth, and some, I believe, foundered in the gale, among which, if I mistake not, was a brig, on board of which my two companies had been first embarked, but were subsequently removed to the *Alfred*, and some of the German Legion, I think, put on board her.

At length we made the Isle of Wight, and subsequently Spithead, which we reached on the 31st, and the next day landed once more on the happy shore of our native Britain.

Thankful indeed I ought to have been for the ever watchful care of an indulgent and kind Providence, who had brought me safely through the toils and sufferings under which so many more robust and hardy than myself had sunk; but, alas! I had then no sense of the gratitude due for such unmerited favours, and instead of rendering thanks to Him who had thus preserved me, I entered, with all the eagerness of a person devoid of reason and religion, into every vice and sensuality that presented itself. I here learnt with sorrow the great loss which my friends in the first battalion had sustained, but glad nevertheless that it was not to the extent we apprehended, and that none of my particular friends had fallen.

We left Portsmouth, and returned to our old quarters at Hythe, in Kent, passing again on the road my native county militia at Battle, in Sussex, as I did at Bury, on my return from Holland; and truly our appearance on this occasion was, if possible, more deplorable than on the former. However, our tattered and worn-out habiliments had the effect of inspiring some of my countrymen in that regiment with a desire of sharing in the glory, as they termed it, of suffering so much in the defence of our beloved country; and they accordingly made up their minds to volunteer into our corps the first opportunity that offered, and which they put in execution that same year, as will be told hereafter. We took up our abode in the comfortable barracks at Hythe, and immediately set about putting every thing in order, and truly much was wanting to fit us again for duty as soldiers.

Chapter Nine
Quartermaster & Back to Spain

In April of this year, an order was issued to allow the militia regiments to volunteer, for the purpose of filling up the regiments of the line; and I was sent by Colonel Beckwith (our two battalions being then both at Hythe) to receive those who chose to volunteer from the Northumberland militia before-mentioned, which had now been removed to Ipswich.

Lieutenant Beckwith had the charge of our party, but proceeded incognito to Ipswich, the general orders not permitting officers of the line to be seen in the quarters of the militia. On our arrival at Ipswich, I had the pleasure of obtaining the names of thirty fine young fellows, among whom the patriots formerly mentioned of course were included. Several other militia regiments in this district also gave volunteers to us, so that in three days, from the commencement of the volunteering, we obtained upwards of 1100 men; and had we not, by an order from the Horse-Guards, been precluded from taking any more, I doubt not we should have obtained several hundreds besides, for our regiment alone had near eighty names down for us, who were not allowed to enter from the above cause.

Indeed the Commander-in-Chief, Sir David Dundas, (afterwards our Colonel,) appeared quite astonished, and not well pleased, that we had run away with so many men when others wanted them so much. He was obliged, however, to grant us a 3rd battalion, as we had so many more men than were required to fill up the 1st and 2nd; and our respected Colonel, Major-general Coote Manningham, dying about this time of the fatigue he had undergone in Spain, Sir David took us to himself, and became our Colonel-in-Chief, giving the command of the 3rd battalion to my respected (and now lamented) friend and benefactor, Major-general the Honourable William Stewart. The

Lieutenant-colonelcy was given to Major Norman M'Leod, our senior Major, and only two or three other steps were given to the officers of the regiment, although it was alone owing to their exertions in obtaining men, and to the high character the regiment had acquired, that such numbers had volunteered into it.

It becomes not me to censure or criticise the measures of government, but I cannot help thinking that more favour was certainly due to the corps as a body. For myself, I ought and must speak with gratitude, not of them, but of that kind Providence which has favoured me so far, so very far, beyond my deserts, for, on the 8th of June following, I was appointed Quartermaster of the 3rd battalion.

Our 1st battalion was again sent out to join the army in Portugal, while mine was sent to Brabournlees to equip and drill our new levies. Every exertion was made to this effect, and the battalion was soon completed and rendered fit for service. Here my wife joined me again, the child to which she gave birth in my absence having died when six weeks old. This was the only child she ever had, and it was perhaps a providential dispensation, for she was extremely delicate, and by no means a healthy person, and it is not unlikely her offspring might have inherited her disease, that is, an affection of the chest. We had only lived a few months together, till another call for service separated us again.

In June 1810, we received orders to send out to Cadiz two companies of my battalion, together with the commanding-officer and staff, three others having been already sent thither in the spring. The melancholy business of parting with my wife was again to be gone through; but on this occasion I was favoured by being permitted to accompany her to London, where, parting from her with a heavy heart, I took my place for Chichester, at which place my detachment would be quartered next day, on their way to Portsmouth. I omitted to mention, that Lieutenant-colonel Barnard of the 1st or Royals, had exchanged with Lieutenant-colonel M'Leod some time previous, and he consequently was now going out as my commanding-officer. We embarked at Portsmouth on the 11th July, on board the *Mercury* frigate, armed *en flute*, and commanded by Captain Tancock.

We had a favourable passage, and landed at Cadiz on the 29th of that month. This city, it may be remembered, was besieged at this time by a French army under Marshal Victor; consequently, when we arrived, we were amused by seeing immense shells flying from one party to the other, but without doing any serious injury to either, the distance being too great to produce any effect of moment.

As we came in sight of Cadiz, the view was most enchanting, for the city appeared as if composed of lofty and elegant snow-white buildings, apparently rising from the bosom of the ocean, for the land on which it is built cannot be seen at a distance; added to which, the numerous and beautiful towns about the bay, and a little beyond it, rendered it a most delightful scene. On the right was Cadiz, with its lofty lighthouse, and its strong sea-walls rising out of the water; on the left was Rota, an apparently neat little town. Farther up the bay, on the same side, was Port St Mary's, and beyond that Porto-Real, both considerable towns. In the centre rises the Isla de Leon, now called St Ferdinand; beyond that Chiclana, composed of the elegant country residences of the more wealthy Cadiz merchants; and, in the distance, towering on the mountains behind, the dazzling white town of Medina Sidonia shining in the sun; indeed altogether imagination can scarcely picture to itself a more interesting *coup-d'oeil*, the scene being closed by the lofty snow-clad mountains of Ronda. We landed at Cadiz, and remained for the night in the barracks situated in the barrier, on the land-side of the town, and which is remarkably strong, the fortifications being composed of solid masonry, and the barracks all bomb-proof. I suffered dreadfully from the myriads of fleas which preyed upon me during the night, and was glad when morning appeared.

We marched next day to the Isla, (be it observed the town is called by that name as well as the island on which it and Cadiz are situated,) distant from Cadiz about seven miles; the island is of a most singular form, being about ten miles broad at the end next the continent, from which it is separated by the river Santi Petri; immediately below the town of Isla it begins to narrow very rapidly, forming from thence to Cadiz nothing more than a narrow sand-bank, in some places not more than a hundred yards across, and on which a causeway has been built to connect the two places. We took up our abode in the Isla, where the Spanish government, such as it was, at this time resided; and here I witnessed the first opening of the Spanish Cortes in 1810, which was attended with all the pomp and show of a truly Roman Catholic people. *Te Deums* and other pompous and brilliant ceremonies marked the event; indeed, here we had an opportunity of seeing a great number of the grandees of the Spanish nation, for, as I said before, the government had retired to this place from Madrid, and most of the courtiers and others attached to the government had assembled here, together with the deputies from the different provinces; altogether the scenes we witnessed here were sometimes very imposing.

The French occupied all the towns before named save Cadiz and Isla, their advanced piquets being thrown forward to near the river Santi Petri, except near the Bridge of Luaza, which is the only communication across from the island to the mainland; here our pickets were advanced a considerable distance beyond the bridge upon a causeway on which is the road leading to Seville, through a broad salt marsh on the banks of the river; it is here about two miles wide, and utterly impassable, except to those who know the footpaths across it, being intersected at every few paces by deep salt-pits or pans.

The enemy, as mentioned before, had their sentries at some parts pretty far into the centre of this marsh, and there were some fellows in the Spanish service called by the name of "creepers," they obtaining their livelihood by killing sea-fowl and other animals in this marsh; and so dexterous were they at this creeping, that they could steal upon the birds unperceived, which enabled them to get them with ease. Sometimes a fellow of this calling would set off on a creeping excursion, and instead of bagging a wild-duck, or some other such bird, would plunge his stiletto into the heart of an unsuspecting French sentry, and leave him weltering in his gore. This was a noble exploit in their estimation, and marks strongly the character of the Spaniard, who, inured to blood by the frequency of their bull-fights and other similar exhibitions, hesitates not a moment at assassination if urged on by what he deems his own or country's wrongs; this inhuman act, of course, was perpetrated in the dark.

I may mention, in connexion with this, that on the Christmas of 1810, it was reported that sixteen people had been assassinated in Isla alone, on the evening or night before; it is probable the number may have been exaggerated, but the thing was such an almost everyday occurrence that it appeared not to excite the least horror at its atrocity. I had occasion to go down the town during the Christmas day, and I saw still lying at the corner of one of the most frequented streets, one of the unhappy beings who had thus fallen. No one seemed inclined to own him; and his body, foul with blood and dust, was thus permitted to remain in the public streets without any enquiry being made with respect to the perpetrator of so foul a deed. In truth they are, as it were, trained up to this recklessness of human life from their infancy, for in the town of Isla there was a sort of naval academy, where a number of boys, from perhaps eight to twelve years of age, were educated; these urchins were permitted to wear swords, and it is really astonishing how desirous they appeared to make use of them, for they could scarcely ever pass along the streets without trying the sharpness of their points upon the backs of pigs or dogs, or any other unfortunate animal that came in their way.

The French also occupied a long low tongue of land which stretches out into the Bay of Cadiz, taking its rise from between Port St Mary's and Porto Real, and extending to within about two and a half miles of Cadiz, and about one from Puntalis, a fort erected on the island opposite the extremity of this low tongue; this is called the Trocadero, since become famous as the field on which the Duke D'Angouleme, and Prince Carignan of Naples, gained so many honours. On the point of this tongue the enemy's principal batteries were erected, and from thence they contrived occasionally, but not often, and never with any great effect, to throw shells into the town of Cadiz. The mortar now in St James' Park, called the "Prince Regent's bomb," was cast at Seville on purpose to enable them to reach the town, no ordnance of common dimensions being capable of throwing a shell so far; but it did not answer the end proposed, or at least the effect expected from it, for it was imagined by them, that if they could once succeed in throwing shells into the city, the inhabitants would become so alarmed that they would compel the military to surrender. This, however, was far from being realized, although they did throw a few in; but the distance being so great, they were necessarily thrown much at random, some of them falling short of the town, others flying completely over into the bay near the lighthouse on the other side, and some few, as I said, falling in the city, but from which very few casualties occurred.* I am told they were obliged to have the mortar slung in chains at the time of firing it, the concussion being so great as to destroy the bed in which it was fixed.

As may be supposed, there was constant war between our fort Puntalis, before mentioned, and the enemy's batteries on this point; in fact our people had orders to throw a thirteen-inch shell every quarter of an hour, besides the occasional firing from the guns and other mortars when any thing appeared on the opposite side; and you may be certain the French were not behind us in the expenditure of ammunition; they were remarkably fond of firing what are termed salvos, that is, volleys of artillery. On one occasion I happened to be looking out from a high tower near Isla, call the Tore Alto, and while all was deep and profound silence, and I happened to be looking towards the point of Trocadero, in a moment the smoke rose from at least 100 pieces of artillery, fired by signal, and the noise they made was tremendous. Our poor little fort of Puntalis appeared almost

---

* *The distance to which the French threw these shells is truly amazing. The longest range of heavy iron sea-mortars is only about 4200 yards, whereas the distance from the French batteries on the Trocadero to the nearest point of Cadiz was, I believe, 4500 or more; but they exceeded this considerably, for, as I said above, some of their shells fell in the sea beyond the town, near the lighthouse, a distance of at least 500 or 600 yards farther. The shells were always half filled with lead, to increase their flight, so that when they burst the mischief they occasioned was never extensive; I believe not more than about half-a-dozen individuals suffered from them in all.*

enveloped in the dust raised by the striking of the shot, and the smoke from them which fell about it, and seemed as if almost deprived of power by so sudden and unexpected a salute; but she began at length to return the compliment, although feebly in comparison of the tremendous volley she had received. This and such like were of frequent occurrence, scarcely a day passing without something interesting taking place.

To enable us to cope in some measure with the French, a large double fortified sea-mortar was brought from Gibraltar, which threw thirteen-inch shells. It was brought up to the back of the town of Isla, near some powder magazines, and an attempt made there to throw some shells over to the Trocadero. The first trial, an empty shell was put in, with not less than thirty-two pounds of powder in the chamber. On firing it, the shell flew all to atoms, from the violent shock occasioned by so great a quantity of powder; and the shell being too weak for that description of mortar, another was tried filled with sand, to give it more weight and solidity; this answered the purpose, for it fell on the land on the opposite coast, but still, from the great range, much uncertainty must naturally attend the practice, and it was eventually given up.

The next day, however, we were saluted from the opposite side with both shot and shell, the French thus showing us that they were better able to play at long bowls than we were; neither, however, did their practice continue, for there was nothing at the point where their shot and shells fell to be injured by them, the magazines before noticed being now empty.

On another occasion an attack was made by our people on the Trocadero itself, where it was reported the French had got a considerable number of boats, &c., laid up on shore, about halfway between the point and Porto Real; our folks took gun-boats and boats with rockets, the intention being to set fire to the enemy's Craft. They accordingly advanced in good style, keeping as far, however, as possible out of the range of the French batteries at the point, which, as they were directed towards Cadiz and Puntalis, could not easily bring their artillery to bear upon our boats. They reached the place where it was said the French craft was lying, and fired a considerable number of rockets, but without being able to effect any thing farther than burning one boat, I believe. As they were returning, however, they met the French commander, who had been down to the point in a light boat, and he, like a brave fellow, determined to run completely the gauntlet rather than return, keeping as close in shore, however, as possible. The whole of our gun-boats fired at him as he passed, and knocked the water up about him in all directions without ever once touching him, although, to look at him, one would have imagined it impossible he could escape; but here the old soldier's adage was verified, for there was still more room to miss than to hit him, and he accordingly escaped scot-free.

While here, I had a most ample opportunity of closely viewing the Spanish army, great numbers being stationed in and about the Isla, and great numbers constantly coming into and going out of the place, after receiving such equipment as the government was able to provide for them. Nothing could exceed the hardy and robust appearance of the men in general; and had they been clothed, appointed, and disciplined like either their enemies or their allies, there could not have been a finer soldiery. I cannot however, say so much for their officers; most of them appeared to be utterly unfit and unable to command their men. Those who had the means, seemed to think of nothing else but dressing like apes or mountebanks, and intriguing with the women. It was really absurd and ludicrous to see the strange figures they generally made themselves. In one regiment alone you might have observed more different uniforms than both we and the French have in all our armies. One would have had on a blue coat turned up with red, with a chaco and a straight sword, the uniform prescribed for officers of the infantry, I believe; the next would have most likely had on a hussar dress, with an enormous sabre dangling by his side; another would have had a red coat, a fourth yellow, a fifth white, and so on. In short, all the colours of the rainbow were generally exhibited in the uniforms of one regiment's officers; and every one of them appeared to vie with the other who could make the greatest harlequin of himself, whilst those of them who were mounted would caper and prance about the streets like so many fools, riding with their legs at full stretch, and the toe of the boot (if they had one) just touching the stirrup, and drawing the reins continually through the fingers of their right hand; and if by any chance an ape of this kind came near the window of his dulcinea, and thought there was a likelihood of her seeing him, I pitied the poor foot-passengers who might happen to be near him, for he would make his unfortunate Rosinante prance and caper by the immense long bit in its mouth, and the pieces of iron in the shape of spurs on his (shoes perhaps), till the poor animal was like to fall under him. In short, they had all the pride, arrogance, and self-sufficiency of the best officers in the world, with the very least of all pretension to have an high opinion of themselves; it is true they were not all alike, but the majority of them were the most haughty, and at the same time the most contemptible creatures in the shape of officers, that I ever beheld. It was, therefore, not to be expected that the soldiers would or could look upon them with that degree of respect and reverence so essential to a due maintenance of subordination in an army.

About the month of February 1811, it was concerted between the Spanish government and General Graham, who commanded us, to undertake an expedition which should land in the vicinity of Gibraltar; and being there reinforced by some troops from that fortress, the whole should move forward in the direction of Chiclana, and, taking the enemy in the rear of his works, compel him either to abandon them or fight a battle. Accordingly, on the 18th of that month, we embarked on board some small vessels that had been fitted up for the occasion in the bay of Cadiz, and, sailing soon after, we reached Algeziras, ten miles on this side of Gibraltar, and landed there on the 24th. Our force consisted of a brigade of artillery, with ten guns; two battalions of Foot Guards; the 28th, 67th, and 87th regiments; a battalion composed of flank companies from Gibraltar; two companies of the 47th regiment, and two of the 20th Portuguese regiment, with six companies of our corps and one squadron of cavalry,—in all about 4500 men. The Spanish army, under the command of General La Pena, (who, being senior officer, directed the whole,), consisted of two divisions,—in all from ten to eleven thousand. We were not allowed to take any baggage with us; consequently we could not expect much comfort during the service, which was expected to be short.

The day we landed we bivouacked on a height near Algeziras, and the next morning moved on towards Tarifa, where we remained for that day and the next, to allow time to get the artillery and cavalry horses on shore. Here I observed a strange custom among the females of this place, the remains, I apprehend, of the Moorish fashion, (which no doubt would continue longer in this place than others, it being immediately opposite to and in sight of Africa.) The Spanish women all wear what they term a mantilla, that is, a kind of scarf made of cloth, generally black, which they throw over their heads lengthwise, letting the two ends come over their shoulders, and meeting and crossing on the breast, it forms a sort of head-dress which shows only the face, and keeps them close and snug about the head; but here, they bring it so far forward as to completely cover the face, leaving nothing but a very small hole in front of their left eye (I think it is), at which they peep out, without showing any part of the face. Colonel Brown of the 28th, who was then a most wild and eccentric character, although now I understand completely altered, could not relish this hiding of their beauty by the modest dames of Tarifa. All, therefore, that he met in the streets he stopped, and made them open the mantilla, that he might have a fair peep at them, to the great scandal of the good ladies of this still Moorish town, and which, had it been on any other occasion, might have been attended with unpleasant consequences to himself.

When every thing was ready we moved forward from Tarifa, and halted for the night on a height about twelve miles distant. The next day we reached Casas Vejas, or "Old Houses," where we bivouacked on a scrubby hill, the weather being very bitter, which we felt in all its force, having no covering whatever. Next day we had to cross a considerable lake of fresh water, by a sort of ford which crossed it about the middle. We had started before day-light, and, through some mismanagement, did not reach this lake till near mid-day, although it was only a few miles distant from our last night's quarters. One division of the Spaniards led the column, and another was behind us, we being thus in the centre, as being the least thought of probably by our Spanish Commander-in-Chief; for indeed we had often heard it said in and about Isla, "what fine-looking and well-disciplined soldiers the British are!—what a pity they cannot fight!" So thought La Pena, probably; but by two o'clock the first division of Spaniards had not near got over the lake, at which the patience of our General was so completely exhausted, that he requested the Spanish General to allow him to bring forward the British troops, to show him the way how he and they would act. My battalion led the van, and were ordered to march straight through it without any picking of steps, and to go forward in regular sections, one man supporting another. They went in and marched right through it, as if it had been plain ground, the water taking them generally about mid-deep. The rest of the British army followed, and were all through in less than half an hour; a one-horse cart, indeed, stuck fast in the middle of it, from the wheels having got entangled between the large stones at the bottom. General Graham seeing this, instantly dismounted, and, plunging in, set his shoulder to the wheel, and fairly lifted it clear of the obstruction.

La Pena, and those about him, after witnessing the example set them by our General and his troops, seemed really ashamed of their former conduct, and, setting to in good earnest, they contrived to urge their soldiers and officers to take the water with more freedom, and before dark the whole army had got over. While we were so long detained by the first division of Spaniards getting across, I, with several other mounted people, rode forward to the ford, to ascertain the cause of our stoppage for so long a time. The Spaniards were going into the water one at a time,—here one, and there one,—while the creatures of officers were making the men carry them on their backs. Had the whole army acted thus, we should not have got over before day-light next morning.

When all were across, and the columns formed, we moved forward, and reached the neighbourhood of Veger, which stands on a high hill not far distant from the memorable Cape Trafalgar. We halted in an olive-grove below the town, and bivouacked for the night; it was bitter cold, and the troops could find but little wood for firing, which they much needed, from having got so completely wet in crossing the lake.

We remained at Veger all the next day, and a little after dark commenced our march. We being now in the neighbourhood of the enemy, it became necessary to conceal our movements as much as possible. During the night we passed the fishing town of Conil, and, keeping near the coast, we arrived the next morning on the plain of Chiclana. I quote from our General's dispatch, as it states the thing in a much more clear and satisfactory manner than I could do. He says:

"After a night march of sixteen hours from the camp (bivouack) near Veger, we arrived on the morning of the 5th on the low ridge of Barossa, about four miles from the Santi Petri river. This height extends inland about a mile and a half, continuing on the north the extensive heathy plain of Chiclana. A great pine-forest skirts the plain, and circles round the height at some distance, terminating down towards Santi Petri, the intermediate space between the north side of the height and the forest being uneven and broken."

The two Spanish divisions had preceded us, who, after having rested a while on the plain, moved down towards the Santi Petri, where a bridge was to be thrown over by the troops in (the Isla de Leon, and thus open a communication between the two armies, that is, between those inside the island and us.

The General goes on to say,—"A well-conducted and successful attack on the rear of the enemy's lines, near Santi Petri, by the vanguard of the Spanish army under Brigadier-general Ladrizabel, having opened the communication with the Isla de Leon, I received General La Pena's directions to move down from the position of Barossa to that of the Torre de Bermesa, about half-way to the Santi Petri river, over which a bridge had been lately established. This latter position occupies a narrow woody ridge, the right on the sea-cliff, and the left falling down to the Almanza creek, on the edge of the marsh; a hard sandy beach gives an easy communication between the western points of these two positions.

My division being halted on the eastern slope of the Barossa height, was marched about twelve o'clock through the wood towards Bermesa, (cavalry patrols having previously been sent towards Chiclana, without meeting with the enemy.) On the march I received notice that the enemy had appeared in force on the plain, and was advancing towards the heights of Barossa. As I considered that position as the key of Santi Petri, I immediately countermarched, in order to support the troops left for its defence; and the alacrity with which this manoeuvre was executed, served as a favourable omen. It was, however, impossible, in such intricate and difficult ground, to preserve order in the columns, and there never was time to restore it entirely. But before we could get ourselves quite disentangled from the wood, the troops on the Barossa hill were seen returning from it, while the enemy's left wing was rapidly ascending. At the same time his right wing stood on the plain, on the edge of the wood, within cannon-shot. A retreat in the face of such an enemy, already within reach of the easy communication by the sea-beach, must have involved the whole allied army in all the danger of being attacked during the unavoidable confusion of the different corps arriving on the narrow ridge of Bermesa nearly at the same time.

Trusting to the known heroism of British troops, regardless of the numbers and position of the enemy, an immediate attack was determined on. Major Duncan soon opened a powerful battery of ten guns in the centre. Brigadier-general Dilkes, with the brigade of Guards, Lieutenant-colonel Brown's (of the 28th) flank battalion, Lieutenant-colonel Norcott's two companies of the 2nd rifle corps, and Major Acheson, with a part of the 67th, (separated from the regiment in the wood,) formed on the right.

Colonel Wheately's brigade, (consisting of the 28th, 67th, and 87th,) with three companies of the Coldstream Guards, under Lieutenant-colonel Jackson (separated likewise from his battalion in the wood), and Lieutenant-colonel Barnard's flank battalion (being two companies 47th, two ditto 20th Portuguese, and four of third battalion 95th) formed on the left. As soon as the infantry was thus hastily got together, the guns advanced to a more favourable position, and kept up a destructive fire. The right wing proceeded to the attack of General Ruffin's division on the hill, while Lieutenant-colonel Barnard's flank battalion, and Lieutenant-colonel Bush's detachment of the 20th Portuguese, were warmly engaged with the enemy's tirailleurs on our left.

General Laval's division, notwithstanding the havoc made by Major Duncan's battery, continued to advance in very imposing masses, opening his fire of musketry, and was only checked by that of the left wing. The left wing now advanced firing. A most destructive charge, by the three companies of the Guards and the 87th regiment, supported by all the remainder of the wing, decided the defeat of General Laval's division.

The eagle of the 8th regiment of light infantry, which suffered immensely, and a howitzer, rewarded this charge, and remained in possession of Major Gough of the 87th regiment. These attacks were zealously supported by Colonel Bilson with the 28th regiment, and Lieutenant-colonel Prevost with a part of the 67th. A reserve, formed beyond the narrow valley, across which the enemy was closely pursued, next shared the same fate, and was routed by the same means.

Meanwhile, the right wing was not less successful The enemy, confident of success, met General Dilkes on the ascent of the hill, and the contest was sanguinary; but the undaunted perseverance of the brigade of Guards, of Lieutenant-colonel Brown's battalion, and of Lieutenant-colonel Norcott's and Major Acheson's detachments, overcame every obstacle, and General Ruffin's division was driven from the heights in confusion, leaving two pieces of cannon.

No expressions of mine could do justice to the conduct of the troops throughout—nothing less than the almost unparalleled exertions of every officer, the invincible bravery of every soldier, and the most determined devotion of the honour of his Majesty's arms in all, could have achieved this brilliant success against such a formidable enemy, so posted. In less than an hour and a half from the commencement of the action, the enemy was in full retreat. The retiring divisions met, halted, and seemed inclined to form; a new and more advanced position of our artillery quickly dispersed them. The exhausted state of the troops made pursuit impossible. A position was taken up on the eastern side of the hill; and we were strengthened on our right by the return of two Spanish regiments, that had been attached before to my division, but which I had left on the hill, and which had been ordered to retire.

An eagle, six pieces of cannon, the General of Division Ruffin, and the General of Brigade Rousseau, wounded and taken; the Chief of the Staff, General Bellegarde, and aide-de-camp of Marshal Victor, and the colonel of the 8th regiment, with many other officers killed, and several wounded and taken prisoners, the field covered with the dead bodies of the enemy, attest that my confidence in this division was nobly repaid. The animated charges of the 87th regiment were most conspicuous. Lieutenant-colonel Barnard, (twice wounded,) and the officers of his flank-battalion, executed the duty of skirmishing in advance with the enemy in a masterly manner; and were ably seconded by Lieutenant-Colonel Bush, of the 20th Portuguese, who (likewise twice wounded) fell into the enemy's hands, but was afterwards rescued.

The dispatch contains many more acknowledgments, which, as they have no connexion with my narrative, I have omitted.

I beg now to make such remarks and observations as may tend to throw light upon the different parts of the foregoing dispatch.

The two Spanish battalions attached to our division, together with Lieutenant-colonel Brown's flank-battalion, were left upon the height of Barossa, when we moved down into the wood, in order to secure that position till we had possessed ourselves of the height of Bermesa; but we had not left the plain more than half an hour, I think, and descended into the wood, till an officer came galloping after us, saying the French had debouched from the wood, and were moving on to the high ground in our rear, and had attacked the troops left there for its defence. Orders were instantly given us to countermarch, and to get on to the plain and into action as soon as possible. In coming about, one of the guns got entangled with a pine-tree; there was no time to disengage it, and setting to with the whip, they pushed the horses forward, and tore up the tree completely by the roots, although one of considerable size. I thought (as our General says) it appeared a good omen, and that a trifling obstacle would not be allowed to impede their career.

When we reached the plain, and perceived the enemy, never did a finer sight present itself. They were manoeuvring on the high ground before us; and as Home says,

"The hill they gained, and moving on its top,
of more than mortal size, towering, they seemed
An host angelic, clad in burning arms."

Those immediately in front of my battalion were the famed 8th regiment, and consisted of two battalions of 700 men each; one was composed of grenadiers, and the other of voltigeurs, or light infantry. The grenadiers had long waving red plumes in their caps, at least a foot in length; while the light infantry had feathers of the same length and make, but green, with yellow tops. The whole of the French army had on their best or holyday suits of clothing, with their arms as bright as silver, and glancing in the sun as they moved in column, gave them really a noble and martial appearance. We had no sooner cleared the wood than we inclined to our left, and went immediately at them. Major Duncan's guns commenced playing upon their column the moment he could get a clear piece of ground. The two companies of the 47th, attached to my battalion, were taken to cover and remain with the guns. Our people extended as we went up the hill, the Portuguese supporting us in the rear; and in a very short time we were hotly engaged with the fellows with the beautiful green feathers, many of which fell on the ground in a short time. As we advanced, the battalions to our right and in rear of us got formed in line, and moving forward

106

in fine style, took up stronger ground in advance; the guns in the centre also moving onward, and causing dreadful havoc in the enemy's ranks.

Early in the action my horse was killed, being shot in the head, which ball, had his head not stopped it, would in all probability have entered my body. He fell like a stone. I then went on and joined the ranks, and finding a rifle of a man that had just fallen, (poor little Croudace's servant, who afterwards fell himself,) I took a few shots at them in revenge for my horse. At this time the grenadier battalion of the 8th, with their waving red plumes, began to advance in close column, the drums beating all the time the *pas de charge*. They were supported by other columns in their rear, together with one, the French 54th, which they sent into the wood to try to turn our left. The 8th advanced, notwithstanding the galling fire kept up by our people and the Portuguese, every shot almost of which must have told, as they were in a solid body, not more than from 100 to 150 yards distance.

Our people were of course compelled to give way to this imposing column, when the regiments on our right and in our rear, opening out upon them a destructive fire, and the 87th and Guards immediately after attacking them with the bayonet, their rout and discomfiture was complete. The 8th, which suffered most, and from whom the eagle was taken, never yet got into line— nor did they intend, I believe—but advanced as a solid body, (occasionally firing from their front,) till, coming in contact with the regiments above mentioned, and in this state receiving the charge, their loss was excessive, for they could not get away.

I understand, when the 87th charged, Ensign Keogh of that regiment made the first attempt to wrench the eagle from the officer who carried it; but in so doing he was run through by several of those who supported it, and fell lifeless to the ground. Sergeant Masterson of that regiment then dashed at it, and was more fortunate, he succeeding in securing it. I understand there was some dispute between them and the Guards, who charged at the same time with the 87th, to whom it properly belonged; but I imagine the 87th must have been the captors, for Sergeant

Masterson soon after received a commission for his gallantry, and is now a captain in that regiment.

The 54th, the French regiment, which had been sent into the wood to turn our left flank, by some means got entangled; for, except their light company, no part of the regiment ever got into action again; and when their columns were routed, they found some difficulty in effecting their retreat.

There is something rather extraordinary and very interesting in the story of the eagle and the 8th regiment, if it he true, and which I see no reason to doubt. They were one of the regiments, it is said, which were, engaged at Talavera, and were particularly distinguished; and it is further said, that the 87th was one of the regiments opposed to them, and over which they gained some advantage; that is, the French troops caused the British brigade, in which the 87th was serving, to retire with considerable loss; and that it was for their conduct in this action that Bonaparte had placed a golden wreath of laurel round the neck of the regimental eagle with his own hand. If such was the case, it is most remarkable that the very regiment by whom they should have obtained this honour, should be the regiment that deprived them of their eagle, which had been so highly honoured. But here, poor fellows, although they did not lose their honour, they lost very nearly the whole regiment; for out of 1400 which entered the field, not more than 200 of them entered Chiclana after the action.

Indeed I never witnessed any field so thickly strewed with dead as this plain was after the action; and I feel confident, and all accounts agree in confirming the opinion, that the loss of the French on this occasion was little short of 3000 men; ours was about 1250. Here then we have a loss of 4000 men in about an hour and a half, out of about 12,000 which composed the two armies.

In this action, Colonel Bush was almost absurdly brave and conspicuous. As soon as he got his Portuguese fairly into action, he rode slowly backward and forward among them, with his spectacles on, crying out as the balls whistled past him, *"Que bella musica!"* what delightful music! Poor fellow, he did not ride there many minutes; for, being within a very short distance of the enemy's tirailleurs so conspicuous an object, it was not to be expected he could escape. He died a few days after the action.

Colonel Barnard, my commandant, (now Sir Andrew,) about the middle of the action, received a severe wound, and was borne away to the rear. Whilst the surgeon was dressing him, another shot struck him, and inflicted, I believe, a worse wound than the former.

The horses of my battalion suffered greatly in proportion to their numbers. We had only four in the field, two of which, Major Ross's and my own, were killed, and Colonel Barnard's wounded; only the adjutant's escaped with a whole skin. Indeed there was scarcely an officer or soldier in the action that had not marks of shot about him. The caps of the tall guardsmen were riddled as it were; while the greater part of the enemy's shot passed over our little fellows, who were both too near them, and too low for their fire.

I may remark on this subject that the French generally fire high, but here I think unusually so; for, after a considerable quantity of ammunition had been expended by my battalion, it became my duty to look out for a fresh supply. I accordingly posted off to the rear, where I expected to have found some mules which had been attached to us, with ammunition on their backs; but on my way thither, the ground was actually ploughing up on all sides by the enemy's large shot, and their musket-balls falling very thick; so much so, that some of our mules far to the rear had been wounded, and the others had dispersed. Hence also the second wound which my gallant commander received, where he ought to have been completely out of danger. Some ammunition for our rifles was, however, found in a one-horse cart belonging to the artillery, and out of it those whose ammunition was expended were replenished.

But during my absence to the rear, the gallant and decisive charge had been made; and when I again reached the front, I perceived the enemy's columns in full retreat, covered by the remainder of their light troops, closely followed by some of my people. The retreat was accordingly sounded to recall them from the pursuit, and our brave and victorious little army cheered the enemy as his beaten and disheartened columns left the field.

Immediately after our army began to move off towards the Isla, our General being, as I understood, so much exasperated with: the apathy evinced by the Spanish General, that he would no longer co-operate with him, and consequently drew off our troops into the Isle of Leon. My battalion, however, was destined to remain on the field all night to protect the numerous wounded from any marauders, or small parties and cavalry patrols of the enemy, which might happen to return. However, not a Frenchman made his appearance there again that night. When it was determined to withdraw the British army, Major Duncan, with great humanity, (approved of course by our excellent General,) cast off from the artillery-carriages all the spare ammunition, in order to make room for as many of our wounded officers and soldiers as those carriages could accommodate, and thus a considerable number of them were carried from the field immediately.

After they had left us, and my battalion was still standing in front of the position last occupied by our troops, all having retired but ourselves, and it now began to draw towards night, and we were preparing to move off, an unfortunate French sergeant attracted our notice. Poor fellow, he had been shot in the small of the back, and (on our surgeon examining him) pronounced to be mortally. He appeared to be a man above forty, and apparently a veteran, who had fought many a hard field; and was, I think, one of the most respectable-looking men of his class that I have seen. When he saw us preparing to leave him to his fate, the expression of his countenance became the most piteous and beseeching imaginable; imploring us in French not to leave him there to perish. My heart bled for him; but unhappily we had no means of removing him, had there even been a hope of his recovery. When he saw that his fate was inevitable, he crawled in the best manner he was able to a broken ammunition-box, and raising himself on his knees, supported by it, besought that Being who never casts out the cry of the unfortunate, and who, I sincerely hope, imparted to him that strength and comfort which his unhappy circumstances so greatly required. I doubt not he was a sincere Christian; never shall I forget the impression his unhappy fate made on my mind. To be left in solitude and darkness on this blood-stained heath, with the prospect of his own certain death before his eyes, and without any to comfort him in his last agony, must indeed' have been a severe trial to his fortitude. Would to God I could have relieved him! His case was not singular, it is true; but none ever presented itself to my view under such truly affecting circumstances as this unhappy veteran's did.

After dark, my battalion retired over the field where the thickest of the dead and wounded were strewed, and many were the dying groans which struck upon our ears, as we traversed this bloody field; but, except these groans, no sound was heard, where lately the din of arms had been loud and fierce, and where war had raged in all its fury; till coming to the house upon the sea-beach, where many of the wounded had been collected, we were formed into square on a sand-hill near it, and in this position rested on our arms for the remainder of the night. On our way from the front, we passed not far from where my horse had fallen; and as saddlery was scarce at Cadiz, I thought it would be prudent to try to recover that on which I had been riding. I found it; but my horse having fallen with his back inclined to the front, it was perforated by shot in five places, and the tree was broken. However, I disengaged it, and giving it to one of the men, whose rifle I carried in return, I got it safely into Isla.

About twelve at night, poor General Rousseau died, a cannon-shot having carried away the greater part of the flesh of one of his thighs; and as no other troops were near, the task of paying him the last sad duty devolved upon me. I went to the house aforesaid, and procured a shovel or a spade, and digging a hole in the sand by the light of the moon, his body was deposited, where it in all probability will remain till the last trumpet shall summon it to rise. Poor drunken Gilles, one of the men I had employed on the occasion, pronounced the only service as he was committed to the dust, which was, "God rest his soul!" I indeed sincerely hope so. Poor Rousseau had been a noble soldier; in his pocket was found a leave which he had obtained to return to France on account of ill health; but in the prospect of the approaching action he had delayed his departure, and thus fell a victim as it were to his patriotism and his sense of honour. He was military governor of Xeres de la Frontera, from whence we have our wine called Sherry, a corruption of Xeres. He was a small slender person, and apparently had suffered greatly from ill health. During the night some Spaniards were sent into the field to look for and bring off the guns we had taken, which they did.

As it approached towards morning, Major Ross, seeing all was quiet, moved us off by the beach towards our former quarters; and passing over the position of Bermesa, which the Spaniards still occupied, and crossing the Santi Petri by the lately erected bridge, we returned weary and hungry to La Isla, and where our friends received us once again with great cordiality.

If my reader is not tired of the subject, I would just beg to draw his attention for a moment to the circumstances attending this action. The French troops were at least 7500 (some say 8000) strong, well clothed and appointed, and apparently well fed, and fresh from their cantonments, none of them probably having marched more than four miles. They were some of the best in the French service, and commanded by one of Bonaparte's ablest generals, a marshal of France, Victor, Duke of Belluno. They occupied a fine position, having the ground completely at their choice; while we did not muster more than 4500 at most. We had been marching for sixteen hours successively through the night over bad roads; and being taken in a manner by surprise, we came out of the wood beneath the enemy, broken and disjointed, and were instantly hurried into action.

The French fought desperately; for when their marauding columns came down upon us with an intrepidity seldom seen in the French army, and opening out their heavy and destructive fire, my heart quaked within me for the safety of our little army, and the honour of our country, for I thought it would be impossible to resist them. However, the steady valour of our troops repelled the assailants, and, taking advantage of their proximity, charged as before stated, and completely overthrew them. It is certain, as General Graham says, that all must have done their duty on this occasion; notwithstanding, we may sing with great propriety, *"Non nobis, Domine"*—"Not unto us, O Lord, but unto thy name be the praise;" for it is certain we must have been specially favoured by a kind Providence, or it is impossible we could have gained such a victory under so many and so great disadvantages; for never was victory more complete. In less than three hours from the first glimpse we had of them as we debouched from the wood, a Frenchman was not to be seen in all the field, save the numerous killed and wounded.

Although our General did not say any thing in his public dispatch of the abominable conduct of La Pena, no doubt he stated truly in his private information how ill that General had behaved; for he and the 10,000 or 11,000 Spaniards he had with him remained within two miles of the field of action, quiet and passive spectators of the scene, without making one effort to support us had we been beaten, or to take advantage of the victory should we gain it; and the consequence was, the French retained their ground arid works by which they invested Cadiz and La Isla, whereas, had he made the slightest movement during or after the fight, they would have all gone off, and the siege would have been raised, for it is evident they contemplated and were prepared for this, the soldiers having each three or four days' bread in his possession.

A considerable number of other officers besides Generals Ruffin and Rousseau were taken. Ruffin was wounded in the neck by a rifle-shot, which touched the spinal marrow, depriving him of the use of his limbs. He was soon after embarked for England, but died as he came within sight of the Isle of Wight. He was an immense and a fine-looking man, about six feet two inches or six feet three inches high, and ate enormously. He every day received a mess from our General's table. The other officers also were treated with the greatest politeness and attention, dining first at one regimental mess, and then at another. They were fully sensible of the kindness shown them, and expressed themselves very grateful. They were afterwards sent to England.

I cannot omit here noticing the high estimation in which General Graham was held by every officer and soldier of this little army. I may truly say, he lived in their affections; they not only looked up to him with confidence as their commander, but they esteemed and respected him as their firm friend and protector, which indeed he always showed himself to be.

In all my fighting I never was in an action where the chances of death were so numerous as in this; and I may say, I never was in an action where I was less prepared to die. It is therefore of the Lord's mercies that he spared me—I hope, for good at last.

Chapter Ten
Ciudad Rodrigo & Badajos

We remained at Isla till June, without any thing of importance occurring, but at this time I was brought nigh to death's door by the bursting of a bloodvessel in the lungs. I was so ill that it was deemed necessary to send me home for change of air, it being exceedingly hot at this time at Isla. I was accordingly removed to Cadiz to wait for the first ship returning to England, and while there I suffered greatly, not being able to lie down in bed.

However, before a vessel could be had, an order was received for my battalion to proceed to Portugal, and our esteemed commander was likewise ordered to proceed to that country. As I felt myself somewhat better, I obtained permission to accompany my battalion to Portugal, and I accordingly embarked with it at Cadiz on the 30th of that month, on board a transport, the name of which I forget.

General Graham intended to have gone in a 50 gun ship that was leaving that port for England, he being to be left at Lisbon in passing. He sent an aide-de-camp on board to prepare for his reception; but he met with such treatment while on board, as induced the General to alter his plan and go in a frigate, on board which some of our people were embarked. It is said, that after the aide-de-camp had been shown the accommodation, the captain intimated to him, that it was expected the military officers would always keep on the leeward side of the quarter-deck. The windward side on board a man-of-war is considered the most honourable,—therefore this was in fact putting the General beneath himself. He suffered, however, for his ill-timed assumption of supremacy, for there was a quantity of specie at Cadiz which was to be transported at the same time for the use of the army in Portugal, and which was intended to have gone in the ship with the General; but after this reception of his aide-de-camp, and the imperious condition attached to his going in this ship, he went on board the frigate with his suite, and took the money with him, thus depriving him of a considerable premium for its transport, to which he would have been entitled had the General gone with him. He, however, being the senior officer, we were all put under his charge, save the frigate before mentioned, and we were greatly annoyed by him during our passage, which our master said he prolonged in looking out for American merchantmen, there being then an appearance of war between the two countries. They said he actually detained one or two which left Cadiz when we did, and that he fired small arms into them to bring them to, although war had not been declared. One day during the passage he made a signal to the transports which we did not immediately perceive. We were astonished at the report of a gun, and at the same time a cannon-shot whizzed past our rigging. This is not, I believe, customary, a blank gun being generally fired first, and when nothing else will do, a shot ahead of the vessel, but he appeared not to stand on any ceremony.

We were glad when the voyage was over, it continuing from the 30th June to the 19th July, although three or four days only is the usual time.

We landed at Lisbon, and immediately set about preparing for our journey up the country to join the army; but Colonel Barnard having received letters respecting the settlement of our late Colonel (General Manningham's) affairs, which could not be easily arranged without my presence, determined to send me home for the purpose, with a promise, however, that I should immediately come out again. I accordingly embarked on board the same transport with a ship full of all kinds and descriptions of people, sick and wounded, and lame and lazy; such a motley group I have seldom seen. Our paymaster also returned home with me, and besides him I did not know a person on board.

We had a long and tedious passage, not reaching Portsmouth till the 27th August, although we embarked on the 1st of that month. When we entered the chops of the Channel, there was a considerable swell in the sea. Our master, for some purpose or other, had got up from the hold a small quantity of ballast (gravel), which was laid upon the quarter-deck. A fine stout young Irishman, an officer on board, came up the companion, and seeing the ballast lying there, asked where it came from.

"Why, don't you see," says the master, "how rough the sea is? it has been washed up from the bottom and thrown upon the deck."

The Hibernian seemed quite astonished at the effect of the swell, but believed the story with all the simple-hearted credulity of a Johnny-raw, as the soldiers term a young and inexperienced soldier. Our paymaster was a little of a gourmand, and having for some time been deprived of luxuries, determined to indulge a little now we had come to the land of plenty. On our road, therefore, to London, (he and another officer and myself posting it,) we stopped at Godalming for dinner; he would needs have a carp, which he happened to see in a pond in the garden, made ready for our dinner. It was prepared according to his request, and with it and other good things we contrived to fare pretty well; although, according to my taste, a fresh herring would have been preferable. But lo, and behold! when the bill was called for, the awful sum of half a guinea for the carp was added to the other items of the dinner, which amounted to quite enough without it. To remonstrate would have been useless; we therefore paid the bill and set off, determined to be more economical in future.

I passed through London, and reached the depot of my battalion, then stationed at Ashford in Kent, where, after having arranged the business for which I had been sent home, I obtained a three months' leave of absence to visit my native place, where I arrived, thank God, in a much improved state of health, and where I found all my friends and connexions as well as could be expected, and no doubt happy to see me.

About the middle of November of the same year, I started once more for foreign service, and embarked at Portsmouth for Lisbon on the 22nd of that month, on board a small brig heavily laden with corn for the army in Portugal. We remained some time wind-bound, but at length got to sea and proceeded on our voyage, but shortly after the wind headed us and began to blow very fresh. We were therefore compelled to run for the Race of Portland, where we came to anchor. But the wind coming more favourable in a day or two, we weighed again, and got as far on our voyage as opposite Torbay; but here again the wind coming foul, we were obliged to enter the bay and drop anchor again. We were detained here a good many days, during which I went ashore with another officer, who was on board with me, and indulged in some Devonshire clotted cream at Brixham.

In about a week we again started, and got about half way across the Bay of Biscay, when a heavy gale overtook us, and in which we lost a considerable portion of our quarter-bulwarks (I think they are called). Indeed, from the brig being so heavily laden, the water being within a very little of her gunwale, she did not weather the heavy seas which struck her very well, for during the night one came clean over her, partly filling the cabin where we lay with water; and I own I had considerable apprehension for our safety, which I believe was pretty universal on board. It pleased Him, however, who ruleth over all things, to bring us through the gale without further injury, although we appeared next morning in a very shattered condition, and after a few more days' sailing, we reached the Tagus, and landed at Lisbon about the middle of January 1812, and immediately commenced equipping for a campaign with the army which was at this time besieging Ciudad Rodrigo.

I had to purchase a riding-horse and a mule to carry my baggage, and a great deal more of essential requisites to enable me to do my duty in the field; and to say truth, I had not, by any means, sufficient funds to meet these considerable expenses, and was consequently forced to borrow, and glad enough to find a friend who could and would lend me enough for the occasion. And here I cannot but remark, that it seemed peculiarly hard on junior officers, on their taking the field, to be compelled to furnish all this equipment at their own expense. I have known several who did not recover from the debt they thus incurred (could they find a friend, as I did, to lend them what they wanted) for a considerable time after they had joined the army; nay, I believe some never recovered it, and the persons who were kind enough to oblige them lost several large sums in this manner. In my own case, I know, I was most wofully put to it to raise a sufficiency for this purpose; and many, I know, have been compelled to take the field without the necessary equipment to render them efficient. They were thus of little service to the army for a considerable time after joining, and many of them were obliged to leave it again, after striving to do their duty, inadequately provided with the conveniences and comforts requisite to enable a man to bear up against the fatigues he had to encounter. It struck me as but just, and in this opinion I am not singular, that all officers who have not sufficient pay and allowances to enable them to provide themselves with the means of transport, ought to be furnished in the first instance at the public expense, and then be afterwards obliged to keep them in a fit state for service at their own.

I set out from Lisbon soon after, and joined my regiment, which was one of those that formed the light division, and found them cantoned in the neighbourhood of Rodrigo, that fortress having fallen some days previous to my arrival. I had not been many days with the regiment till the division was assembled at a village called Ituera, on the banks of the Azava, to carry into execution the sentence of a general court-martial, before which seven men of the division had been arraigned for desertion to the enemy, they having been taken in Rodrigo at the capture of that place.

They were of course all found guilty, as they were taken as it were out of the enemy's ranks, and never attempted to plead not guilty; but they had said in palliation of their heinous crime, that they were forced to desert from want of food and clothing; indeed the army had not been so well supplied for a short while previously, as they had been accustomed to, but there never was any thing like want. I understood the clothing also was getting bad, but the men could not be got up the country for want of transport, and they were no worse off than their comrades. Indeed, from all I could learn, they had acted in a most diabolical manner; for at the attack of the breaches in assaulting the place, they were distinctly heard crying out to one another, "Now here comes the light division; let us give it them, the rascals," or something to that effect, and had, it is said, done more injury to the assailing party than twice their number of Frenchmen.

Death of course was their sentence, and now the wretched victims of delusion were to atone with their lives for one of the greatest crimes known in the criminal code of the army. The division was formed into three sides square, on a plain in front of the village, the graves of the hapless beings occupying a part of the fourth face of the square. When all was ready, and a firing party from each regiment had been formed in the centre, the provost-marshal went to the guard-tent, where the prisoners were in waiting, to conduct them to the place of execution.

They soon after appeared, poor wretches, moving towards the square, with faces pale and wan, and with all the dejection such a situation is calculated to produce. Their arms had been pinioned one by one as they came out from the guard-tent, and all being ready, the melancholy procession advanced towards the centre of the square. The proceedings of the court which tried them, together with the sentence, and the approval of the Commander of the Forces, was read by the Assistant Adjutant-general, in the hearing of the whole division; which concluded, the prisoners were marched round in front of every regiment, that all might see and avoid their unhappy fate. They were then moved towards their graves. I ought to observe that the chaplain of the division had been with them in the guard-tent some little time previously to their leaving it, and when they quitted as above described, he followed them at a considerable distance, apparently ashamed of his peculiar calling, and the duty incumbent on him in such a conjuncture. They were led, as I said before, towards their graves; and when they reached the bank of earth in front of each, they were made to kneel down with their faces fronting the square, and then being one after another blindfolded, and left for a few moments to their own reflections or their prayers, the provost-marshal proceeded to the firing party, who had been previously loaded, and directing the men of each regiment to fire at their own prisoner, he advanced them to within about ten or twelve paces of the wretched men, and giving the signals by motion for their making ready and firing, the whole fired at once, and plunged the unhappy criminals into eternity.

There was, indeed, one melancholy exception to this. One of the prisoners belonged to the troop of horse artillery attached to the division, and it seems the provost, in giving his orders for the soldiers of each regiment to fire at their own man, had not recollected that the artillery had no men there to fire. He was thus left sitting on his knees, when the others had fallen all around him. What his feelings must have been it is in vain to guess; but, poor fellow, he was not suffered long to remain in suspense, for a reserve party immediately approaching, they fired and stretched him also along with his companions in crime and misery; and in such of the others as they perceived life still remaining, they also immediately put an end to their sufferings, by placing their muskets close to their body, and firing into them. One poor man, when he received his death wound, sprung to a considerable height, and giving a loud shriek, he fell, and instantly expired.

When all was finished, the division was formed into column, and marched round in front of the bodies, where each soldier might distinctly perceive the sad and melancholy effects of such a fatal dereliction of duty. They were then, without more ado, thrown into their graves, which were filled up without delay, and the division separating, each regiment marched to its quarters.

I cannot describe the uncomfortable feelings this spectacle produced in my mind—nay, not only there, but in my body also—for I felt sick at heart; a sort of loathing ensued; and from the recollection of what I then suffered, I could not easily be persuaded to witness such another scene, if I had the option of staying away. Death in the hundred shapes it assumes on the field of battle seems honourable, and not near so revolting to the feelings, and withal comes suddenly; but to witness the slow and melancholy preparations for an execution such as this, is productive, in any heart that can feel, of the most unpleasant sensations, I think, imaginable.

One of the poor wretches was the little shoemaker of our Highland company, by name M'Guiniss, whom I had known for many years, and who formerly bore an excellent character; but he had most likely been seduced by some of his companions to commit this heinous crime.

Not many days after this, the whole army began to move towards Badajos. On the 26th of February we left our cantonments, and passing by way of Castello Branca and Villa Velha, we reached a village not far from Niza, called Povo das Meadas, where my battalion took up its quarters for a time.

From hence I was dispatched to Lisbon for the regimental clothing, which had then arrived at that port; but being unable to procure the means of transport, I was obliged to return without it. I rejoined them in the camp before Badajos about the 15th of March, and witnessed the siege of that fortress from this period to its fall on the 6th of April. The breaches having been reported practicable by the engineers on the 5th, in the evening the army was assembled for the assault, and was disposed as follows: the 3rd division under General Picton was ordered to attack the citadel, and to endeavour to establish himself there by escalade; the 4th and light divisions, the former under General Colville, and the latter commanded by Colonel Barnard, were destined for the breaches; the 5th division, which had not co-operated hitherto in the siege, but brought this evening into the neighbourhood, was ordered to occupy the ground in front of the town by way of reserve. One brigade of that division was ordered to make a false attack on a work called the Pardeleras, which was connected with: the town, although not actually belonging to it. Another brigade of the same division was ordered to make another false attack round towards the gate near the river Guadiana, which latter was to be turned into a real attack, if circumstances permitted General Walker, who commanded it, to do so. There was also a brigade of Portuguese, which was ordered to attack St Cristoval, a fort on the other side of the river. Every thing was arranged in the clearest and most satisfactory manner; all knew what they had to do, the point they were to occupy in the attack having been pointed out to most of them the day before. Soon after dark, the different divisions began to move towards their destined posts, all elated with the certainty of success.

I was then in the mess of the senior captain of my battalion, who commanded it on this occasion; and my other messmates were poor little Croudace and Cary, both lieutenants, the latter acting adjutant, and another. We had taken a farewell glass before we got up from dinner, not knowing which of them would survive the bloody fray that was likely soon to commence. Poor Croudace, a native of the county of Durham, and consequently a near countryman, put into my hand a small leather purse, containing half a doubloon, and requested me to take care of it for him, as he did not know whose fate it might be to fall or to survive. I took it according to his wish, and put it into my pocket, and, after a little more conversation, and another glass, for the poor little fellow liked his wine, we parted, and they moved off.

Although I had thus, as it were, settled it in my mind that I would not go with them on this occasion, for my services could have been of but very little utility, yet, when they went away, I felt as if I was left desolate as it were, and was quite uneasy at parting from my beloved comrades, whom I had always accompanied hitherto. I therefore slung over my back my haversack, containing my pistol and a few other things, and moved forward, to try if I could find them; but falling in with some of my friends, staff-officers of the 43rd, who were in the same brigade, they strongly dissuaded me from it, representing to me the folly of uselessly exposing myself, and the little service I could render there; and one of them requested me to accompany him to a hill immediately in front of the breaches, where we could see the business as it proceeded.

We waited till about ten o'clock, when the fire first commenced from the castle upon the 3rd division, as they approached it; but the fire from thence did not appear very heavy. Not long after it opened out at the breaches, and was most awfully severe; indeed it was so heavy and so incessant, that it appeared like one continued sheet of fire along the ramparts near the breaches, and we could distinctly see the faces of the French troops, although the distance was near a mile. All sorts of arms, &c. were playing at once, guns, mortars, musketry, grenades, and shells thrown from the walls, while every few minutes explosions from mines were taking place. The firing too appeared to have such a strange death-like sound, quite different from all I had ever heard before. This was occasioned by the muzzles being pointed downwards into the ditch, which gave the report an unusual and appalling effect. This continued without a moment's cessation, or without any apparent advantage being gained by our struggling but awfully circumstanced comrades. Lord Wellington had also taken his stand upon this hill, and appeared quite uneasy at the troops seeming to make no progress, and often asked, or rather repeated to himself, "What can be the matter?"

The enemy had adopted an excellent plan to ascertain where our columns were posted; they threw an immense number of light balls on all sides of the town, and when they found out where there was a large body, a rocket was fired in the direction of where it stood, and instantly every gun, mortar, and howitzer, not previously engaged, was turned in that direction, and grievous was the destruction their shot made in the ranks of these columns. Still our people at the breaches did not get forward, although we distinctly heard, with emotion, the bugles of our division sounding the advance. His lordship seemed now to lose all patience, and aides-de-camp were sent to ascertain the cause of the delay. They flew like lightning, while the whole rampart round the town seemed enveloped in one name of fire. Our brave but unsuccessful comrades were heard cheering every now and then; but still the fire at the breaches did not slacken. At length a dispatch arrived from General Picton, stating, that he had established himself in the castle. This was cheering news to his lordship, who expressed very strongly the gratitude he felt for that gallant General.

During the reading of the dispatch, which was done by torchlight, the enemy, perceiving the light, and that a number of people had assembled on the hill, directed a shell in that direction; but it fell short, and did us no injury. His lordship now rode off, and ordered our people at the breaches to retire, as the town was now perfectly secure. I also set off to inform my people of the happy circumstance. I found them drawn off from the glacis a few hundred yards; but, oh! what a difference in their appearance now from what they were previous to the attack. The whole division scarcely mustered at this time 2000 men, so many had been killed and wounded, and many had been sent to the rear with the latter. I informed them that General Picton had got possession of the castle, but my story appeared to them an incredible tale; for it was actually impossible, they thought; and although they made me repeat it over and over again, they could scarcely bring their minds to credit such unexpected news.

It was now dawn of day, and the firing had ceased at every point. Here I learnt the fate of my two beloved friends and messmates: Croudace had been shot through the body, and carried to the rear; Gary had fallen, but they could not tell what had become of him. I now went forward towards the breaches, where I found that several men of both the 4th and light divisions had remained; and when General Picton moved from the castle towards that point, which I believe he stated in his dispatch to be his intention, the enemy, finding themselves attacked in rear, began to abandon the defence of the breaches, and our people were then enabled to enter.

Never did I witness any thing like the artificial impediments which the enemy had here thrown up, which, added to the natural ones, that is, to the breaches not having been so perfectly practicable as was desirable, rendered it next to impossible to enter, even after all opposition on their part had ceased. In one breach (the large one) this was literally the case; for at the top of it was fixed a *chevaux-de-frize* extending the whole width of the breach, and composed of a strong beam of wood, with sharp-pointed sword-blades fixed in every direction, they being generally about three quarters of a yard long, and so closely set together, that it was impossible either to leap over them or penetrate between them, and the whole so firmly fixed to the works at the top, that it could not be moved. In addition, they had fitted a number of long and thick planks, with spikes about an inch or more in length, and laid them all down the breach, but fixed at the top, so that it was impossible for any one to get up without falling on these. Beyond the *chevaux-de-frize* several ditches had been cut, into which those must have fallen who surmounted the obstacles on the breach; but I believe none did, although I saw one Portuguese lying dead upon the ramparts; but I imagine he must either have been thrown up there by some explosion, or been one of those of the 3rd division who came from the castle. In addition to all the above, from the covered way down into the ditch was, I should imagine, at least thirty feet; our people had descended by ladders, and, I doubt not, in the dark, and, in the hurry and confusion of the moment, many were thrown down and killed. In the middle of the large ditch a smaller one had been cut, which was filled with water, and in which, added to the inundation close to the right of the breaches, (which had been caused by bringing the river partly into the ditch,) numbers were drowned. Small mines had been constructed all along in the ditch, which were exploded when it was filled with people, and which produced infinite mischief.

On the top of the ramparts the enemy had a considerable number of shells of the largest size, ready filled and fused; and when our people had filled the ditch below, these were lighted, and thrown over on their heads, each shell being capable of destroying from twelve to twenty men or more. They had beams of wood also laid on the ramparts, with old carriage-wheels, and every sort of missile imaginable, which were poured upon the unfortunate people below.

When these things are taken into consideration, added to the incessant and destructive fire of from 3000 to 4000 men, all emulous to do their duty, at the short distance of perhaps twenty yards, with the ditch as full as it could possibly stow, the reader will be able to form some idea of the destruction that must naturally ensue: and awful indeed it was, for, within the space of less than an acre of ground, I should imagine not less than from 1200 to 1500 men were lying: it was a heart-rending sight. I learnt afterwards that many were the desperate efforts that had been made to ascend the breaches, but all in vain; that many had nearly reached the top, but they being either shot or blown up, the others were forced down again. Another and another trial still was made, but each succeeding party shared the fate of their predecessors. At last the bottoms of the breaches were nearly blocked up with the bodies of those who fell.

By this time, General Philippon, the French governor, had surrendered. When he found the 3rd division had got possession of the castle, and were preparing to move down to second the attack of the breaches by taking the enemy in rear, and that General Walker, with a part of the 5th division, had escaladed, and established themselves at the other end of the town, he deemed further resistance useless, and retired, with the garrison, to St Cristoval, on the opposite side of the river; and shortly after the whole surrendered prisoners of war, the troops, after being stripped of their arms and accoutrements, being marched along in the ditch to one of the gates, from whence they were escorted on their way to Elvas. They passed near the breaches while I was there, and I had a full view of them as they moved along. I thought they seemed under great apprehension for their safety, as they appeared quite downcast and dejected, which is not generally the case with French prisoners, who will shrug their shoulders, and tell you it is the fortune of war; but these poor fellows, who certainly had made a noble defence, seemed low-spirited and timid to a degree. Certainly by the rules of war, I believe, they might have been put to death, for having stood an assault of the place; but a British general does not resort to the same measures which their Marshal Suchet did at Tarragona, when he put all, both soldiers and inhabitants, to the sword.

Soon after daylight, the remaining men of attacking divisions began to rush into the town, in hopes of sharing, with those who had already entered, the plunder they imagined it would afford; and though every thing was done by Colonel Barnard, aided by the other officers, to keep out those of the light division, it was useless, although he even risked his life to prevent their entering. He had bravely, during the attack, repeatedly ascended the breach, in hopes of overcoming the obstacles which presented themselves, but he had always been driven back, although he escaped unhurt where all was death around him; and now his life nearly fell a sacrifice, in endeavouring to restore that discipline in his division which this unfortunate and unsuccessful assault had considerably impaired. He opposed his personal and bodily strength to the entrance of the plunderers, but in vain. They rushed in, in spite of all opposition; and in wrenching a musket from one of the soldiers of the 52nd, who was forcing past him, he fell, and was nigh precipitated into the ditch. He, however, finding resistance here in vain, set off, accompanied by several other officers, into the town, to endeavour to restrain, as much as lay in his power, the licentiousness of those inside, whose bad passions, it was but too evident, would be let loose upon the defenceless inhabitants.

I had been in company with Captain Percival, my commanding-officer before alluded to, from the time of my first coming down to the division before daylight; and now he and I, hearing the heart-piercing and afflicting groans which arose from the numbers of wounded still lying in the ditch, set to work to get as many of these poor fellows removed as was in our power. This we found a most arduous and difficult undertaking, as we could not do it without the aid of a considerable number of men; and it was a work of danger to attempt to force the now lawless soldiers to obey, and stop with us till this work of necessity and humanity was accomplished.

All thought of what they owed their wounded comrades, and of the probability that ere long a similar fate might be their own, was swallowed up in their abominable rage for drink and plunder; however, by perseverance, and by occasionally using his stick, my commandant at length compelled a few fellows to lend their assistance in removing what we could into the town, where it was intended that hospitals should be established. But this was a most heartrending duty, for, from the innumerable cries of,—"Oh! for God's sake, come and remove me!" it was difficult to select the most proper objects for such care. Those who appeared likely to die, of course it would have been but cruelty to put them to the pain of a removal; and many who, from the nature of their wounds, required great care and attention in carrying them, the half-drunken brutes whom we were forced to employ exceedingly tortured and injured; nay, in carrying one man out of the ditch they very frequently kicked or trode upon several others, whom to touch was like death to them, and which produced the most agonizing cries imaginable.

I remember at this time Colonel (the late Sir Niel) Campbell passed out at the breach, and, as he had formerly been a Captain in our regiment, many of the poor fellows who lay there knew him, and beseeched him in the most piteous manner to have them removed. He came to me, and urged upon me in the strongest manner to use every exertion to get the poor fellows away. This evinced he had a feeling heart; but he was not probably aware, that for that very purpose both my commanding-officer and myself had been labouring for hours; but it soon began to grow excessively hot, and what with the toil and the heat of the sun, and the very unpleasant effluvia which now arose from the numerous dead and wounded, we were both compelled, about mid-day, to desist from our distressing though gratifying labours.

It was now between twelve and one o'clock, and though we had had a great many removed, a much greater number lay groaning in the ditch; but our strength was exhausted, for he was lame and unable to move much, and I had been obliged to assist in carrying many myself, the drunken scoundrels whom we had pressed into the service seldom making more than one or two trips till they deserted us. But my lamented friend and messmate, poor Cary, was still to search for, and, after a considerable time, he was found beneath one of the ladders by which they had descended into the ditch. He was shot through the head, and I doubt not received his death-wound on the ladder, from which in all probability he fell. He was stripped completely naked, save a flannel waistcoat which he wore next his skin. I had him taken up and placed upon a shutter, (he still breathed a little, though quite insensible,) and carried him to the camp. A sergeant and some men, whom we had pressed to carry him, were so drunk that they let him fall from off their shoulders, and his body fell with great force to the ground. I shuddered, but poor Cary, I believe, was past all feeling, or the fall would have greatly injured him. We laid him in bed in his tent, but it was not long ere my kind, esteemed, and lamented friend breathed his last. Poor Croudace had also died immediately after reaching the hospital, whither he had been carried when he was shot.

Thus I lost two of my most particular and intimate acquaintances, from both of whom I had received many acts of kindness and friendship. They will long live in my memory. Cary was buried next day behind our tents, one of the officers (my other messmate) reading the funeral service.

I cannot help adverting to some of the scenes which I witnessed in the ditch, while employed there as above noticed. One of the first strange sights that attracted our notice, was soon after our arrival. An officer with yellow facings came out of the town with a frail fair one leaning on his arm, and carrying in her other hand a cage with a bird in it; and she tripped it over the bodies of the dead and dying with all the ease and indifference of a person, moving in a ball-room,—no more concern being evinced by either of them, than if nothing extraordinary had occurred. It was really lamentable to see such an utter absence of all right feeling.

Soon after this the men began to come out with their plunder. Some of them had dressed themselves in priests' or friars' garments—some appeared in female dresses, as nuns, &c.; and, in short, all the whimsical and fantastical figures imaginable almost were to be seen coming reeling out of the town, for by this time they were nearly all drunk. I penetrated no farther into the town that day than to a house a little beyond the breach, where I had deposited the wounded; but I saw enough in this short trip to disgust me with the doings in Badajos at this time. I learnt that no house, church, or convent, was held sacred by the infuriated and now ungovernable soldiery, but that priests or nuns, and common people, all shared alike, and that any who showed the least resistance were instantly sacrificed to their fury. They had a method of firing through the lock of any door that happened to be shut against them, which almost invariably had the effect of forcing it open; and such scenes were witnessed in the streets as baffle description.

One man of our first battalion, I am told, had got a hogshead of brandy into the streets, and, getting his mess-tin, and filling it from the cask, and seating himself astride like Bacchus, swore that every person who came past should drink, be who he may.

His commanding-officer happened to be one who came that way, and he was compelled to take the tin and drink, for, had he refused, it is not improbable the wretch would have shot him, for his rifle was loaded by his side, and the soldiers had by this time become quite past all control. Another, who had been fortunate enough to obtain a considerable quantity of doubloons, put them in his haversack, and was making his way out of the town, but was induced, before he left it, to drink more than he could carry. He laid him down somewhere to take a nap, and awoke soon after without even his shoes, and not only were the doubloons gone, but all his own necessaries also.

In short, a thousand of the most tragi-comical spectacles that can possibly be imagined, might be witnessed in this devoted city. The officers did all they could to repress these outrages, but the soldiers were now so completely dispersed that one quarter of them could not be found; and indeed the only benefit almost that the officers could render was, by each placing himself in a house, which generally secured it from being broken open and plundered. The different camps of our army were for several days after more like rag-fairs than military encampments, such quantities of wearing-apparel of all kinds were disposing of by one set of plunderers to the other. But they were not content with what they had brought out of Badajos; they had now got such relish for plunder, that they could not leave it off when driven out of the town.

A night or two after the surrender of the place, they stole no less than eight horses and mules belonging to my battalion, and took them to some of the other divisions, where they sold them as animals captured from the enemy. I lost on this occasion an excellent little mule, worth at least L.20, and for which I of course never obtained a farthing. We used every exertion to discover both the perpetrators and the animals, but without success.

An English army is perhaps, generally speaking, under stricter discipline than any other in the world; but in proportion as they are held tight While they are in hand, if circumstances occur to give them liberty, I know of no army more difficult to restrain when once broke loose. A reason may perhaps be assigned for it in part. On such occasions as this siege, where they were long and much exposed to fatigue almost insupportable, to the most trying scenes of difficulty and danger, which were generally borne with cheerfulness and alacrity, they perhaps reasoned with themselves and one another in this manner,—that as they had borne so much and so patiently to get possession of the place, it was but fair that they should have some indulgence when their work and trials were crowned with success, especially as the armies of other powers make it a rule generally to give an assaulted fortress up to plunder. They had also become quite reckless of life from so long exposure to death; but an English army cannot plunder like the French. The latter keep themselves more sober, and look more to the solid and substantial benefit to be derived from it, while the former sacrifice every thing to drink; and when once in a state of intoxication, with all the bad passions set loose at the same time, I know not what they will hesitate to perpetrate.

The reader will judge of the state of our soldiers who had been engaged in the siege, when Lord Wellington found it absolutely necessary to order in a Portuguese brigade to force the stragglers out of the town at the point of the bayonet. At this time I think I was fairly tired of life, so disgusting and so sickening were the scenes the few last days had presented. I had also lost two of those for whom I had a great regard, together with several others of my brother officers, all excellent young men, with still a greater number wounded,—in all, in our fifteen companies, to the amount of twenty-six,—and men in equal proportion. It was indeed a trying time.

Notwithstanding what has been said above of the bad conduct of the British troops on this occasion, I am fully persuaded there is more humanity and generosity to be found in the breast of an English soldier than in any other in the world, for, except when inflamed by drink, I am confident it would be most revolting to his feelings to be ordered to proceed with cool deliberation to the execution of such horrid butcheries as we read of in the armies of other nations.—No! When calm and sober, no man acts with more tenderness towards those in his power than an

English soldier. Bonaparte would not have found in them the willing actors, in his political tragedy in Egypt, when he coolly fusiladed several thousands of his unfortunate Turkish prisoners, as related by Sir R. Wilson.

If I may be permitted to make a few remarks on the taking of this strong fortress, and of the conduct of the besiegers, I would say that never in the annals of military warfare was greater devotion shown by those of all ranks, from the General to the common soldier. The arduous and dangerous service of the trenches was cheerfully performed by every individual whose duty called him there; but the most conspicuous gallantry was manifested in the assault. Conceive of the heroic Picton and his brave division escalading a wall probably forty feet high, built on the summit of an almost inaccessible rock, and with troops at the top of all to oppose them as they reached its summit. It is true the enemy were not numerous here, having only about 200 men in the castle, but still one man in this situation was able to destroy probably twenty of the assailants, by throwing down a ladder after it had been set up; most of those ascending would be crushed to death by the fall over such a precipice. But he carried every thing before him, and after establishing his own division in this commanding-situation, he either actually did, or prepared to move upon the body of the enemy, who were defending the breaches.

General Walker also, who commanded a part of the 5th division, bravely forced an entrance into the town at the opposite side, overcoming every one of the numerous barriers and obstacles which presented themselves; and where he himself, in the act, I believe, of mounting the rampart, received a most desperate wound. It was said, but I know not how truly, that when he fell, the French soldier who wounded him was about to repeat the blow, which in all probability would have deprived him of life, but that the General, whether intentionally or not it is not said, made the masonic sign, which was understood by one of the Frenchmen, and that he instantly interfered in his behalf and stopped the blow. They say the General some time after found out that his brave deliverer had been sent to Scotland with his fellow-prisoners, and that he had him searched for and handsomely rewarded, and, I believe, procured him his liberty.

It is well known, I believe, to be the rule in all services like the assault of fortresses, &c, that those, both officers and men, who form the forlorn hope and the storming party, are volunteers, these being services of extreme danger, and which generally provide for the officers who survive a step of promotion; but it might as well have gone (in the light division at least) as a tour of duty, for on all occasions of this nature, with only one or two exceptions, the senior officers of each rank insisted upon being sent on that duty. Nay, in one instance this heroic feeling was carried to an almost censurable excess. Lieutenant Harvest of the 43rd having been some time the senior of his rank in that regiment, and there being a vacancy for a captain, he had been recommended for the company; and although he had not been gazetted, yet it had been intimated to him through his commanding-officer that his name should shortly appear as captain. Thus his promotion was perfectly secure; notwithstanding, when volunteers were called for for the storming party, he insisted on his right of going as senior lieutenant; so over scrupulous was he that his permitting a junior officer to occupy this post might be construed to the detriment of his honour. He went, and fell; and thus not only lost his company but his life, and by his too refined sense of honour deprived another officer, probably, of that promotion which would have been the consequence of going on this duty had he survived.

Among the men also the same noble enthusiasm prevailed, for he who was selected for this dangerous service out of the superabundant numbers who always volunteered, was envied by his comrades as truly fortunate. In fact, it required a character for good conduct to entitle a man to this honourable employment. Whatever, therefore, their other faults might be, a want of bravery was not one of them.

Chapter Eleven
Salamanca

On the 11th April we left Badajos to return again to the neighbourhood of Rodrigo, the French having, during the absence of our army from that frontier, made an irruption into Portugal, and penetrated as far down as below Castello Branca, completely ravaging the country. Our first march was to Campa Mayor, where we were quartered in the town. We next day reached Arronches, where we bivouacked in a wood near it. The following day we marched into Portalegre, and on the 14th, Niza; the 15th we crossed the Tagus at Villa Velha, and moved on to Lamadas. Here we began to perceive some of the effects of the reoent visit from the French; but at Castello Branca, which we reached next day, the devastation they had caused was truly deplorable. We halted here one day to refresh the troops and get forward our supplies, and the next day reached Escallas da Cima. Here we began to get very close upon the rear of the enemy; it therefore became us to move forward with circumspection, for our force on this side the Tagus was yet but small. We advanced, however, and occupied successively St Miguel d'Arch, Penamacor, and St Bartholomo, near Sabugal, which last town we passed through on the 23rd, and bivouacked that night at Alfyates. The utter desolation of Sabugal was beyond conception; filth and misery presented themselves in every direction. It had been made a depot for provisions by the French, I imagine, for on all sides the entrails and other offal of bullocks and sheep polluted the atmosphere by the abominable stench they caused, and had attracted multitudes of vultures and other birds of prey, who had by this time become horribly tame and familiar: one vulture sat so long upon a dead horse as I was riding along the road, that he allowed me to come near enough to make a cut at him with my sword, as he stretched his enormous wings to mount up from his prey.

On the 24th we reached Ituera, where we halted for two days. We had now entered Spain, and it not being intended as yet to commence another active campaign, we moved into quarters near the river Agueda, my battalion and the 43rd occupying the village of La Encina, or "The Oak." Here it was necessary that every exertion should be used to re-equip and prepare the troops for service, as it was intimated that another campaign would speedily commence.

All the winter and spring hitherto had been spent in active service, consequently much required putting to rights before we again took the field; all hands were therefore employed to patch up and repair our clothing and shoes, and to get every thing in good order when our services were again to be called for.

While we were here, I began to experience some of the ill effects of a deep-rooted enmity which one of my brother officers had conceived against me, though till now partly concealed. I was unconscious of having given him any cause for this; but he, without ever giving me any opportunity for explanation, used all his influence in endeavouring to injure me in the opinion of two of my superior officers, who had hitherto been friendly to me; and not only with them, but, I have reason to believe, with our acting brigadier, whose mind, with the others also, he completely estranged from me for a time. But though he misled them then, they did not retain the ill opinion of me which his misrepresentations had produced. I was not so fully aware of his dislike of me, till one day I was dining at the table of our acting brigadier, when he and one of those before noticed were also guests. I overheard him telling this officer, (with an intention, I almost imagine, that I should hear,) that I must be a bad man, for that I was sitting silent when all the rest were talking, in order that I might listen to their conversation. But I was the junior officer there, and it did not become me to be talkative; besides, I never was loquacious. I said nothing, (although some may blame me for it, but I loved peace,) trusting that one day such forbearance would not be forgotten; but I felt it deeply, and mourned over it in secret with great bitterness of spirit.

In this place also I began to receive very pressing letters from the merchants in England, from whom I had purchased a quantity of goods when last at home, but which, for want of transport, could not be got up to the army in order to their being disposed of; and, in short, scarcely a post arrived that did not bring some unwelcome and distressing tidings. I had purchased a fine mule in place of that stolen from me at Badajos, for which I had given about £30. I sent him down to Lisbon with my batman, to bring up as many of the goods as the mule could carry; but he had not been long gone till I had the mortification to learn that this mule also was lost. The man said he had been stolen, but I had every reason afterwards to believe that he had sold him. Be it observed, I could but very ill afford losses of this extent out of my pay and scanty allowances; but I endeavoured to bear up as well as I could against these misfortunes, although it is certain I was not able to bring religion to my aid" at this time of trial, for I had lived hitherto in total neglect of that most momentous of all concerns, and, although I endeavoured to amuse myself occasionally by fishing in the Agueda, my mind began to be greatly depressed.

About this time an order was issued for each British regiment in the Peninsula to endeavour to enlist fifty Spaniards to be incorporated in the regiment. I was sent in company with another officer into the mountains of Gata, not far from the city of Placentia. We were not successful, for although we obtained the names of some who promised they would follow us to La Encina, they never made their appearance. However, the beauty and magnificence of the mountain scenery amply repaid us for our trouble. From this village also I had the pleasure of visiting, for the first time, the lately captured fortress of Ciudad Rodrigo, and some of my brother officers who had shared in the toils and dangers of the siege, pointed out to me the most remarkable scenes about it. Like Badajos, it had been battered till practicable breaches were made to admit the besiegers, and then stormed in the same manner, but its defence was feeble compared with Badajos; and yet, to look over the ground in the neighbourhood of the trenches, one would imagine it impossible for troops to have lived, so completely was it ploughed up with shot and shells, each of the latter generally making an excavation sufficiently large in which to bury a horse.

Whilst we remained in these cantonments, the officers of the division once or twice got up a sort of "picnic," every one contributing something towards the feast, which was held in a large wood in the neighbourhood of Ituera. On our way from La Encina to this assembly, we passed over the ground where the 5th and 77th regiments had so distinguished themselves in September 1811, against a very superior force of the enemy's cavalry. The bones of the combatants lay bleaching upon the plain, the flesh having been very soon devoured by the innumerable birds of prey, which appeared as if collected from every part of the Peninsula. Indeed so numerous were the battles and skirmishes which took place along this frontier, together with the offal from the animals killed for the use of the armies, that they were no doubt better fed than they had in general been accustomed to.

But the period of our stay in this vicinity drew to a close, and on the 11th June we broke up from our cantonments, and passing the Agueda, the division assembled in a wood about a mile or two in front of Rodrigo. While we were here a rather remarkable phenomenon appeared about midday, or soon after; the sun, which shone most brightly, and the moon, with several stars, appeared all at the same time, the latter being distinctly visible. This of course attracted great numbers, and many were the sage remarks that were made, some believing it ominous of disastrous events; and indeed very shortly afterwards a circumstance occurred which in some degree confirmed their prediction. A grenadier of the 88th regiment (I think it was) had come over from his own division, to endeavour to prevail upon his wife, who had deserted him and taken up with a sergeant of our first battalion, to return with him, she having, as I understand, left him with one or more children, the first of their marriage, which he was anxious she should come and take care of. They had often, I fancy, quarrelled, and he had probably used her ill, but he was now desirous of a reconciliation, and entreated her to return with him to his regiment. He prevailed upon her to accompany him to some distance from the bivouack, that they might the more freely discuss the subject, for she had hitherto refused to agree to his request, being probably better provided for by the sergeant than she had been with him. While walking in a field close to the wood in which the bivouack was situated, and arguing the point with some heat, and she still persisting in remaining where she was, he became so exasperated at her continued refusal, that he, in a rage of jealousy and anger, drew his bayonet and plunged it in her bosom. Her cries soon brought people to the spot, who at once secured him, and he was instantly committed to the provost prison tent, and her body of course brought in and buried. Poor creature! she was one of the gayest of the females which graced our rural balls near Ituera only a short while previous, and had often danced with old General Vandaleur on those occasions. I believe he was not brought to trial for it, as her ill conduct probably had been considered as in some measure palliating what he did, and that he might be supposed to have been irritated to a degree of madness when he perpetrated the fatal act. I subsequently learnt that he was a brave soldier, and that he afterwards fell in the hard-fought battle of the Pyrenees.

We moved forward the next day in the direction of Salamanca, halting on the 13th at Alba de Yeltes, on the 14th at Sancho Bueno, the 15th at Matillo, in a large plain in front of which we bivouacked, where were the most luxuriant meadows I think I ever saw, the horses on our arrival being literally up to their bellies in fine rich grass. What a pity the natives know nothing of hay-making. This fine herbage is permitted to stand there till it perishes, and yet in the winter they are frequently very ill off for provender for their cattle; indeed I do not exactly know how they contrive to feed them in that season, but I know we were always greatly put to our shifts to procure any sort of long forage for our animals, being generally compelled by necessity to resort to this grass, rotten and dead as it was. I believe they use a considerable quantity of straw, which they chop very short, and which in truth is no bad substitute for hay; but when it is so very plentiful and so good, common sense, one would imagine, would induce them to preserve it.

LordWellington in the following season caused a considerable quantity of hay to be made in Portugal, getting scythes, &c. out from England, but we never returned that way afterwards to reap the benefit of it. All this immensely rich and extensive plain is in a complete state of nature—no enclosures to mark the different boundaries of the proprietors, should it have any, but where there are "landmarks," the mode of ancient days is resorted to.

On the 16th we moved forward to within about five miles of Salamanca, and bivouacked near a range of low hills extending from the Rio Valmuso (which we had just crossed) to the city. In front of this place our cavalry fell in with that of the enemy, with whom they had a petit affaire, and had captured a few of them, who, in the afternoon, passed our bivouack, on their way to the rear. We observed as they passed that they wore long queues, which had an odd appearance in our eyes, the British army haying for so many years left them off.

Next morning we advanced towards the city. We had gone, I think, about three miles, when ascending one of those heights over which the road passes, we had a most interesting view of this beautiful place. It seemed thickly studded with elegant and highly ornamented spires, springing from the numerous cathedrals and colleges, &c. which it contained; but what heightened the effect was an immense column of smoke rising from some magazines which the enemy (not having time to carry off) had set on fire. We feared it was but the prelude to the whole city sharing the same fate, for their barbarous conduct in Portugal during Massena's retreat, rendered it but too doubtful they were resorting to the same mode of warfare here. They still retained possession of a portion of the town, in which they had constructed three forts; one very strong, and capable of containing about 500 or 600 men; the other two were smaller, to cover and act as supports to the principal one. In constructing these works they had destroyed the greater part of the colleges, and a considerable number of other public buildings, besides several extensive streets which Salamanca had formerly contained; but even now it was still a beautiful and interesting city. One of these works commanded the bridge, which rendered our crossing the Tonnes here impracticable. We were in consequence moved about a league higher up the river, where we crossed by a rather deep ford. However, all got safely over, and we halted for the night on a small plain, a short distance from the ford, the main body of the enemy having retired and left 800 men in the forts before mentioned. These occupied but about one-third of the town, of course the remainder was open and free, and, as might be expected, every one was anxious to have a peep at this famous university. Consequently away a number of us scampered, and soon entered the city, the inhabitants of which were overjoyed to see us. The nuns were seen waving white handkerchiefs out of their iron-grated windows, and the Padres and other respectable inhabitants welcomed us with a thousand vivas, embracing us, and using every means of testifying their joy at our arrival.

I need not attempt to describe the place, for I am not able, and it has so often been described that my reader will not be disappointed at my declining to do it here; suffice it to say, the buildings in general, and the religious edifices in particular, were most superb; but the Goths had destroyed the finest portion of the city.

The forts were immediately invested, and we went and had a look also at them. They seemed remarkably strong, having been constructed principally of hewn stones, taken from the buildings they had destroyed; and on all sides of them a space of perhaps two hundred yards or more was cleared away to make room for the play of their artillery, and to prevent a lodgement being made by the besiegers.

We next day moved from our bivouack near the ford, and marched to the village of Aldea Secco, in front of which our cavalry and the enemy had a rencontre, after which the latter retired: this was about a league and a half in front of Salamanca. Next day we were suddenly assembled in consequence of the enemy, in great force, making his appearance at some distance in front of our bivouack. We were then removed from the plain, and took up a position on a height called Monte Rubio, or Red Hill, a little to the right. Soon after, also, the other divisions of our army began to assemble on the height, and our Chief arriving on the spot, every thing had the appearance of something serious being about to take place.

Here also, for the first time, I saw Don Carlos de Espagna with his few followers. These were better clothed, and equipped than almost any other Spanish troops that I had seen. The day passed over, however, without the French making any attack, and without any movement being made on our side, farther than putting the different divisions into position as they arrived on the ground. The French were continually receiving reinforcements, or rather their different divisions were rapidly arriving in succession, when they all bivouacked in the plain in front of us, at perhaps a mile and a half distance, and near to the village of Morisco. This they very soon gutted of every portable article, whether it was food, clothes, furniture, or whatever they could carry off; nay, they unroofed the greater part of the houses for fuel for the troops, but this latter proceeding could not be avoided, there being no wood near them. Englishmen may well feel thankful that their dwellings have not been exposed to such visitors, who, in half an hour, will convert a comfortable and smiling village into a heap of ruins.

We remained in this position for some days, the two armies, like two experienced pugilists, each waiting for the other to strike the first blow, by which he would in some measure lay himself open. It was not, however, Lord Wellington's game to commence operations, seeing a part of our army was then employed in the siege of the forts in Salamanca; besides, it is said, when some one ventured to hint that we should attack the enemy, that his lordship judged it would make a difference of 3000 men less on the side of the attacking army. I know not if this story be true, but certainly great prudence was displayed on both sides. However, the enemy had occasionally cannonaded us a little from the first; but about three days after their arrival, they made a very brisk and vigorous attack upon a conical hill immediately in front of our position, and a little to the right of Morisco. It was defended by the seventh division, which repelled the attack with great gallantry, driving the enemy down the hill again with great precipitation. The 68th regiment distinguished itself greatly, but in their pursuit of the beaten enemy, they advanced too far into the plain, and which the French observing, a forward movement was made again by them, and before our people could recover the high ground, Captain M'Kay and Lieutenant M'Donald, with a considerable number of their men, were made prisoners. Poor M'Kay received I know not how many bayonet wounds on this occasion, I believe not less than ten or twelve, but none of them very serious of course, or he could not have survived. He, with the others, were taken into the French lines, but he was so ill when they retired a few days after, that they were obliged to leave him in Morisco. The enemy's artillery played upon our line during the greater part of this attack, and caused us some loss, but not of any consequence, the horses appearing to have suffered more than the troops.

The French seemed disappointed and annoyed at our sticking so pertinaciously to the hills on this occasion, and told M'Donald (from whom I afterwards had this information) that it was only when we had every advantage on our side that we durst give them battle. Our armies were, I think, pretty nearly equal, each having perhaps about 40,000, but they were, I believe, superior in cavalry, and of course the plain was the very ground for them. Marmont seeing himself thus foiled, withdrew from before us, and made a movement to his left, crossing the Tormes with a considerable part of his force, and advanced on the other side of the river towards Salamanca. Our heavy German cavalry, under General Baron Back, opposed them here, and greatly distinguished themselves, driving the enemy's cavalry from the field. Our army made corresponding movements with the enemy, changing in parts our position.

Meantime the siege of the forts had been proceeding with from the first day of our arrival, and as the distance from Monte Rubio to the town was not great, several of us rode in to see how the siege was progressing, as the Americans have it. An attempt had been made to carry them by escalade, but it had failed; General Bowes, who led the attacking party, with several officers and men, having fallen in the attempt. His lordship now deemed it necessary to batter them regularly previous to another assault being made upon them. Heavy ordnance was therefore got into battery, which not only effected a breach in the smaller fort nearest the principal one, but which also threw a considerable quantity of hot shot into a building in the centre of it, which served as a barrack to the troops, the roof of which was presently set on fire, and the only shelter they had was thus destroyed. They thus were compelled on the 27th to surrender prisoners of war.

It is not easy to describe the effect produced on those inhabitants who lived nearest to the forts while the siege was going forward. Just as I entered one of our batteries, which had been established close behind a street, still occupied by the people, one of our artillerymen was carried out shot by a musket ball in the breast, and dead; the poor people when he was brought out into the street assembled round his body, and set up the most piteous lamentations imaginable. This impressed me with the good feeling which must have existed in their minds towards the English, for they are not a people, as the reader will be aware, who are very susceptible of horror at the sight of blood. A few hours after these forts surrendered, I went to visit the principal one—the devastation caused by our hot shot on the house before mentioned was awful. They had been obliged to make this their hospital also as well as barrack, and it was really lamentable to see the poor wounded Frenchmen lying there in, house that was literally falling about their ears, the roof having been completely fired, while burning beams and rafters were continually dropping upon these poor helpless beings. A French surgeon was still in charge of these men, and he had the politeness to show us all over the fort. As it had appeared from the outside, it was in reality remarkably strong, and the place where our people had made an attempt to escalade it, was pointed out to us; he said it was heavily mined, and that if our people had carried it by escalade, the mines would most likely have been sprung. There was fixed immediately opposite the gate a beam of wood, with holes bored in it, and about twenty

144

musket barrels fitted into them, so as to command the entrance. These, I imagine, it was intended to have fired by a train, as our people forced the gate, and it would have been like a little volley, which must have swept away the first of the assailants. The inhabitants seemed greatly rejoiced when this business was concluded, and peace once more established in their city, and they vied with each other in showing us every mark of attention and kindness, looking upon us as their deliverers.

If I am not mistaken, it was here where our illustrious Chief played off a sort of innocent ruse upon some of the Padres of the place. Soon after our arrival, and before the attempt upon the forts had failed, he went to visit some of the principal cathedrals, &c. which remained entire; the priests of course were proud to show their churches on such an occasion. He admired them greatly, and praised them much; but what seemed particularly to attract his attention was the extreme whiteness and cleanness of their walls and ceilings, although they were so very lofty. He enquired how they managed to get up to them to keep them so; and the unsuspecting Padre, without hesitation, led him to where they kept the immensely long ladders by which they ascended. This was just the very thing he wanted in his meditated attempt upon the forts, and of course they, with others of a similar description, were procured for that service. I will not vouch for the truth of the above, although I heard it, and I think it was not unlikely to have taken place. Indeed had he made a formal demand for such things, it is not improbable they might have denied they had them; but his having seen them himself precluded this.

The forts surrendered on the 27th, and on the 28th the enemy's main body retired altogether; for they soon learned the fate of the besieged, as they had occasionally communicated in some measure by rockets thrown up, and answered. On the same day, our division moved forward to Castilbanos; and the day following to Parada de Rubiallis. On the 30th, we reached Castrillo de Aguerino; and on the 1st of July, the town of Ravel-del-Rey. The next day, we moved on towards Rueda, a considerable town. Here we found the French in some force, their main body having retired across the Duero to Tordesillas.

The force in and about Rueda consisted of both cavalry and infantry, and seemed to act as a rearguard till the enemy's columns had time to file over the bridge at Tordesillas. I was at some distance in front of our division, the cavalry having preceded it, with whom I went forward. As we approached the place, a pretty large column of the enemy's infantry left it, and moved in the direction of the bridge. Some of our horse-artillery at this time came up, and fired Shrapnel shells into it, which did considerable execution; one shell particularly having killed and wounded great numbers, among whom was an officer, I think one of the handsomest men I had almost ever seen.

Our cavalry had a little brush with some squadrons of the enemy a little further on in the plain, and captured a few prisoners. One of these was the sergeant-major of one of their hussar regiments, and of all the men I ever saw taken, this man evinced the greatest trepidation and alarm. He was absolutely like to sink to the earth, either from fear of what awaited himself, or from the effects of the contest in which he had been engaged. He had lost his cap in the fray, and seemed like a person deprived of his senses. He must, notwithstanding, have been looked upon by the French as a good soldier, and a valuable non-commissioned officer; for I learned afterwards that they sent in a request that he might be exchanged for one of our sergeants whom they had captured, as it was intended immediately to promote him to the adjutancy of his regiment; of course this was immediately complied with. The enemy retired to Tordesillas, and we bivouacked near Rueda, a part of the officers being permitted to go into houses in the town during the day.

In this situation we remained for a day and a night; but the sun being so powerful, the troops began to feel the ill effects of the heat. They were accordingly brought into the town and quartered in the houses. Here I experienced more of that hostility before spoken of, on the following occasion. In the number of houses allotted to my battalion, there happened to be some of the best of them without stables; but as there was not time to examine farther than their outward appearance, this could not be known by me. I therefore marked off the houses according to custom, giving the best, in point of appearance, to the senior officers in succession, and so on till all were served. It so happened that the house allotted to this officer, who had nearly the best in the battalion given him, had no stable. This I was, from the fore-mentioned cause, totally ignorant of. Neither had I any stable in the house I occupied, but, after some trouble, I had found one in a house occupied by some of the men, where I had put up my horses and mules, and went about the other duties of my station. In the evening I was informed by my servant that my animals had been turned out by this officer, and his own put in, in their stead; and that mine were running loose in a yard, he not caring what became of them. My saddlery, and all the mule-apparatus, (precious articles in this country,) had also been cast out. He was my senior officer, and I was consequently obliged to bear this ill-treatment.

I mention this little circumstance, because it will show with what determined and unrelenting hostility he pursued me. Indeed it might not have been so trifling an affair, for had I not heard of it in time, I might have lost every horse and mule I possessed, which would have been one of the most serious disasters that could have befallen me. I could obtain no redress, for the captain before mentioned, who commanded the battalion, and this officer, being on rather unfriendly terms, he felt delicate in interfering in my behalf. Indeed I have some reason to believe, that it was partly on account of his enmity to this captain (with whom I still messed) that he so persecuted me.

I own I was on this occasion strongly tempted to demand that satisfaction which the rules of honour (as they are termed) dictate, for I then had not a Christian feeling on this subject; but after consideration and consultation with some friends, it was feared he might take advantage of his superior rank, not only to decline giving me that satisfaction, but to report me, and thus destroy my prospects for life, for he would have been compelled to the latter step had he not acceded to my demand; and from the feeling he displayed towards me, there is not the least doubt he would have rejoiced at such an opportunity of ruining me. At this time, also, I had very few real friends who would have

147

stood by me; for his secret machinations, and his having the ear of our brigadier, tended greatly to estrange my former friends from me.

All this, as might be expected, tended powerfully to depress my spirits, and to cast a gloom over a mind but too susceptible of impressions of that nature; for there is not any thing almost I would not do or submit to, to live on good terms with those I associate with, and indeed with all men. My mind was also much harassed at this time by receiving very unpleasant letters from England on the subject of the goods I before mentioned, and which had not yet reached any farther than Abrantes; and as the men began to be ill off for want of clothing, I obtained leave to proceed forthwith to Abrantes, to endeavour to get both the clothing and goods brought up to the regiment. I therefore set off, accompanied by one servant on a mule, leaving the other animals with the battalion, and proceeded on the 16th on my journey, and passing through Ravel-del-Rey, I halted for the night in a village where the seventh division was quartered. As I knew some of the officers of the 51st, I took up my abode with them for the night, and they indeed received me very kindly. My friends spent the evening very merrily; but, about midnight, they were called out and put under arms, expecting shortly to turn in again, as they told me; but they were marched off, and left the place entirely, leaving only my servant and myself in occupation of the town.

It seems that Marmont, with his whole force, had moved from Tordesillas, and had threatened Lord Wellington's communication with Salamanca. In order, then, to keep up a corresponding movement, and be ready to take advantage of any false step the enemy might make, his lordship withdrew his whole force, and began to retire as Marmont advanced. Thus, in the morning, to my surprise, all the army had left the neighbourhood, and as I was not certain who the next visitors might be, I quickly decamped from a village now left open to the enemy. I got on at a considerable pace, as both my servant and myself were riding, and on the 19th I reached Salamanca.

During yesterday's march I heard a considerable cannonade

to my right and rear, and I afterwards learnt that the two armies had come nearly in contact with each other, and some skirmishing and exchange of shots had taken place. I did not stop in Salamanca longer than to draw rations for ourselves and animals, being anxious to get on as fast as possible, to try to get up the supplies while the army remained near the frontiers, for it was still expected they would advance into the heart of Spain, notwithstanding the present partial retreat. I accordingly moved on that evening to Matilla, and continued thus making stages of thirty or forty miles a-day, and on the 25th I reached Abrantes; but on the preceding day I was overtaken by Lord Clinton, going home with the dispatches relative to the glorious and decisive battle of Salamanca, which took place on the 22nd. His lordship was nearly worn out, being actually asleep on his horse as he rode past me, for he had never once stopped from the time he first set out. I learnt the news from the person who accompanied him. It is impossible to describe the joy this information created among the Portuguese inhabitants of the village. I stopped for the night at Gaviæ.

I found at Abrantes a detachment of our second battalion proceeding to join the army; but, to my sorrow, learnt there was no chance of procuring transports for the clothing, &c, for months to come. This was distressing information to me, and of course added to the despondency already preying upon my spirits; for the merchants letters I was continually receiving began to be most importunate, and indeed attributing the non-remittal of their money to a want of principle, and talked of reporting my conduct to the Commander-in-chief.

Want of a proper religious feeling, under such circumstances, as might be expected, laid me open to great temptations. I therefore, to drown sorrow, and because I had always been too much addicted to it, began to give way to intemperance, and, falling in with a number of officers of very dissipated habits, I was led on to indulge in the most vile and abdminable of all vices, drunkenness, to an excess almost incredible. But the gloom still seemed to thicken, and a dark cloud seemed impending over me, of which I was fully aware, and wrote home to my friends to that effect.

At length my birthday, the 4th of August, arrived, and which must, as my unhappy companions in sin urged on me, be kept with all due jollity. Accordingly, a dozen of strong port-wine was procured, and we boozed away most joyfully, the whole being drank by about four or five of us. This produced constipation in the bowels, and had nigh brought me to my end; but my mind was more affected, if possible, than my body.

I arrived at Galigao, the place of my intended rest for the night—and here I was attacked with ague and fever in addition to my other disorder—this was the effect of my exposure to the sun in so weak a state. Here I felt myself extremely ill, and believed I could not survive till morning. I consequently got my servant to make down my bed in a corner of the room I occupied, with his own near it, and told him to leave the candle burning, for that my time could not be long.

I reached Lisbon in two days from this time, having taken a boat at Santarem. I ate nothing, with a trifling exception. I had no inclination for food, nor did I think I ought, for the reason before given; my only sustenance was a little water which I kept in a bottle, and with which I now and then moistened my parched lips.

I arrived at Lisbon about daybreak in the morning, and proceeded as well as I was able to a friend's house, and knocked at the door; but shocked indeed were he and his wife, when they saw me standing below, more like a ghost than an inhabitant of this world. Indeed it is not easy to describe my looks at this time; there must have been much of that spiritual misery depicted in them which a confirmed despair no doubt produces. They took me in, and after hearing my woful tale, prepared to do for me the best that lay in their power; they gave me their own bed, taking a pallet for themselves, and treated me as if I had been their brother.

My health now gradually improved, under the kind and fostering attentions of my warm-hearted host and hostess, and it became necessary that I should resume my station at Abrantes, which I did, in hopes of being able to obtain transport from thence, although the army was at this time in the neighbourhood of Madrid. But after returning to Abrantes I suffered a relapse, and was again brought to the borders of the grave.

During my stay at Lisbon, my batman, whom I before mentioned as having lost, or rather sold, my mule, and who had here rejoined me to take care of the horse and mule I had with me, either from remorse, or some other cause, made an attempt to cut his throat, and succeeded so far as to sever the windpipe, I believe, but did not quite effect his purpose. He was found in a field near Lisbon bleeding nearly to death, and brought into the hospital, where, with great care, and after some time, he recovered. Indeed 1812 was a sickly year, and many were affected strongly in the mind, several having committed suicide, I believe.

While I lay here ill the second time, I received a letter from the regiment telling me that the paymastership had become vacant, the poor old gentleman with whom I returned to England last year, having come out again to the Peninsula, and got as far as Rodrigo on his way to the regiment, and there, being attacked with the same disease I had suffered so much from, died; and that as General Stewart, our colonel, had arrived at Lisbon, I was to go and wait upon him, and that letters would be written from the regiment requesting him to recommend me for the situation.

I with great difficulty again reached Lisbon, and waited upon the general, but to my great mortification I found the promised letters from the regiment had never been received, and that another person had, in consequence, been recommended, he being the son of the late paymaster, and had applied some time before. My disappointment did not prey upon my mind, for at this time I set very light indeed by the good things of this world, and felt conscious that I already possessed much more than I deserved. I was compelled through illness to remain again in Lisbon some time, but found great difficulty to obtain permission from the commandant for so doing. My general, however, procured me leave to stay till I should be able to resume my post at Abrantes. Here, not only myself, but all the officers who were then in Lisbon, and also at the army, suffered much from the want of subsistence. I had at this period seven months' pay due me, and could not obtain a dollar from the public chest, although I wrote a note to the commandant showing him how I was suffering from want of money.

The army had in the meantime pursued the French, as before noticed, on one side to Madrid, and on the other to Burgos; but the attempt to take the latter by storm having failed, and the enemy having been able to assemble a more numerous force than Lord Wellington had before it, he was obliged to retire from both those places to the frontiers of Portugal. The division from Cadiz, the siege of which having been raised by our forward movement in summer, had joined the army at Madrid. Much was suffered, I understand, during this retreat, the troops having been exposed to great privations, and the weather being exceedingly wet and unpleasant. My division, after the retreat, took up its quarters again in the villages on the Portuguese side of Rodrigo—my battalion being stationed at the village of Espeja. The army, as might be expected from the late severe and harassing service they had been engaged in, began to be extremely ill off indeed for want of clothing, many of the men being nearly quite naked; in consequence, the most pressing orders were sent from head-quarters to use every means possible to have the supplies immediately forwarded, for Abrantes at this time contained stores belonging to almost every regiment in the army. My health having been considerably improved, I again returned to that depot, and, after waiting a few weeks, the-means of transport were at last given me by the commissary there. I need not say with what alacrity I prepared for and commenced my long wished for journey. I had got a sufficient escort assigned me, from a detachment of our men. being about to join the regiment.

We started about the beginning of January 1813, and proceeded on our route by way of Niza, &c. I had been obliged to buy another horse from some cause which I do not now recollect, but when we were leaving the town just named, I found, on turning out to move off, that a large nail had been driven right up into the centre of one of his feet. Whether this was done accidentally, or by design, I never could learn, but the consequence was the loss of the horse. I had great trouble also to keep the convoy, which consisted of about a dozen bullock carts, with as many soldiers as an escort, together; the drivers, if they were not strictly guarded, very often made their escape, taking their bullocks with them during the night, and leaving the cart in our possession, glad, I dare say, that they got off so cheaply, for they seemed to have a great antipathy to go with us. I was therefore compelled to collect them all together near Castello Branco, and making the soldiers load their rifles before them, told them as well as I was able that they had orders to shoot the first who attempted to desert with his bullocks. This had a good effect, for I believe we lost no more till we reached the regiment; but, as we approached the frontiers of Spain, several of the drivers ran away without their cattle, preferring the loss of both bullocks, cart, and payment, rather than enter that country, of which the peasantry in general seemed to have a great dread. Those who stuck by us to the last, were rewarded with the bullocks and carts of the deserters; but I think we did not take more than two or three out of the twelve to the regiment, the rest had all made their escape. Nothing can be conceived more tiresome than travelling with such a convoy.

The carts are all constructed upon the principle of the Irish car; that is, the axle rolls round with the wheels, they being firmly united; consequently the creaking noise created by the friction is loud and most unpleasant, and they have no idea of grease or tar to diminish this, but believe in many parts, if not in all, the noise to be a sort of holy noise, which keeps the devil from them. I found, in removing these stores, that great robberies had taken place upon them, several of the bales having been opened while on board ship, great quantities of goods taken out, and their place filled up with old transport bedding, &c. I found it necessary, however, to endeavour to bear up against all this, for my mind would not suffer me to dwell too much upon such misfortunes. At length I arrived at the regiment, where indeed I was a welcome guest, for they were greatly in need of all kinds of equipment.

The officer who had rendered my life so unhappy before, had left the regiment, and gone into another far distant from my present place of abode, for which I was truly thankful, and his absence I found produced a great change in my favour; for every one seemed glad to see me, and sympathized with me in my late alarming illness; in fact, the face of things was entirely changed for the better. I myself had benefited much by my late chastisement. I had learned to think meanly of myself, and to be kind and submissive to all to whom I owed submission; a virtue which, I fear, I was but too deficient in before.

All things now went well with me. The goods, which before had been such a source of uneasiness and trouble, were rapidly disposing of, and thus the prospect of my soon being able to pay my creditors became every day brighter. But, in the mean time, what I had hinted at before took place: one of the merchants had actually reported me to his Royal Highness the Duke of York. This might, indeed, have deprived me of my commission, had his Royal Highness been harsh with me; but he caused a letter to be written to my commanding-officer, (now Sir Andrew Barnard,) to call on me to explain why I had not remitted the merchant what I owed him, and to account for my not answering his letters, which he said I had failed to do for several months. My answer was very simple, as the reader is aware; but, with respect to the letters, I showed the colonel one, in which the merchant acknowledged having received one from me a short time previously. This also was satisfactory, and I had moreover remitted him a short while before L.300 of the money I owed him. The colonel was fully satisfied, and wrote off to his Royal Highness accordingly, and I heard no more of the business. Soon after the captain, who had been acting as paymaster, was obliged to return to England, on account of ill health. After some necessary steps I was appointed to this duty, it being an addition of 10s. *per diem* to my pay. According to the army regulations, a person in my situation could not be appointed acting paymaster; but a committee of three captains was formed, who took all the responsibility of my transactions upon themselves, giving me, as before said, the whole 10s. *per diem*. This showed, at least, that they were not afraid to trust themselves in my hands; for I might have involved them deeply. In short, whatever I did (almost) prospered, and a kind Providence seemed to smile upon me; and I believe that from this to the close of the Peninsular campaigns was the happiest part of my life. I have reason, therefore, to bless God for his unbounded goodness to me.

Chapter Twelve
Vittoria

As the officer whom I have had occasion so often to mention owed me a trifle of money, I wrote to him, in as friendly a manner as I could, hoping, now we were separated, that his enmity would cease, and I was desirous of being at peace with all mankind; for, as I said before, I never yet knew why he was my enemy. He wrote back, with an order for the money, telling me, he hoped never to hear from me again, for that he was anxious to forget that such a person had ever existed in the world. This, as might be supposed, wounded my feelings deeply, but I remembered that I had myself sinned as deeply against God, and that He might raise up such instruments for my correction as seemed good to Him. My feelings, therefore, towards this person were more of regret and pity than of resentment, and I think I did not forget to pray to God for him. Poor fellow, he has a good while since been called to his account, and that in rather an awful manner; he fell in a duel, but which (from all I could learn) he was engaged in from the best motives, that of endeavouring to prevent the seduction of a young female belonging to his regiment. I hope he is at peace.

During our stay in winter-quarters every exertion was made to put the troops in a proper state to take the field again, so soon as the season was sufficiently advanced. While we remained here also every sort of innocent amusement, at least generally innocent, was had recourse to, both by officers and men, not only to pass the time of inactivity with pleasure, but to keep up that readiness for action always so necessary in a state of warfare. We accordingly had races, balls, plays, and every other description of pastime our situation admitted of. We in Espija established what was termed a trigger club, each one in turn giving an entertainment at his house, and at which, as the name would imply, as much game was produced as our sportsmen could procure. The plays were generally held at Gallegos, the quarter of the 43rd, and which were indeed got up in a surprising style, considering the means of doing so. A walking club was established in our 1st battalion, which was quartered at Alamada; we were of course frequently favoured with the company of its members, for they thought nothing of setting out, each with a long pole in his hand, and walking twenty or more miles to dinner. Thus harmony and a brotherly feeling was promoted amongst the officers of the division,—a thing of great moment where regiments have to act together, as well as pleasant to all parties. Some of our people also occasionally had a wolf-hunt, for these animals were quite numerous in this part of the country; nay, so bold were they when pressed with hunger, that they did not scruple sometimes to enter our villages, and devour whatever fell in their way that they could master. An officer of ours had an ass or a mule torn to pieces one night while standing in the yard behind his house. The mode of hunting them was, to have a certain number with arms stationed at the different passes in the wood, whilst a large party of drivers scoured the wood in line, driving every thing before them, when the animals, coming upon the armed people, were shot; but I do not think they were at all successful: it requires people accustomed to the business to enable them to kill many. There is a premium given for every wolf's head, but I forget how much it is.

I sometimes took a trip to the Azara, or the Agueda, on a fishing excursion; but I was ill off for fishing tackle: the hooks the Spaniards make are the clumsiest things imaginable, and would not, I am persuaded, be made with less dexterity by the natives of New Zealand. Those which we were forced to use for fly-hooks had a hole-or eye at the top, like the crook which you will sometimes see in a butcher's shop, intended to be hung upon another, which was formed by turning the wire down again, and through this they run their line; besides, they almost invariably broke, and I have been wofully tantalized sometimes by having the hook break off the only fly that the fish were taking; notwithstanding, I caught some very fine trout in the Agueda, this river abounding with them. I sometimes also caught barbel in that river; but it was literally swarming with a sort of roach, or what some of our people called rock-fish: they generally feed from some stuff they find on the large stones. But as the season approached which was to call us to the field, a review of the whole division was ordered to take place on the plain of Espija, and which, I think, was as brilliant a spectacle of that description as it was possible for 5000 men to make. Every regiment was in high and complete order, the whole having by this time been fully equipped for the campaign: the movements, too, were beautiful, and executed with great precision and promptitude, and, as might be anticipated, called forth the unqualified approbation of our illustrious Chief.

A new and different arrangement was made this campaign with respect to both officers and men in their field-equipment. Experience had proved that constant bivouacking injured the men's health, as the mode they had adopted last year, though very ingenious, was not calculated to protect them sufficiently from exposure to the weather. They had last campaign been ordered each man to have loops sewed on at the corner of his blanket; thus, when in the field, two of these were united, and spread over two stand of arms set up at the ends for poles, and being fastened down at the other corners with bayonets, they formed a sort of tent, into which perhaps four men might creep; but then they had thus only two blankets to serve as a bed for the whole four men; consequently they would, in cold weather, be much exposed. This campaign each company received four tents; thus allowing about twenty men for each, and the officers of each company had one among them, and the field and staff officers in like proportion. These were carried on mules, which before had carried the camp-kettles; but these being exchanged for smaller ones, the men carried them in turns upon their knapsacks. Thus it rarely happened that the tents were not on the ground nearly as soon as the men; but strict orders were given always to encamp out of sight of the enemy, if practicable, that they might not be able to calculate our numbers. How very different from the ancient mode of encamping! each of which being more like a town laid out with regular streets, &c. &c. But war was a very different thing in those days, and could Marlborough have risen to see one of our straggling and irregular mountain camps, I know not what his feelings would have been: he would, I fear, have thought we had sadly degenerated.

All being now ready for opening the campaign, a part of the army, under Sir Thomas Graham, crossed the Douro low down in Portugal, and proceeded up the right bank, while we, with Sir Rowland Hill's corps, moved forward in the direction of Salamanca and Toro. On the 21st of May, our division broke up from its cantonments, and assembled at the village of St Felices el Chico, a few miles below Ciudad Rodrigo, each regiment having had the Agueda to ford in its march to this camp. Our division at this time consisted of the following corps:—viz. the 1st brigade, under General Kempt, was composed of the 43rd regiment, 17th Portuguese, and the 1st and 3rd battalions of my regiment; the 2nd brigade, under General Skerrit, contained the 52nd regiment, 1st and 3rd Portuguese Cacadores, and the 2nd battalion of my regiment; one troop of horse artillery, under Colonel Ross, was attached to the division; the whole being under the command of General Charles Alten. On the 22nd, we moved on to Martin del Rey, near the river Yeltes, by the side of which we encamped. On the 23rd, we marched to and encamped near San Munoz, where the division had, I understand, suffered considerably during the retreat of last year, from the French having gained ground upon them, and severely cannonaded them from a height near this village. On the 25th, we moved on to Robliza, having halted the day before to enable the other division to come up with us. We next morning moved forward to the little river Valmuzo, a few miles on the Portugal side of Salamanca, and alluded to in my former advance. Here we halted for three hours during mid-day and cooked, and in the afternoon advanced to the ford of El Canto, on the river Tonnes, and about two leagues below Salamanca. Here we encamped for the night, and remained next day also. Lord Wellington, with some cavalry we understood, had entered Salamanca, where only a small force of the enemy's cavalry had been found, and which retired immediately; but I believe some little skirmishing took place between the parties. On the morning of the 28th we forded the Tonnes, and advanced towards Aldea Nueva de Figuera, which we reached late in the day, the distance being about twenty-four miles.

While we lay at El Canto, a few of our officers visited Salamanca, in hopes of meeting some of their old friends of last year; but not a viva greeted their ears on entering the city; a sort of suspicious look of recognition was all they could obtain from those people, who had received us only last summer with such extravagant demonstrations of joy. No doubt they had been made to suffer for their former expressions of attachment to us, for the French had in almost every place their partisans, who doubtless would not fail to give them, on their return, an account of the manner in which the English had been received, and the contributions would be laid on accordingly.

We remained at Aldea from the 28th May to the 2nd of June, waiting for information from the corps under Sir Thomas Graham, it being intended to form a junction at or about Toro, where it was expected the enemy had a considerable force; this was distant from us about thirty miles. While we continued here, I took a trip to Sir Rowland Hill's division, where I had a townsman, an officer in the 28th, but had not the satisfaction of seeing him. I had other friends in that division, however, with whom I and my companions spent the day in great harmony and satisfaction, and at evening returned to our camp, about four miles distant, highly gratified.

On the 2nd of June, we set off early in the morning, and arrived at Villa Buena about mid-day, where we halted for three hours to cook and refresh, after which we continued our march towards Toro, which we reached in the evening, but the enemy having destroyed the bridge across the Douro at this place, we encamped for the night in some fields on the left bank of the river. We learnt here that the hussars attached to Sir Thomas Graham's division had attacked a corps of French cavalry soon after their having quitted Toro, and with whom a very smart affair had taken place, the enemy being completely routed, and about 150 prisoners taken from them. Our cavalry, I believe, lost an officer on this occasion, who fell into the hands of the enemy. Nothing could exceed the miserable appearance of the horses taken from the French on this occasion; they appeared really half starved, although at this season there was plenty of green forage to be had; they must either have been sadly neglected, or have been doing exceeding hard duty.

The bridge having been rendered passable for the men, the division crossed on the following morning, the horses and mules fording the river. We left Toro immediately, and moved on in pursuit of the enemy, and encamped that night at Terra Buena. On the 4th, we reached the convent of Espinar, and encamped on a height just over it. It was a most picturesque and beautiful piece of country around this convent, but itself appeared to have been lately rendered uninhabitable. I believe the monks had been driven away by the French, but not a soul remained to enquire of; all about the building was desolation. We next day advanced to the village of Muderra, and on the 6th to Amperdia, and on the 7th we marched through the city of Palentia, and encamped outside the walls, on the banks of the river Carrion.

Here the inhabitants evinced the same degree of enthusiasm on our entrance as we had been accustomed to witness in other large towns, till the French had taught them a little more circumspection, and which the good people of Palentia would have been most probably fully taught, had these good friends of theirs ever got possession of their city again. Some time after we had pitched our camp, and were strolling about the city, the Lifeguards entered, and were of course saluted with repeated vivas. One of the men, a rather country-looking young fellow, cried out, "Ay, the folks be always glad to see we Lifeguards," happily supposing, no doubt, that they were intended as a particular compliment to his corps alone. All the country through which we had marched for several days past, was one continued plain of waving corn, mostly wheat of the very finest description. There are no hedges or dikes, but, as before noticed, only landmarks to divide the different fields, so that its appearance is like an immense sea, stretching as far as the eye can reach, the long corn undulating with the wind as the waves in the ocean.

On the 8th we marched forward and encamped at the village of Tamara, the weather having, from being exceedingly fine, and indeed rather hot, set in extremely wet and cold, and thus rendered marching very unpleasant. We next day reached La Pena, (the name, it may be remembered, of the Barossa Spanish hero,) the weather continuing very coarse and stormy. On the 10th we continued to advance, and marching through the village of Framosa, and passing over a canal which crosses here, we halted for the night on the right bank of the river Pisuerga, near the village of Lantadilla. In all these late movements, we had experienced a great deficiency of fuel for cooking and drying our clothes when wet, neither forest nor bush-wood being to be seen for days together, and indeed scarcely one solitary tree to be met with nothing but corn; so that we were occasionally compelled to resort to the cruel and unchristian like expedient of pulling down houses to obtain the timber with which they were built for the purpose of cooking, or we must have eaten our food raw. This, however, was done in a regular and systematic order, the Alcalde of the village pointing out such of the houses as were to be doomed to the fire, and the troops taking no more than was absolutely necessary. It is astonishing to me how the natives themselves exist for want of this article of first necessity.

From this village we moved forward on the 11th, and crossing the Pisuerga, marched on the town of Pallacio, which we passed, and reached the village of Landrino, near which we encamped for the night.

From the time we left Toro, the enemy had been gradually retiring before us, having withdrawn his forces from all the strong places on the Douro, and seemed concentrating somewhere in the direction of Burgos or Vittoria. Excepting our cavalry, no part of our forces ever had the satisfaction of seeing a Frenchman hitherto during the whole of this long and rapid march; but on the morning of the 12th, as we now approached Burgos, it was fully expected that we should be able to get a sight of the fugitives; and accordingly, after we had left our last night's quarters, and marched a few miles in the direction of the city, a pretty strong body of the enemy's cavalry was seen drawn out on a high plain, a little above the village of Hornilla de Camino. These were supported by a division of infantry formed in square, and occupying the outer edge of the high plain facing the way we advanced, and apparently observing our motions. On discovering this force, our division was halted to give the cavalry attached to us time to ride forward to reconnoitre, and ascertain more exactly the force before us, than could be done while we were on the low ground.

I rode forward with our cavalry, which, passing by the enemy's square of infantry, approached the main body of their cavalry. It not being, however, the intention of the French to fight here, they slowly and orderly retired before us across the plain; but as we had left the square of infantry nearly behind us, the guns attached to our cavalry turned in that direction, for this body seemed indifferent about the movements of our cavalry, and it was not till our division began to ascend the hill that they evinced the slightest intention of stirring. On seeing them, however, they quickly decamped, and as they had to pass within 150 yards of the position our guns had taken up, I imagined considerable execution must have been done upon them before they got out of our reach. But, strange to say, I believe only one single man was knocked down by the great numbers of shot fired at them. It must have been owing to the relative situations of the two parties; they passed down a hollow way which led from the high plain in the direction of the Burgos road, and which covered them completely till they came immediately below our guns, when it became a difficult matter to depress them so as to bear upon the enemy's square as they passed us. However the whole turned round and gave us a regular volley, for, as we were so much above them, there was no danger from their firing in square; but this, although the shots flew pretty thick about us, was not productive of any mischief that I remember. They retired across the plain below us, pursued by another division of ours which had advanced on our right, and between whom and the French a pretty smart skirmish took place. So soon as their infantry were clear from us, their guns opened out from the opposite side of the river upon us on the height, but, the distance being considerable, their shot did little execution. It was evident this force was only left here as a rearguard, to ascertain our movements and force, &c. We encamped far the night near the road by which we had ascended the high plain; but were awoke early next morning by a tremendous explosion which shook the earth beneath us, although at the distance of 6 or 7 miles from Burgos, the castle of which the enemy had blown up, and retired altogether. We soon after commenced our march, and, leaving that city to our right, made a long march in the direction of the Ebro, and halted for the night near the village of Tovar. The next day we moved on to Quintanajar, and on the 15th, after a long march, we reached the Ebro, and halted at the village of Puente Arrenas, situated in the delightful valley of Veras. This is one of the most picturesque and beautiful valleys in Europe, I dare say. When you arrive at the brow of the high ground over the Ebro, a sight breaks upon you all at once which is indescribably grand and beautiful;—a large river rolling under you, beyond which a rich and fertile valley, laden with the fruits of a hundred orchards, with charming villas and farm-houses dispersed through all the lawn; a stupendous bridge, of I know not how many arches, leading you across this magnificent river; and the whole closed by high and beetling rocks jutting out of the high woody bank on the opposite side. It really appeared like enchantment when we first arrived within sight of it, from the long dreary plains we had been so long traversing. Here, for the first time since we entered Spain, did we meet with *"manteca de vaca,"* or "cow butter," all the other we had been compelled to use hitherto for want of better, was what they call *"manteca de puerco,"* or "hog's-lard." The women who brought it wore a quite different dress from those we had seen in the parts we had passed through; the women had on generally yellow stockings, with abundance of petticoats of red, yellow, green, &c. &c, and were all very stout-made; they were, I believe, from Asturias. Poor creatures, many of them followed us with loads of butter, wine, cheese, &c. &c, even into France, so pleased were they with the excellent prices their merchandise brought amongst us;

indeed, we had been so long debarred the enjoyment of butter and cheese, that we would have given almost any price to get them sweet and good. They carried their loads (and tremendous ones they were) as the flesh-wives in Newcastle carry theirs, that is, by passing a broad leather belt across the forehead and over the shoulders, and so underneath the heavy load upon their back. They were a civil and obliging race of beings, and apparently much more industrious and cleanly than the rest of their country people.

We left this delightful spot on the morning of the 16th, following the course of the river upwards for about a league, then turning short to the right, passed through an enclosed country, and halted for the night at the town of Medina del Pomar. This is a considerable-sized place, in which was a nunnery, the inmates of which greeted us with hearty welcomes and vivas, with waving of handkerchiefs, &c, through their strongly iron-grated windows, where they more resembled criminals of the worst description shut up in a strong prison, poor things, than people who had devoted themselves to the service of their Maker. Next morning, we moved forward through a country almost without roads; we were, in fact, crossing the country in order to get nearer to the great road leading from Madrid to Vittoria, and on which the enemy's army was then retiring. We encamped for the night, after a fatiguing day's march, on a woody height near the little river Loza. We took the high ground on this occasion for our encampment, although extremely inconvenient' and uncomfortable, being among stumps and brush-wood, where there was scarcely room to pitch our tents; this was in consequence of being in the neighbourhood of a considerable force of the enemy, which was retreating, as before noticed, along the great road.

The next morning, the 18th of June, we started pretty early, and calculating that we should this day come in contact with the above force, we marched in such a manner as to be ready, when that event took place, to take advantage of any favourable circumstances that might offer. We had in our front a squadron of Hussars belonging to the German Legion, and which were generally attached to our division. About mid-day the squadron in front of us reached the village of San Millan, where the road on which we were then marching, and the great road on which the enemy was retreating, unite; the latter descending from a high tableland just above the village, and passing a narrow defile between two high rocks. Our cavalry, on reaching this village, descried the advance of the French, composed also of cavalry; and what was not a little singular, they also were Germans in the French service. Our brave Hussars instantly charged those of the enemy, and immediately overthrew the body opposed to them, and in the charge captured several men and horses, which they brought in prisoners.

By this time the head of the division had reached the spot, (my 1st battalion leading,) which in a few minutes got warmly engaged with the enemy's voltigeurs, a considerable number of whom had advanced to oppose us, in order that the main body of their division might be enabled, under cover of their fire, to pass through the village on the way towards Vittoria. Our people, however, pressed them so hard, that the whole of their leading brigade was obliged to join in the action. At this moment our illustrious Chief came galloping up; for, whenever any thing was to be done, he was always present. He had also taken care to have our 4th division moved so as to arrive at the village of Espija, a town about a league in front of us on the great road, nearly about the same time, so that, should the French contrive to get away from us, they might fall into their hands. He immediately sent me off to the leading company of our people who were engaged, for the guide they had had with them, in order that he might conduct his lordship to Espija; but that was no place for a Spanish peasant who had neither honour nor glory to gain, and he had accordingly made his escape the moment our folks got into action. His lordship instantly dashed off without a guide, while our two battalions, that is, the 1st and 3rd of my regiment, kept advancing upon the enemy, and fairly drove them through the village, being supported by the other regiments of the brigade, but who had not any occasion to come into action.

The first brigade of the enemy being thus beaten, retreated

along the great road in the direction of Espija, leaving their second brigade and all their baggage to their fate. These latter being pressed by our second or rear brigade, and seeing us in possession of the village, and the road they had to pass, immediately broke in all directions, and dispersed themselves in the mountains over the village, each man making the best of his way. This their baggage could not do, and it consequently fell into the hands of the captors, an easy and valuable booty; but although my brigade, by beating and dispersing the enemy at the village, had been the principal cause of its capture, yet those whose hands it fell into had not the generosity to offer the least share of it to us, but divided it amongst themselves.

During the skirmish in the village, a French hussar chased one of our officers several times round one of the trees growing by the side of the road, and repeatedly cut at him with his sabre, and it is likely would have cut him down at last, had not the officer seen a rifle lying near, belonging to a man just killed; and luckily it was loaded when he picked it up. He waited for the Frenchman, and coolly shot him through the body, and instantly seized his horse as lawful prize; had the rifle missed fire he was gone. We had not rested long after this brush till we heard a firing in our front, where indeed it was expected. The troops which had just left us, I imagine, had been attacked by the 4th division, and we, the 1st brigade, were instantly ordered to their support should they need it; but before we reached Espija, the enemy was completely beaten, and had retired in the direction of Vittoria. We had to retrace our steps and join our other brigade, and encamped for the night in the neighbourhood of San Millan.

Our loss on this occasion was but trifling, considering the smartness of the affair. An officer of my regiment, of the name of Haggup, a countryman of my own, received a most dangerous wound in the abdomen, of which it was feared he would die, but he soon after completely recovered. An aide-de-camp of the French General was wounded, and taken prisoner, but he soon after died, poor fellow. Along with the captured baggage were a number of Spanish ladies, who had been attached to the French officers to whom it belonged, but they did not appear over faithful to their protectors, for most of them, I believe, preferred remaining in the hands of their captors, to being forwarded after their beaten and now ill-provided former companions; such is generally the fidelity to be expected from that sort of people.

On the 19th we advanced by the same road the French had retired, till we reached the town of Salinas, where there were very extensive salt-works, as the name of the place denotes. We encamped for the night near the village of Pobes, on a small rivulet named Bayas, I believe. Near the end of our march to-day we had a view of the enemy's rear-guard, as they rounded the end of a mountain, which lay immediately before us, and over which the road to Vittoria passes. After rounding the mountain, this part of the enemy's force fell in with our 4th division again, which had been moved forward from Espija by another road. A very smart skirmish was the consequence, which we distinctly heard, and in which a good number fell on both sides. The French retired from hence into their position in front of Vittoria. During the next day, while we halted here, it began to be whispered that the enemy had concentrated his forces in and around Vittoria, which was distant from us perhaps about ten or a dozen miles, and that the divisions of our own army had that day approached nearer together, which indicated a determination on the part of our Chief to try his hand with King Joseph, should he be bold enough to stay where he then was.

Many, of course, and various would be the reflections which occupied the minds of the different individuals composing the two armies; but I can speak from experience, that those are of a much more pleasing nature which a consciousness of superiority and a good prospect of success inspires, than those which a retreating army are compelled to entertain.

Pretty early in the morning of the 21st, we fell in and moved forward by the way the French rearguard before-mentioned had taken, and after having passed the end of the mountain and descended into the valley on the other side, we saw evident proofs that the affair between our 4th division and the French, above alluded to, must have been pretty warm. We continued to advance on the road to Vittoria, till, on ascending a rising ground, the French army appeared in position immediately in front of us. It was a noble and animating sight, for they appeared as numerous almost as grashoppers, and were posted as nearly as I can recollect in the following order. Immediately before us ran the river Zadora, passing from our left and front to our right and rear. In the centre of an extensive plain rose a pretty lofty conical hill, from which extended to their left a sloping plain, through which the great road lay, and terminated by a long range of mountains, stretching from Puebla de Arlanzon, just above the river, to a considerable distance beyond Vittoria. The city was shut out of our view by the conical hill before mentioned, and was distant from it about four or five miles; to the right of this hill, along the bank of the river, it appeared broken, and not easily approachable. On the face of the conical hill, and to its very summit, it appeared as thickly set with troops as if they had been bees clustering together; it was also thickly studded with batteries and other field-works. On the plain between that and the long range of mountains, the. troops appeared to stand so thick that you might imagine you could walk on their heads. There did not appear any great force on the mountains to their left, and what they had to the right of the conical hill and towards Vittoria We could not discern, but it turned out they had a strong force there. There were several small villages in the plain and on the side of the mountains; the largest stood rather to the right of the plain, with a wood immediately behind it; this, I believe, is called Subijana de Alva. On the bank of the river also were three or four villages, most of them on our side, with a bridge at each village. The French army did not extend immediately to the river bank, but was placed at some little distance beyond it. The river was easily fordable.

Our army began to arrive by divisions, and was posted as follows—General Hill with the 2nd division, consisting of about 12,000 men, was on our extreme right, except about 3000 or 4000 Spaniards under General Morillo, who were still more to the right, and facing the long range of mountains before mentioned. In the centre was his lordship with the 3rd, 4th, 7th, and light divisions, perhaps 25,000 strong, with the main force of artillery and cavalry. Sir Thomas Graham had been early detached to our left with the 1st and 5th divisions and some Portuguese, about 12,000 in all, to turn the enemy's right flank, and to try to cut him off from the great road leading from Vittoria to France, which ran in that direction.

Whilst this movement was executing, and the different divisions were getting into their several stations, we, who had arrived first, were allowed to pile our arms and sit down. His lordship, with a numerous staff, went down a little nearer to the river to reconnoitre the enemy's position. I wandered down with them, and got as near as I could in order to ascertain the opinion of the big-wigs as to the business about to take place. One staff-officer, after carefully examining the position of the enemy through his glass, gave it as his opinion, that we should scarcely be able to make any impression upon so numerous an army, and so very strongly posted; but this opinion must have been dictated, I think, by his rather desponding temperament, for I believe it was entirely singular.

The enemy, however, did not fail to notice this movement of our General and his staff, and instantly detached a corps of voltigeurs, who, rushing down to the river, dashed across the bridge at the village of Villoses, and immediately took possession of a small woody height on our side of the river,. from whence they opened a fire on his lordship and those that were with him. This of course could not be borne; and as my battalion was the leading battalion of the column and nearest at hand, we were ordered (with two companies of our 1st battalion, which stood next to us) to take our arms, and drive those fellows across the river again. Thus we had, I believe, the high honour of commencing the action on that memorable day. We soon chased the voltigeurs from the woody height, down through the Tillage, and over the bridge, where they took post and remained, we not having orders to pursue them any farther. We took possession of the village, and continued skirmishing with the enemy, a good many men falling on both sides, as the river was not more probably than thirty or forty yards wide, and a constant fire was kept up by both parties till the French were afterwards driven away by our divisions crossing lower down the river.

After we had chased the enemy along the bridge, and they were fairly clear of the village, a French battery, situated a little above the river towards the conical hill, opened its fire upon us, from which we suffered a good deal, one shot having taken our people, who were lining a garden wall, in flank, and swept away five or six at a stroke; after this we kept more under cover.

Almost the first person who fell on our side was a lieutenant of the name of Campbell. He had, I am sure, a strong presentiment of his death, for he had, I believe, made his will the evening before; and when we first came in sight of the French army, and the others were all animated with life and glee at the prospect of gaining laurels in abundance, he, poor fellow, sat down by himself quite pensive, and seemed lost in thought. He received a shot in the forehead which terminated his career in a moment as it were, and plunged him into an eternity of bliss or woe. I hope he was prepared, but scarcely dare say I believe he was. Our duty having been accomplished by taking possession of this village, and keeping the French from coming over, we had now leisure to look round us and see what was going forward; and we had certainly a noble field for observation. My commanding-officer with the rest of the staff-officers and myself, together with half a company of men, took up our station at the church, which, standing high, gave us a fine opportunity of witnessing the movements of both armies.

A short while after we had taken post here, we observed the smoke to arise in dense columns in the direction which Sir Thomas Graham had taken, which showed he had commenced the attack on that flank of the enemy, and this was the signal for commencing operations on our right and centre. Sir Rowland Hill's people, with the Spaniards, instantly forded the river, and advanced along the top and side of the mountains before mentioned; and as this was done in considerable force, it seemed to disconcert King Joseph a good deal, for instantly his aides-de-camp were seen galloping in every direction, and the troops which stood upon the plain began to move in that direction, while those upon the conical hill began to descend in great numbers into the plain. This was precisely what our Chief had calculated upon; and now, by a rapid movement, he threw the centre divisions across the river, by the bridges of Trespuentes and Nanclara, a little below our village, and attacking the remaining troops upon the conical hill, they were overthrown as fast as our divisions reached them. The 2nd, Sir Thomas Picton's division, here particularly distinguished itself.

General Hill's people were by this time very warmly engaged, for the enemy having, as stated above, strongly reinforced that point, they made a rather obstinate defence, particularly at the village and wood of Subijana de Alva, which latter was filled with their light troops, and where our 28th regiment, which was opposed to them, suffered considerably, and were not able to make much impression. The action had now become general, and our people on every side advancing; at this moment old Douro, who never failed to inspire confidence wherever he appeared, came dashing down into our village, and seeing the light troops which had been opposed to us had retired, instantly ordered us to advance, and join our division on the other side of the river. We accordingly moved forward, and marched with all expedition to reach our point; but the French had now begun to retire, and our people to follow them, so that we found it difficult to overtake them, and did not do so till they had passed the conical hill. When we came near that eminence, I rode up to have a peep at the field before us, and never did I witness a more interesting and magnificent sight. A beautiful and extensive plain lay before me, covered with the cavalry, infantry, and artillery of the contending armies; while the noise and din, occasioned by repeated volleys and rolls of fire from the infantry, with the rattle of upwards of 200 pieces of artillery, almost stunned the ear. Near the end of this plain, and to the left, arose the lofty spires of Vittoria; and beyond that again, the smoke arising from the attack of Sir Thomas Graham's people added animation to the scene.

I had not contemplated the scene before me above a minute or two, till a howitzer-shell from the French fell close at my feet. My horse's bridle was hooked on my arm, and I was standing looking through my glass; but when this unwelcome visiter descended so near me, I thought it high time to be packing. My horse, however, not having the same fear of the consequences that I had, would not move but at a snail's pace. I was, therefore, constrained to leave him to take his chance, and get myself out of the way. It burst, but providentially without injuring either horse or man, but in the scramble I lost the top of my glass, which I could not afterwards find.

I got down the hill, and joined my people, who had by this time passed it; and just at this juncture I observed a body of troops a little to our right, moving in the same direction we were. They were dressed in blue, and had caps covered with white canvass. I took them for Spaniards; but upon consideration that no Spaniards ought to be there, and a closer inspection, I found they were a battalion of French, and most likely those who had been so warmly engaged with the 28th at the village of Subijana, and who having stood perhaps too long, and afterwards having the wood to traverse, they had been detained considerably behind the rest of the army; for by this time our advance, and consequently the French rear, could not be less than half a mile in front of us.

I pointed them out to one of our lieutenant-colonels; but as we had received orders to push on with all haste, and he not liking to disobey his orders, and withal a ravine being between them and us, which would have prevented our closing with them, they were allowed to move quietly off, which they did with a pretty quick but steady pace. Before we reached our division, we had to pass a village, over against which was a very strong French battery, and where they peppered us considerably, but without doing much harm, I believe. We here joined our brigade.

Immediately in front of this village the enemy made one of his longest stands. Our brigade non-formed lines of battalions, and lay down in some ploughed fields, while their artillery kept playing upon us. On our left the 3rd division was warmly engaged. In about half an hour we moved in that direction. The 45th we found posted behind a thin thorn hedge, with its commanding-officer poor Colonel Ridewood, whom I had known before, lying on its right, gasping in the agonies of death. A great many men of this regiment had fallen here. We passed them, and continued to advance along the plain by brigades and battalions; but we found the ground much intersected with ditches, which would have retarded us had we wished to advance rapidly; but from some cause or other, which we could not then comprehend, we never pressed upon the enemy closely, but gave them time to get quietly away.

We were still, however, in expectation of their making their final stand; for at every short interval a beautiful little position presented itself, which the French invariably occupied in the finest style possible, forming their lines on these little eminences with the greatest precision, and in beautiful order; but they never stood to let us get at them, for the moment we began to come within musket-shot, they instantly began to retire to another, which they took and abandoned in like manner. All this time, indeed, there was continual skirmishing going on between the light troops of the two armies, and a constant cannonade, and occasionally the heavy lines came in contact; but their infantry appeared to us to leave the field in the main unbroken.

We continued these movements till near dark, by which time we had considerably passed Vittoria, and the enemy's artillery had nearly ceased. Our cavalry now got at them; and although, from the nature of the ground, their movements were greatly cramped, yet they continued to charge, and nearly captured King Joseph. We halted when we had got about four miles beyond Vittoria, which we passed on the left hand. We thought we had indeed gained a victory, but it appeared to us to be a most barren and useless one; and many were not over well pleased that the enemy had been allowed to get off so easily. But our noble Chief knew well what he was about, for he reaped all the fruits from this that could have been possibly gained from the most bloody battle. Indeed it was far from being a bloodless victory, but he certainly did not sacrifice one half the men that some in the action would have done: they thought we should have pressed the enemy far more, and brought him to closer action.

After we halted, I (being the only quartermaster present)

174

was sent in search of the baggage belonging to the division, and which had followed as far as they could along the great road. I passed through Vittoria on my way to the rear in search of it, and saw as I entered it several of Morillo's men, who had descended from the mountains and come into the town. From the vivas and other marks of gratulation which some of the inhabitants were rendering these ragged ruffians, a stranger would have thought that Don Morillo, with his 3000 or 4000 Spaniards, had achieved the whole victory themselves. It is certain they are a vainglorious people.

I passed through the town, and, taking the great road, I soon had ocular proofs of the value of our day's work; the road being literally blocked up with every description of carriage-guns, tumbrils, waggons, &c. &c. which filled the great high-road for nearly two miles to the rear of Vittoria. I found it difficult to make my way through them, but at last fell in with the baggage; I could not, however, get it through, and was obliged to leave it, after giving directions where to find the division in the morning. I again passed through Vittoria in returning to the division; but oh, what scenes had I now to witness! The followers of an army are sometimes very numerous, and here they were abundantly so; muleteers, Portuguese and Spanish concubines, with every description of vagabond you can imagine. These were by this time all labouring hard in their avocation of breaking open and plundering the carriages and waggons, &c. that had been left by the enemy. Among these were hundreds of soldiers, who were now beginning to feel the effects of the wine, &c. which they had found in the enemy's baggage; and such a Babel was here to be witnessed as is not easy to conceive.

I had some difficulty in forcing my way through the town, at the end of which I was accosted by five or six soldiers' wives, belonging to one of our light cavalry regiments, who wished to accompany me, in order that they might find their husbands, as that regiment was attached in some measure to our division. Of course it would have been cruel to refuse them; and as they were all mounted, away we posted, but had great difficulty to make out where the division now was.

Many were the waggons and other carnages we passed on the road, either broken down, upset, or with people plundering them; and I did not reach the division till 10 o'clock at night. I was very glad when I found them, being then excessively fatigued and hungry; and just as I reached my people, I found the mess to which I belonged cooking a piece of thin mutton, which they had cut off from a sheep that had been taken from the enemy. This was all the plunder I got that memorable day, although, had I done as many others did, I might have obtained a great deal both of money and other valuables; for, as I said before, the numerous carriages I passed gave me an opportunity which many would have rejoiced at of possessing myself of immense wealth; but plundering never was my forte. One officer whom I knew got, I believe, near L.1000 worth of money, and other valuable property; and innumerable others got considerable sums, more or less. I am glad now that I refrained from what might have been accomplished with ease and safety, but what also might have entailed upon me disgrace and ruin. One officer I heard of, who, while in the rear, where he ought not to have been, found a box full of money, most likely silver, but very heavy. A German dragoon coming up at the same moment laid claim to half of it, and when this officer took hold of it to remove it, the German also laid hold to prevent him. A sort of scuffle ensued, when the German made use of most abusive and mutinous language, with threats, which the officer was obliged to submit to, knowing, as both of them did, how far he had descended from his station, thus putting it in the power of the soldier to treat him as a brother plunderer. Surely the mention of such an occurrence is enough to deter any man who possesses the least spark of honour from ever putting it in the power of a soldier to treat him so. Besides, if an officer plunders before his men, what may not soldiers be expected to do?

In looking back upon the events of this day, I cannot help being struck with the bad generalship of those who commanded the French army. Marshal Jourdan, I understand, was Joseph's adviser on this occasion. He had always borne the character of an able General, but here he showed but little ability. Why did he so much weaken his force on the conical hill to support his left? Had he maintained his ground there, which is strong by nature, and they had rendered it stronger by art, he might have completely checked us on the right; for if we had advanced too far on that side, our wings would have been separated, which would have been a dangerous experiment; and I think Lord Wellington would not have hazarded it. And after leaving his first position, why did he not fight at every one of the beautiful little positions which he afterwards took up but never defended? This conduct is most unaccountable, for had he made a longer stand, even although he should be beaten, which no doubt he would have ultimately been, yet, by making this stand, he might have got off the greater part of his materiel, instead of which he carried off with him one gun and one howitzer only, leaving upwards of 250 pieces of ordnance in our hands. Most of his infantry left the field apparently unbroken; for only here and there they had stood to let our people get at them. It is true Sir Thomas Graham early cut off their retreat by the great road to France; but what then? This ought to have made them fight the more desperately, to enable them to get off the better by the Pamplona road. The infantry should have stood till the last, and not retired till fairly beaten out of the field. Nothing could be finer than the movements of our army.

Every thing our Chief attempted succeeded to a tittle. The only thing I did not like was the delay we occasionally made in following up the enemy; but I could not, of course, comprehend the general movements, from seeing only a small part of them, and I believe the victory would not have been more decisive by being more bloody. We lost in the village, where we first began the fight, nearly thirty men, with the officer before' mentioned as killed, and a considerable number wounded. There was something remarkable in the fate of one of the men who were killed by the cannon-shot I before noticed. This man was remarkably averse to fighting and had shown, on all occasions, a disposition to leave that kind of work as soon as practicable. Poor fellow! his failing was known to all; and on this occasion those about him had orders to watch him, and keep him to his duty. They had not been in the village many minutes when this fatal shot swept him and about five others into eternity in a moment. It has often been remarked, that this description of people are generally the first to fall.

It may not be generally known, perhaps, that a battle was fought on the 3rd April 1367, a little higher up this river, near the village of Novarete, between our Edward the Black Prince, and Henry the Bastard, who had usurped the throne of Don Pedro, King of Castile. The history of it is given by Froissart, who says, "a little before the two armies met, the Prince of Wales, with eyes and hands uplifted towards heaven, exclaimed, 'God of truth, the Father of Jesus Christ, who hast made and fashioned me, grant, through thy benign grace, that the success of this battle may be for me and my army; for thou knowest that in truth I have been emboldened to undertake it in the support of justice and reason, to reinstate the king upon his throne, who has been disinherited and driven from it, as well as from his country.' This zealous prayer was immediately followed by the onset, the Prince crying aloud, "Advance banners, in the name of God and St George!"

"At the commencement," says Froissart, "the French and Arragonese made a desperate resistance, and gave the good knights of England much trouble; but at last, when all the divisions of the Prince were formed into one large body, the enemy could no longer keep their ground, but began to fly in great disorder; and Henry, the usurper, perceiving his army defeated, without hope of recovery, called for his horse, mounted it, and galloped off among the crowd of runaways. The English pursued them through the town of Najara, where they gained considerable plunder; for King Henry and his army had come thither with much splendour, and after the defeat they had not leisure to return to place in security what they had left behind them in the morning."

There is a striking coincidence in many parts of the two actions and their consequences, which the reader cannot fail to notice. The most material difference, I think, in the two stories is, the offering up of the prayer by the Prince, and the modern practice of not recognising, publicly at least, the hand of God at all in any of our victories. This is to be lamented.

Chapter Thirteen
To the Pyrenees

We remained in bivouack all night where the battle had terminated; and did not begin to move till near mid-day on the 22nd, when we set off in the track of the enemy, and at night reached Salvatiera, where King Joseph had slept the night after the action.

The poor beaten French must have had a long march after the fight, for this was probably sixteen or eighteen miles from Vittoria. We started early on the morning of the 23rd, and very soon began to overtake the rear of the enemy. They now resorted to a system of retarding our march, at once both cruel and cowardly; every village they passed through they set on fire. Of course this caused us some delay, as the road generally ran through the middle of the village, and the country on each side was enclosed, but still nothing could justify such barbarity to the unoffending natives, who were thus deprived of house and home, and probably all they possessed in the world. We overtook their rearguard near a village about two leagues from Salvatiera. They attempted to make a stand while the village was in flames, but a shrapnell shell from our horse artillery set them instantly in motion. We came upon a considerable body of them again near the village of La Cunca, where we again cannonaded them, and where our people had some slight skirmishing with their rear.

We encamped for the night near this village, and again started after them in the morning early. My battalion led the column to-day, the post of honour. We had marched, I think, about eight or ten miles without overtaking any of the flying foe before us, but at last we came to an open country, that which we had traversed being pretty thickly enclosed, with bad roads and wet weather, which rendered marching very uncomfortable. Here a halt was ordered, as the enemy was in front in some force; here for the first time we got upon the great road leading from Pamplona towards Bayonne; and here, where it turned the corner of a mountain, forming a pretty acute angle, they had the only gun and howitzer they had saved from the fight in position, and ready to receive us. The men of my battalion, and a part of our 1st battalion, were ordered to put their knapsacks up behind the hussars of the German Legion, as it was not expected they would be wanted, and it thus rendered our people better able to run. The enemy appeared to have two battalions here, one of which remained on the great road near the two pieces of artillery, while the other moved off more to our right, down a valley which they imagined would, at the other end, let them out into the great road again.

We now began to move forward, and as I happened to be the first mounted person who left the enclosed road we had been in, I was honoured with the first shot from their gun, which, although a good shot, did me no injury. Our people now pushed on at them pretty smartly, which caused them, after firing a round or two more, to limber up and retire with their artillery, though they of course retired as leisurely as possible, to give time for their troops, whom they were covering, to get away. The skirmishing between them and our people continued for about two miles, they gradually retiring before us; but when they came to a sort of pass in the road, formed by two rocks nearly meeting in the middle, their bugles or trumpets sounded first the halt to their troops, and afterwards the advance upon us. We could not comprehend the meaning of this, till in a few minutes the battalion which we had observed go down towards the right, suddenly made its appearance out of a wood among our skirmishers. Of course a sharp contest now took place, and the firing on both sides became more brisk; this battalion, it appears, had miscalculated on getting out of the valley, down which it had retired, and had been compelled, at whatever risk, to make the great road again before they passed the rocks before mentioned; and in order to let it do so, the other skirmishers had advanced to cover its movement. This battalion suffered considerably before it reached the road, and we did not get off

181

scot-free, having lost out of our five companies about twenty-four men.

Our artillery being pretty near at hand, Colonel Ross brought up two guns, and fired into their retreating column, doing considerable execution. We now moved forward in close pursuit of the enemy for about two miles farther, when a shot from Colonel Ross's guns having struck one of the leaders in their gun, and our people at this time pressing them so closely as not to give time to disentangle the dead horse, they unwillingly were compelled to throw their only gun into the ditch, and there abandon it. We continued the pursuit till we drove them under the walls of Pamplona, which I understand, poor wretches, they were not allowed to enter, on account of the scarcity of provisions in that fortress, and which after events proved was the case. We retired to the village of Aldava and others in the neighbourhood, where we remained for the night.

On the morning of the 25th, we advanced on the road to Pamplona, the enemy having all retired towards France, till we came within about one mile and a half of it, when we branched off to the left, and moved along a range of hills at about a mile distant from the works of the place, till we reached the town of Villaba, on the mountain-road from Pamplona to France; thus cutting off all retreat from the garrison, and thus in fact investing the place. During our movements to-day, my people being in the rear of the 17th Portuguese regiment, I was riding in company with my commanding-officer at the head of the battalion, when the horse of the Portuguese major threw out with both his hind feet with all his might, and struck me with one foot on my thigh, and the other on the calf of the leg. The blow was so severe that I nearly fainted, and was obliged to dismount and throw myself on the ground; but as no bones were broken, I gathered myself up again, and mounted and set off after the troops.

We encamped on the Pamplona side of Villaba, distant from the former about one mile and a half. The captain in whose mess I was, with his company, was that night ordered on picquet with in about three quarters of a mile of the city. I went there to get my dinner, during which several poor people, who had made their escape from the place, came and welcomed us in the name of the people, telling us they were heartily tired of their present lodgers; of course there would be different opinions among them, but I believe the generality at that time hated the French most cordially.

There was a division of the French army under General Clausel, which had not partaken of the flight at Vittoria, being then stationed at Logrona, and he having learnt the fate of his companions in arms, and their retreat into France was moving through the country to our right, in order to effect his retreat also. Next morning, therefore, the 3rd and our divisions were despatched in pursuit of this French corps. We marched that day to near Taffala, and halted at the village of Muro, at the junction of the great road from Logrona with that we now occupied, but we learnt that Clausel had kept more to his right, and was directing his course towards the mountain-road, which passes near Caceda and Languessa, into France.

We accordingly passed through Taffala and Olite, and encamped for the night. Next day we started early, and moved on till mid-day, when we halted for an hour or two to cook and refresh near the village of Murillo del Fruto. We here came upon the river Arragon. This had been already a long day's march, and the greater part of the division were ready to lie down now, but a much longer portion still remained to be accomplished. Accordingly, we set off after a short rest, and traversed the right bank of this river for about ten hours longer. Night marches at all times are unpleasant, but much more so on such a road or path as this was, and every one so nearly tired before beginning it.

We crossed the Arragon at the village of Galla Pienzo, and lay down in a field not far from the village of Caseda. Very few of the division reached this place until daylight next morning. But when I got in I unfortunately lay down on a ridge immediately behind our column, and where, had I given it a thought, I was continually liable to be disturbed. And indeed I was most wofully disturbed, for every fresh batch that came in tumbled themselves down upon me, or in blundering about in the dark were sure to stumble over me. It must be observed that my leg by this time, instead of getting better, had begun to swell dreadfully and to suppurate, consequently I was in a high state of fever; and to the thumps and kicks which I received in the dark during this uncomfortable night, I cannot but attribute much of my subsequent suffering. Next morning we discovered that all our labour had been in vain, for Clausel had got the start of us, and had got off by another road into France.

We next day moved into Languessa, from which we were not far distant, but I could no longer accompany or precede the troops, my leg was now so bad. I was therefore obliged to get a pillow laid on my holsters, and then ride with my leg resting upon it, (a most uncomfortable position, could I have found a better,) while one of my men led my horse, and thus follow them as well as I was able. We rested in Languessa all the 30th and 1st July; and on the 2nd reached Deriza, having passed through Monreal. Here I was obliged to be lifted off my horse, and put to bed. I was almost stupid from the pain I suffered; for my leg was now swoln as large as my thigh. We next day moved into Villaba, from whence we had started in pursuit of Clausel, and thence into some villages on the plain, close to Pamplona. Here I believe some works were thrown up to shelter the troops, either against the shot from the fortress, or a sally from the garrison. This continued all next day. I remained very ill in bed.

On the 5th, the division left this quarter, and set off on the road towards France; but I could not follow them. I got with great difficulty from my present station, which was now occupied by other troops, and stopped at a village, the name of which I forget, just over the ridge where I received my hurt, and a few miles distant from Villaba. Here I found out that Dr Jones of the 40th regiment was in the latter town; and, as he had formerly been in our regiment, I took the liberty of requesting he would come and see me. This I found out by my servant going in for provisions. He very kindly came, and gave me the best advice he could. By this time my leg had burst, and had discharged a prodigious quantity of matter.

I remained in this village till about the 10th, during which

184

time a priest had shown himself remarkably kind and attentive; there were very few inhabitants remaining besides him. He told me in one of the conversations that I had Vera, the last town on the Spanish frontier. Here the enemy had taken up a strong position, both in front and rear of the town; the front position was on Santa Barbara, an exceeding high and almost inaccessible mountain. They were dislodged from the position before the town by my brigade, and retired into the Puerta, or Pass of Vera. I was not present on this occasion, having been again compelled to stay behind on account of my leg. While I remained at Sumbilla, I had been obliged to have my horse shod by a Spanish blacksmith, who drove a nail right into the quick. This I did not discover till several days after, when I found my horse quite lame.

On the 18th, I again crept on after my people, whom I found encamped on the height of Santa Barbara, from which I before said they had driven the enemy. Here we remained till the 26th. During this time my horse's foot had also suppurated, and he was quite unable to move. My leg also was daily discharging a vast quantity of matter, so that I felt at this time very uncomfortable; particularly as very stormy weather came on while we were here, which killed a great number of our animals, horses and mules, I believe not fewer than seven or eight in one night.

It will be known to the reader perhaps, that on the 25th, Soult (who had now been appointed to the command of the French army) made an attack upon our posts at Roncesvalles and Maya, and had driven the divisions stationed there from their posts. He moved on towards Pamplona, in hopes either of beating back our army to Vittoria, (as he vainly talked,) or of being able to supply Pamplona with provisions, which it greatly needed. In consequence of this movement of the enemy, we also were compelled to fall back, although the troops in front of us made no demonstration of advancing.

Accordingly, on the 26th, we began our retrograde movement, being myself at that time in as pitiable a plight as can well be conceived. My horse was so utterly lame, that he could scarcely hop on three legs, while I was totally unable to walk a step. My

185

kind friend Captain Perceval, with whom I had long messed, helped me out of my trouble, by dividing the load of one of his baggage-ponies among the other animals, and lending it me to ride upon. We retired from the height, and crossed the river Bidassoa, near Lizacca, through which we passed, and kept along the mountains on the left bank of that river till we reached a height opposite Sumbilla, where we pitched our tents, and remained for the night. We did not move all next day; but just as night set in, we were ordered under arms, and continued our retreat. This was a still more distressing night-march than any I had previously witnessed.

We were now, it may be noticed, in the midst of the mountains of the Pyrenees, where precipices abound; consequently the precaution to avoid falling over them would be doubled. One little streamlet, I well remember, delayed the division probably two hours. It came down from the sides of the mountain which overhung the road, and crossed it at a very dark and ugly-looking place, making a considerable noise as it fell from rock to rock. This of course made every one extremely cautious; and in consequence a poor good-natured corporal, who was killed soon after, got himself into the middle of the streamlet, and took bold of every person's hand as he passed, conducting him safely to the other side. Poor fellow, he was extremely anxious to help me and my miserable little pony safely over. This and a few other places, something similar, prevented us reaching our destination till an hour after daylight next morning, although the whole distance was not more than ten miles.

We arrived at Zubietta in the morning. This place is about a league to the right of St Estevan, more into the mountains. Here we remained that day, and the next day moved higher up the mountain, behind the town, where we encamped, and remained till evening, when we again commenced our retreat. We had not quite so bad a march of it this night, the road being much more even, although, just at the outset, our adjutant, in riding along, had his cap pulled off by the bough of a tree, and in endeavouring to save it from falling, he pulled his horse right over a small precipice, which the two rolled down together.

Luckily it was not a deep ravine into which he fell, or he would not have escaped so well: neither man nor horse were much hurt. We reached the village of Saldias in the morning, where we remained for the day. Last night my servant told me he had been obliged to leave my little horse behind, as he could not get him to hop any farther. I felt grieved at this, for he had brought me all the way from Lisbon, and shared both my good and bad fortune; however, it was no use to fret, for that would not improve my situation, which indeed was not an enviable one, my leg all this time being extremely painful.

On the 30th, we made an excessively long march, (by day,) and at night reached Lecumberg, where we encamped. During the latter part of this day's march, we had heard an incessant cannonade and firing of musketry in the direction of Pamplona, from which we were apprehensive that Soult had penetrated too far; but as it did not appear to recede, we believed our people had been able to hold him in check at least. We were now on the great road from Bayonne to Pamplona, in order to keep up the communication between our right, where the fighting was now going on, and Sir Thomas Graham, who was besieging St Sebastian. We were here also to intercept any of the enemy's columns that might either advance or retreat by this road. Towards evening of the 31st, an aide-de-camp arrived from Lord Wellington, more dead than alive from the excessive fatigue which he had undergone for the last three or four days, with news of the total defeat of Soult in the several actions near Pamplona, termed the Battle of the Pyrenees, and ordering us to retrace our steps, and again advance. We set off in the evening, and reached Larissa, where we halted for the night. It was whispered that it was expected we should have gone much farther this night, but I am not certain whether it is true; but certainly we might have proceeded to Saldias, if absolutely necessary.

On the morning of the 1st of August, we again started pretty early. It was again reported this morning that another dispatch had been received during the night, directing us to proceed with all haste, as the enemy were retreating by St Estevan, and that we were to attack them wherever we met them. We now of course stepped out very freely, and presently gained Zubietta. Here I had ridden forward to get a shoe fastened on, my horse having cast one in coming over the mountains; during which time the quartermaster had been called for some purpose or other, as I was not there.

My General was not well satisfied: he saw me in this village, and asked me why I had not been present when I was wanted. I told him the cause, but he still did not appear satisfied, and, by way of punishment, directed me to remain in the village till the baggage came up, and show them the way the division had gone. I may here observe, that it was a little unreasonable in my General to find any fault with me on this occasion; for, had I not got the shoe put on my horse, I could not have been of any use at all as a quartermaster. My punishment indeed was slight, and I rather think he was glad to find any excuse to delay me for the purpose for which I was left. I am confident the officers of the infantry suffered more anxiety and even loss on account of the great want of farriers or horse-shoers in their regiments, than from almost any other cause. Without the officer was pretty high in rank, he had not only to pay most exorbitantly for any thing of this kind which he got done, but to beg and pray, and to look upon it as a favour conferred on him. Most of the good shoers were taken by the staff or general officers, consequently only the inferior ones were left for the regimental officers, and in several cases none at all. The consequence of all this was, the loss of several valuable animals, both horses and mules; besides, in some cases, the officers being rendered incapable of performing their duty as they otherwise would have done. To this I attribute a considerable loss in animals during this service. It might easily be remedied by each infantry regiment having a proper establishment of farriers, (say two,) with tools, &c. in proportion, and the means of carrying them; and then every officer, whose duty requires him to be mounted, might be served. I myself bought tools to the amount of L.4, and never had but one horse shod with them. I could not get a man to do it. As soon as I saw the baggage on the right way, I pushed forward, and joined the division again. We were literally at this time climbing up a mountain, where I could not ride, but was obliged to crawl up, and pull my horse after me. My leg by this time had much improved. We followed the road by which we had retreated a few days before, and at length came to the rivulet that had so alarmed us all on our night-march. It was really surprising that we should have been stopped so long by such a trifle; but in such a situation, and at such a time, things of that kind are magnified a thousand fold by the imagination. We passed our old camp ground opposite to Sumbilla, and here we came in view of the enemy's columns retreating along the road on the opposite bank of the Bidassoa. This gave our men new life; but here the 52nd and other regiments of the 2nd brigade were obliged to halt: they could proceed no farther.

We had marched by this time to-day two and a half of the stages we made in retreating; but the 2nd brigade had been in the rear of the column all day, and had consequently suffered much from stoppages, &c. My battalion, our 1st battalion, and the 43rd regiment, continued to move on, and as they approached, the enemy seemed to acquire fresh vigour. At length we reached the point of attack,—the bridge of Yanzi,—and here the 1st battalion turning down towards the river, at once left the wood and ground above the bridge to be occupied by us. The enemy sent a pretty strong corps of light troops across, which got engaged with our people; but we soon drove down through the wood again towards the bridge. At length, we got two companies posted just over the bridge, in front of which all the rear of the French column had to pass. Poor creatures I they became so alarmed, that they instantly began to cut away and cast off, all the loads of baggage, and both cavalry and infantry, &c. to make the best of their way. But the mountain on their right was inaccessible; consequently they had all, as it were, to run the gauntlet. Great was the execution done amongst the enemy at this bridge, and many were the schemes they tried to avoid passing. At length they got a battalion up behind a stone wall above the road, on the opposite side, from whose fire we received some damage; consequently those poor people who had afterwards to pass were not so much exposed. Just about the close of the business, my kind friend, Captain Perceval, received a shot through his right wrist. His left hand had been closed for a length of time before, in consequence of a wound through that wrist, which had contracted his fingers, besides being lame from a wound in the hip. Now he was rendered completely useless. Towards dusk I went with him a little to the rear, and got his tent pitched, and made as comfortable as circumstances would admit. I pitied the French on this occasion, they seemed so much alarmed. The whole of their baggage fell into the hands of our 4th division, who were closely following them up on their side of the Bidassoa.

In this affair, the French were reduced to a dreadful dilemma; great numbers of their wounded had been brought off from the battles of the 28th, 29th, and 30th, near Pamplona, which were carried on biers or stretches by men of this division. When they saw us in front of them, where they had to pass, as it were, immediately under the muzzles of our pieces, they were compelled to adopt the cruel alternative of either throwing their wounded men down to perish, or run the risk of being shot or taken themselves. I believe the former, shocking as it seems, was generally adopted; and I have reason to believe that the greater part of them were thrown into the river; for, from the point where we first came in view of them to near where this affair took place, the Bidassoa was literally filled with the dead bodies of Frenchmen, and they could have come into it in no other way. We lost only a very few men on this occasion, not more than six or eight, while that of the enemy must have been extremely severe. Here the effects of rifle-shooting were plainly visible.

In remarking on this affair, I beg to draw the reader's attention to the following circumstances; viz. probably never troops made such a march over such a country before. We travelled at least thirty-two miles over mountains such as I before described, where you were sometimes nearly obliged to scramble upon your hands and knees. The day was exceedingly hot, and occasionally there was a great want of water. I am told that one of the regiments in our 2nd brigade, which, it may be remembered, were obliged to halt, as they could go no farther, had no less than 200 men fell out, unable to keep up, and that some of them actually died of fatigue. I heard of one poor fellow, who, when he came to water and had drunk, lost his senses, fell to the ground, and shortly after expired. I have reason to be proud of my battalion on this occasion, which, when the roll was called, just before the action commenced, had only nine men fallen out; but they had been in the front all day, a great advantage in marching, particularly over a mountainous country.

This day's work gave me a higher idea of the powers of human nature, when properly trained, than ever I possessed before; for when you consider that each of those soldiers carried a weight of not less probably than forty or fifty lbs. and some much more, it cannot but be surprising that men should be able to sustain such fatigue for such a length of time—at the end of which to fight, and gain a victory.

Next morning were clearly observable the effects of the evening's work. In the house, the yard, and on the road opposite the bridge, were a great number of dead Frenchmen; and to the rear, by the way they had advanced, the road was literally strewed with baggage, and equipments of every description. Some of our people picked up a number of visiting cards, with General Vandermason on them, very elegant; so that his baggage, no doubt, had been cast off, as well as that of inferior people.

Soon after daylight, we were ordered to fall in, and move forward towards Vera. Just as we cleared the bridge, old Douro, with his staff, came riding up, who, when he saw how we had handled the enemy the night before, gave his head a significant nod, and smiled, which conveyed most intelligibly his approbation. We soon reached the neighbourhood of Vera, behind which, in the pass of that name, as before stated, the enemy took up a strong position, from which their picquets had never yet been driven. We were ordered to encamp a little below the bridge leading to Lezacca, between that and Vera, while the other regiments were intended to occupy the heights of Santa Barbara, from which we had before retreated. But towards mid-day it was discovered that the enemy still had a considerable body of troops in and about the pass of Echallar, a few miles to our right. Our brigade was therefore ordered again under arms, with the intention of co-operating with the 7th division in an attack upon those people. It was a thick mist, so that we could scarcely see twenty yards before us; but when we reached the bottom of an immensely high hill, on which the enemy were posted, we presently discovered whereabouts we had them.

Our 1st battalion extended to the right, and my battalion moved straight forward up the hill. For a considerable time the enemy's fire did us no injury, being deceived, I imagine, by the denseness of the fog. They fired almost always over our heads, some of which shots struck the men of the 43rd, a considerable way below us. At length we began to approach the, summit of the mountain, where the enemy were of course much more condensed, the ground they had to occupy being much smaller. Our people were advancing regularly up the hill, when we run right up against a rock, on the top of which was collected an immense body of the French, and from whom our people received a most destructive fire, knocking down fourteen men in an instant. This unlooked-for circumstance checked our people, and made some of them retire for an instant behind a broken part in the mountain, from which they kept up the best fire they could. During this transaction, the French, who were not more than ten or twelve yards distant, were calling out to us in Spanish to advance, and abusing us most lustily. A Spaniard (one of the recruits I formerly mentioned) was so much annoyed, that he began in his turn to abuse the French; and, as if words were not enough, accompanying them with the best shot he could give them. Poor fellow, he was instantly shot through the body, and fell to rise no more.

They now began to get courage, and made a show of advancing upon us: they did do so on the right against our 1st battalion, but my commanding-officer calling out to cheer our people, set up a shout, which had the effect of intimidating them, and they did not dare to advance. I was now sent away by Colonel Barnard to request the 43rd (who were behind us) to send a company to support our 1st battalion, which they instantly did; and just as I returned, I found the French had evacuated the rock from which they had annoyed us, on the top of which we found a great number of caps and pouches, &c, belonging to men who had fallen there. We followed them over the hill, but they now gave us leg-bail, posting down into the valley towards France with all expedition.

The 7th division had some pretty sharp work before they dislodged the people in front of them, and had suffered very severely in effecting their object. When every thing was settled, one of our men thought he saw a man hiding behind a tree just below us: he went to see what it was, and dragged out by the neck a French soldier of the 2nd light infantry. Poor fellow, he came out shrugging his shoulders, and, putting on a most beseeching look, begged we would spare him, as he was only a "pauvre Italien." Of course no injury was done him, only the soldier who took him claiming and taking from him his knapsack, which appeared a fine full one, and which he appropriated to himself. I thought it cruel, and would have prevented it, had my voice been of any weight; and yet, had it not been taken from him now, it would very soon after, when he became a prisoner.

One battalion was ordered to remain and occupy this hill, which dreadfully alarmed me, lest it should be ours, for it was bitter, bleak, and cold. Luckily a Portuguese battalion was ordered up, and we returned to our snug camp by the river side; and here, as if to crown our good fortune, one of our men, who had been left behind in charge of the tents, had got some meat roasted for our mess, of which we all partook with great delight and thankfulness.

A friend of mine of our 1st battalion, during the advance the French had made upon that battalion, was nigh falling into their hands. They rushed at him, but he perceiving, and endeavouring to avoid them, fell into a bush, which scratched him most wofully, and in the fray lost his cap and sword. They grasped at the latter, (which was not drawn,) but which luckily broke loose from the belt, or they would have had him. This hill was always known afterwards by the name of Barnard's Hill, in honour of Colonel Barnard, who commanded on the occasion.

Chapter Fourteen
The Pursuit into France

We remained at rest here for some time, during which I, as acting paymaster, had several trips to Tolosa, a considerable town on the great road from Bayonne to Madrid, where the paymaster-general had taken up his residence with the military chest. In one of them I went and had a peep at St Sebastian, the siege of which was then going on. While here, I received directions from General Sir William Stewart to attend him at Villaba, where he lay wounded, he having received two balls in the late actions. I set off, directing my servants with my baggage to follow close after me: by some means they were delayed a few minutes, and, supposing I was going again to the paymaster-general at Tolosa, went off in that direction, without asking any questions. I imagined they knew very well where I was going, and still went on slowly, every now and then looking back to see if I could descry them coming; but although there was no appearance of them, I simply enough continued my route till I reached St Estevan; and here I put up for the night, thinking, of course, they would come by and by. In the morning, I was fully convinced they must have gone some other road, and as all my books, &c, from which I wanted information, were in my baggage, I thought it useless to proceed any farther. In retracing my steps, which I did leisurely, I had an opportunity of seeing the great number of bodies which the French had thrown into the river, the road running close by its brink nearly all the way. It was really shocking to behold such numerous wrecks of mortality, with the disgusting appearance which most of them had assumed; many of them were half eaten by the fish, and of others the flesh was hanging in rags, and bleaching in the stream. Of course I returned home, but did not see my servants again for several days, as it took three or four to accomplish the journey to

Tolosa and back, and they had waited there a day for me.

On the day that I was absent, all the officers of my corps had had a sumptuous and splendid entertainment, it being the 25th August, the anniversary of the regiment's first formation. They had dug a ditch in an oblong shape in the middle of a field, the centre of which served for a table, while they sat with their feet in the ditch. I am told the French, who were just above, and overlooked them from the heights behind the town, assembled and viewed them, as if in astonishment to see them regaling themselves with so much glee in the midst of the wild Pyrenean mountains. No doubt the wine went merrily round, and many were the toasts which were drunk with three-times-three.

During this interval, I often amused myself with fishing in the Bidassoa, in which there were many excellent trout, and I was pretty successful, for I had got some tackle from one of our captains, which he had brought from England. On one of these occasions, while I was wading in a pool, I spied a fine salmon laying just below me; I threw in and brought my flies right over him, at which he instantly rose, but I missed him. I tried again, and hooked him, but in a moment he plunged right across the river, carrying with him all my flies and part of my line, for I had no reel. I might have calculated upon this, if I had thought for a moment; but the opportunity was so tempting, that I could not resist it.

At length the 31st of August arrived, the day on which St Sebastian was to be stormed. We knew this, for we had furnished a number of volunteers, both officers and men, to take part in the assault; many of our higher officers had gone to witness the glorious spectacle. But early in the morning, we were all astonished at the bugle sounding through the camp the alarm, or assembly, and instantly orders were given for the tents to be struck, the baggage to be packed, and to set off with it to the rear without a moment's delay, for the French were advancing; of course all this was done in as short a time as possible, and the troops were ordered to move on to a hill just over the bridge of Vera. A detachment of ours had joined the evening before, and it cannot easily be conceived the strange effect this sudden alarm had on some of them. One of them, a lieutenant, was all in a bustle getting his pistols put in fighting order, and came to me begging I would take some money to keep for him. I told him that it was likely to be in as much danger with me as with himself, and of course declined. The old hands, on the contrary, were as cool and quiet about it as if it was an everyday occurrence. We moved to the height before mentioned, and saw a cloud of fellows with white caps coming down to the left of the town, and of course prepared to give them the best reception we could. I was sent with orders to my commanding-officer from the General, 'that he was, when pressed, to retire till he got on the ridge just over his house, (which was on the road a little to the rear of where we then were,) and that he was to stand there as long as it was possible.' I thought something very warm was going to occur; seeing such a cloud of Frenchmen were then approaching us, but we were all disappointed; they went quickly to their right after descending from the heights, and forded the river below the town, setting their faces towards St Sebastian. All this was effected under a cannonade from the heights.

Our 1st brigade (except my battalion) was then ordered to cross the river by the Lezacca bridge a little behind us, and to move parallel to the enemy along the ridge above that town, which had all along been Lord Wellington's head-quarters. As soon as they got across, they sent a body of troops to the bridge of Vera, close to which some of our people were stationed, and from thence they kept firing on us all day from some small mountain guns, which they had brought down with them, and occasionally with musketry. We were now somewhat curiously situated. The French position was on the side we occupied, while the other side of the bridge had been fortified by the Spanish General Longa, to protect himself during the last excursion of the French towards Pamplona; but now they occupied the side on which the intrenchments had been thrown up, and turned them against us of course; they did little execution by their fire. Lord Wellington, seeing the intention of the enemy, assembled all the British troops he could easily collect, and brought them in rear of a corps of Spaniards, which met the French in this direction; and finding this a fair opportunity of seeing what the Don could do, withheld the British, and let the Spaniards attack them by themselves. They had now the best chance of showing their valour that ever had or might present itself; they had the high ground, and the enemy had to climb up on their hands and knees to get at them; besides, they had behind them backers that would not see them get foul play. So away they set at them, and indeed they did tumble the French down in good style, upsetting them in all directions; so that our English division had nothing to do but to look on. This was the only time I ever knew the Spaniards act in a body like good soldiers.

The enemy, being beaten, were obliged of course to retrograde; but it came on one of the bitterest nights I have almost ever witnessed; the rain fell in torrents, and the lightning was very vivid. The French endeavoured to retrace their steps during the night, fording the river where they had crossed it in the morning; but the heavy rain had so swoln the river by midnight, that they could not continue any longer to wade it.- A considerable number of them still remained on the other side, and no way presented itself of extricating themselves, but by forcing their passage across the bridge, near which a company of our 2nd battalion, under Captain Cadoux, was posted, with one of ours, a short distance in the rear, to support him. Captain Cadoux's people were stationed in houses about thirty yards from the bridge, and had a double sentry on the bridge. The enemy's column approached very quietly, and then made a rush; but the rain having wet the priming of the sentries' rifles, they could not get them to go off to give the necessary alarm, and were in a moment driven from their post. The French then, seeing they had effected a passage, set up a shout, and rushed towards the houses where Cadoux's people were, who turned out at once, and with the supporting company, opened a deadly fire upon the enemy's column; but poor Cadoux fell instantly almost, as he had imprudently mounted his horse on the first alarm; his lieutenant also was severely wounded. The firing of course soon brought the whole brigade to the spot, which kept up a constant and well-directed fire during the whole of their progress along the little plain towards Vera.

The enemy suffered dreadfully on this occasion, leaving the ground literally strewed with their dead, who, like the others before mentioned, were next morning thrown into the river; so that the fish had ample feeding for some time after. Some people afterwards reflected upon General Skerrott, who commanded here, for not posting a stronger force at the bridge, and for not blocking it up with an abbatis; the former he might and ought to have done; but the latter was impracticable, from the enemy holding the breastwork at the other end of the bridge, which was not more than about thirty yards long. Had a battalion been posted there, it is probable the French, who were compelled to have recourse to this daring attempt, might have been induced to surrender; but I believe the General never imagined they had need to make such an attempt. Our loss on this occasion was rather severe also. A great many of Captain Cadoux's men fell; Lieutenant Travers, who commanded the company of my battalion, was wounded, and a considerable number of men were killed and wounded; among the former, some of the poor fellows who had joined from England only the day before.

Thus was Soult's second attempt frustrated, and St Sebastian fell into our hands. As I was not present at that glorious exhibition of British valour and prowess, I cannot take upon me to give any account of its capture. The volunteers who went from our division to assist in the storm or assault, sustained their full share in the casualties attendant thereon. The field-officer, Colonel Hunt of the 52nd, was severely wounded; a lieutenant of the 43rd, brother to Mr O'Connell, the famous Roman Catholic advocate, was killed; two lieutenants of our first battalion, named Perci-val and Hamilton, were severely wounded. The latter, I believe, was a volunteer on the occasion, not being entitled, from his standing, to take it as a tour of duty. He was conspicuously brave, and received two severe wounds, from which it would scarcely be imagined possible any one could recover.

A few days after the surrender of St Sebastian, I had again occasion to go to Tolosa for money, and took the road by Passages, the port where we now received all our supplies from

England; and also to see the ruins of that late formidable fortress. When I reached it, the houses were still on fire, and not I believe half-a-dozen in the whole town that remained habitable, or the inhabitants had quite deserted it. I went up to the citadel and examined it, and I believe this, with proper casemates or bomb-proofs, might be rendered one of the strongest places in Spain, next to Gibraltar; but the French had suffered dreadfully from our shells, which had literally ploughed the ground on the top of this naturally strong height, and from which cause they had been compelled to surrender.

St Sebastian was indeed a melancholy spectacle at this time. I returned from Tolosa by a part of the road which we had traversed in our late retreat and advance again, as I now began to hope I might perhaps recover my little horse, for I suspected from some cause that my servant, instead of having been obliged to abandon him, because of his lameness, as he told me, had sold him at that time; and this I actually found had been the case. I compelled him to tell me where he had disposed of him, and, with my broken Spanish, traced him from thence for near twenty miles farther into the mountains, where I found him in a village, the name of which I do not recollect, but where a squadron of our German hussars were quartered. I of course claimed and took possession of the horse, giving the person the amount he had paid for him; but he being still lame, the commanding-officer of the hussars kindly permitted me to leave him with his farrier till he got well. He afterwards sent him to me, and would not even allow the farrier to receive any remuneration for his trouble, so kindly and politely did he behave.

September passed away without any thing remarkable occurring. My friend Captain (now Major) Perceval had been obliged to return to England, and Captain Balvaird succeeded him as senior captain of my battalion. I still continued in that company's mess. At length it was determined to attack the Puerta, or Pass of Vera, which the enemy had rendered exceedingly strong. The left of our army, under Sir Thomas Graham, were ordered to attack in their front, and force the passage of the Bidassoa, and establish themselves in France. We were merely to drive them from the heights above the town of Vera, taking possession of all the strong ground between that and France. The fourth division was brought up to support our attack, and formed immediately in rear of the town. One of the captains who formed the Committee of Paymastership, and who, it may be remembered, were held responsible for my accounts, and the due appropriation of all public money which might come into my hands, took a fancy that I exposed myself too much, and requested the commanding-officer, Colonel Ross, to prohibit my again entering into action, except for the purpose of bringing ammunition, &c, when my duty required me; in consequence of which the adjutant was sent to me this morning, previous to the operations commencing, with an order for me not to accompany the battalion. It may seem to the reader perhaps like affectation when I tell him I felt hurt at this order, and determined not very strictly to comply with it, for I believed that my respected commanding-officer had no objection that I should accompany him, did not this untoward circumstance interfere with my so doing. Accordingly I remained a looker-on among the fourth division. My battalion was destined to commence this attack by driving the enemy from a high and rugged hill on the right of the Pass, which was a necessary operation before the Pass itself could be attacked. Accordingly he extended the battalion, and encircled its base on the side next to Vera; and I believe, without firing a shot almost, he marched right up to the top of the hill, notwithstanding the sturdy resistance made by the enemy, and in a very short space of time completely cleared this formidable height.

This operation was the admiration of the whole fourth division, (for it was clearly observable by every one,) and they were most lavish of their praises for such a workmanlike movement. When my people approached the top of the hill, I felt alarmed for their safety and their honour, for the French commander closed all his force to one point, and, forming them into line, made them fix bayonets, apparently with a determination to charge them down the hill again; and I saw that my people, for they could not perceive what the French were doing, were likely to be taken by surprise. Whether the Frenchman's heart failed him I know not, but when Colonel Ross reached the top of the hill, the enemy went to the right about, and instantly retired.

I felt proud of belonging to that corps, and happy at such a termination of this dangerous operation, and feeling a desire I could no longer resist, I set off to join them. By the time I reached the height just mentioned, the attack of the Puerta was going on, and a most arduous undertaking it was. My brigade attacked the right or strongest pass, which they carried in fine style, without much loss, although the enemy had a breastwork at every available point of ground. Our 2nd brigade did not attack the left Pass quite so soon as the other, and when they had got about half way up they encountered the most formidable opposition.

A redoubt which the enemy possessed was filled with men, who waited till our battalion came within a few yards of them, and then poured in the most destructive fire imaginable, making the battalion recoil, and leaving one-third of its numbers on the ensanguined ground. But the 52nd regiment being close behind, promptly supported them when rushing on together to the charge, and the French, after some hard fighting, were finally driven from this stronghold. After this they never made any obstinate stand, although there was occasional fighting all the way from the Pass down into the plain below, where some of our people followed them; but it not being intended to quit for the present this high and formidable barrier, they were afterwards recalled. The boundary lines passed along this ridge.

We lost a few men on ascending the first hill, and a few in skirmishing afterwards, but our loss was not severe. But that of the 2nd battalion, before noticed, was awful; several of that battalion who fell in this action had only a few days before joined from England, and this was their first action. On looking at the ground on which this affair took place, one would imagine it almost impossible that any army could force a passage through such innumerable difficulties. The hill itself was nearly impassable, and with the numerous redoubts and breastworks, with which it was literally covered, no troops in the world, I think, but British, would have dared to attempt it.

We found that the French, who occupied this station, had rendered themselves extremely comfortable, considering the kind of country and ground where they were posted. They had been at great pains in building very convenient and substantial huts in lines and streets, the same as an encampment, and which were indeed remarkably clean and neat. They had even built arm-racks at the end of each line, where their arms were stowed away most securely, and where they were preserved from the effects of the bad weather. Indeed, from the pains they had taken to render themselves comfortable here, it would appear as if they had not expected to be driven from it so soon.

The left of our army, under Sir Thomas Graham, also established themselves within the French territory. A corps of Spaniards on our left, between us and Sir Thomas, had likewise made a forward movement corresponding with the British. Some Spaniards were on the right of our division also, and were destined to drive the French from La Rhune, an exceeding high rock, which overlooks all the other mountains, as well as the plain below. This they failed to accomplish, the enemy keeping possession all that night, and the skirmishing between the two forces continuing till after dark.

My battalion was sent on the outpost duty in the evening down into the French plain below, and relieved the Spanish General Longa, whose corps, with our 2nd brigade, were ordered to assist in the morning in dislodging the enemy from La Rhune. I will not say whether the sight of the red-coats coming against them the next morning had the effect of alarming them, but they certainly evacuated that exceedingly strong post without much farther opposition, and established themselves on a similar rock, but lower, on the French side, and called by them Petit or Little Rhune. But the possession of this lofty peak gave us the power of overlooking all their movements for miles around us, as well as of surveying La Belle France as far as the eye could see, and indeed, compared with the bleak and barren mountains in which we had so long been residing, it did appear a beautiful country, although, in reality, it is far from being such: But we gazed upon it with strange and mingled emotions, hardly believing it possible that we had now reached and entered the territory of that once formidable nation whose victorious armies had penetrated to the farthest confines of Europe, who had overrun and subdued some of the most warlike nations of the continent, and who had so often threatened, and as often alarmed, the inhabitants of England with the invasion of that sacred soil, on which never yet a Frenchman has dared, in hostile array, to set his foot since the days of the Norman William, but who met there either with a prison or a grave.

We now pitched our camps by battalions, each occupying a post more or less important, and the enemy began again to construct their huts, and make themselves as comfortable as their circumstances would admit; Soult, no doubt, being mightily chagrined that we had now fairly beat them out of Spain, when he (as we now learnt) had promised his followers that he would soon lead them again to the plains of Vittoria, where they might again retrieve their lost honours, and at which city they would celebrate the Emperor's birthday. He thus boasted, and no doubt would have effected his purpose, had he not been so promptly met near Pamplona by his never-to-be out manoeuvred antagonist.

We now began to suffer greatly from the severity of the weather. It became exceedingly wet and stormy; and not infrequently the tents were blown away from over our heads, or the pole was forced up through the top, letting the wet canvass fall comfortably down about our ears while we were perhaps in a sound sleep. I had two streams flowing past my head, one went round the trench outside my tent, while the other I was fain to let pass through it; their murmurs lulled me to sleep, and I do not remember that ever I slept sounder than I did here, having made my couch comfortable by gathering dry fern, and spreading my mattress upon it.

Whilst we remained here, a few officers were appointed to watch the motions of the enemy from an old work which we understood had been constructed by the Spaniards and emigrant French against their revolutionary neighbours, whom they endeavoured to keep from entering Spain; and, of course, this was the daily lounge of those who had no better employment, not only that they might themselves see, but hear also from others what of importance was passing. On one of these occasions, a vessel was descried (for the sea was not more than five or six miles from us) making for the harbour of Bayonne, or St Jean de Luz, with a small schooner following her in chase, and every now and then giving her a shot. The vessel, (which turned out to be a French brig going with provisions for the few Frenchmen who still retained the castle of Santona,) seeing she could not get clear of her unwelcome neighbours, her crew set her on fire, and taking to their boats, abandoned her, and escaped on shore—she soon after blew up with a tremendous explosion.

On the 31st of this month Pamplona surrendered, the garrison, consisting of 4000 men, under Major-general Cassan, the governor, becoming prisoners of war. They had been compelled to adopt this measure from sheer starvation, of which they, I understand, had suffered dreadfully. I happened to be at Passages on the day they reached that port, where they embarked, on their way to England. The General was a stout, handsome, and intelligent-looking man, and such a one as I should imagine would make a noble officer. The soldiers seemed quite unconcerned about their fate; whether from the change being actually an improvement of their condition, or from the lightness and gaiety of their natural temper, I know not, but they were jesting and making as merry as if nothing had happened.

During the time we lay on these mountains, I regret to state my gallant and respected commanding-officer, Colonel Ross, suffered so much from rheumatism, that he was compelled to leave the regiment, and take up his abode at Rentaria, a village near to Passages.

It was reported that Lord Wellington intended attacking the enemy along his whole line, early in November, but the weather having rendered the roads impassable, it was postponed. On the day previous to the intended attack, the commanding-officer had been taken up to La Rhune, and the post that each corps had to occupy, with the movements they were intended to make, were clearly pointed out to them; an excellent plan, when practicable, as it leaves no one any excuse for mistakes or blunders during the action.

At length, on the 10th of that month, I believe, it was settled to take place; but on the 9th I was ordered to set off with the mules of the battalion, to fetch corn from Passages, a distance of about thirty miles. I suspected this was a scheme of the captain I before mentioned, as one of the committee of paymastership, in order the more effectually to keep me out of danger, for certainly had any thing serious happened me, they would have had some difficulty in rendering their accounts. It was not quite certain the attack was to take place next day, although it had been so rumoured; however, I was determined to try and reach the division as early as possible on that day. I accordingly got my business done in Passages as early as I could get the commissary to work; and having got the corn, and come on to Rentaria, which I reached about mid-day, I took the liberty of leaving the animals in the charge of the noncommissioned officer who had accompanied me; and calling on Colonel Ross, obtained his permission to let the sergeant proceed in charge of them to the regiment, while I might, if I chose, push on at a quicker rate. I had heard by this time, that the action had commenced by daylight that morning.

I accordingly set off at as quick a pace as my starved animal could carry me; and passing Iran, and crossing the Bidassoa, and keeping along the great road for a considerable distance, I then inclined to my right, and skirted the Pyrenees along the whole plain. I had thus an opportunity of witnessing the conflict carrying on by the left wing of our army, as I passed along towards La Rhune, but with every exertion of myself and my poor jaded horse, night closed in upon me before I had nearly reached the station of the light division. I was compelled to work my way through a country which I had not hitherto passed, and which having been the scene of a sanguinary combat, presented no very pleasing aspect. At last I heard some strange and foreign voices before me, for it was now quite dark, on which I turned into a field, and waited till they passed, by which I learned they were

Spaniards. I was apprehensive I might have kept too far to the left, and had got into the French lines, which would not have been so comfortable; but after finding them to be men of General Frere's Spanish division, I then had hopes of shortly meeting with my own people. Directed by those good Spaniards, I at last reached Petit La Rhune, the late formidable position of the enemy, on which the blazes from a thousand of their huts were rising to the clouds, and enlightening the atmosphere around. But it being now ten o'clock, I found myself incapable of proceeding farther, more particularly as the Portuguese, among whom I now found myself, could not give me any certain directions which way my division had gone. I was fain therefore to take up my abode, and gladly did so, in a cottage with Colonel St Clair and several other officers of the sixth Cacadores. Let it not be supposed that a fighting disposition induced me to use so much exertion to reach my division on this occasion—no; but as I considered that a sort of trick had been played off upon me, I did what I could to render it nugatory; no man liking, as I imagine, to be the dupe of any other party's manoeuvres, with whatever friendly intention these may have been put in operation. I arose next morning early, and hastened to the point where I expected to meet my brave comrades, anxious to learn the fate of all I loved amongst them. I saw them and the third division at a considerable distance, each on a height in front, appearing like flocks of sheep huddled together as close as possible. I soon reached them, and learned with sorrow, that the brave Colonel Barnard was, as they supposed, mortally wounded, the ball having passed through the chest, and that little Lieutenant Doyle was killed.

This was a most stupendous action; the scene of operations extending from right to left, embracing, I imagine, not less than thirty miles of country. The centre had fallen to the share of my division, which, in the eyes of the best judges, was the strongest part of the enemy's line, for it had been fortified with the most consummate skill, and no labour had been spared to render it impregnable, as the enemy had been busily employed in the construction of forts, redoubts, and other fieldworks of every denomination, from the day we drove them from the Pass of

Vera; one in particular, a stone built fort, in the shape of a star, was exceedingly strong, and which was attacked and carried in the finest style possible, I understand, by the 43rd regiment; the 52nd also surrounded a fort in which the French 88th regiment was posted, the brave commander of which not having received any orders to evacuate it, remained till the retreat of the French left him no other alternative than to surrender at discretion. The part my battalion had to play, was to cross the valley separating the two La Rhunes in double quick time, and attack the French rock by a gorge, which allowed a passage from that valley into their position. This was to be in conjunction with the attack of the Star Fort by the 43rd, as it in some measure took that work in reverse. In short, every corps in the division, and I believe in the army, had a most arduous duty to perform, and most nobly did they execute it. The left of our army, under Sir Thomas Graham, did not succeed in driving the enemy from his innumerable works which covered St Jean de Luz, and which he retained possession of till the next morning; when the centre, that is the 3rd and light divisions, together with the Spaniards on our right and left centre, made a movement in advance, and crossed the Nivelle river, from which this action derives its name. Our movement, which threatened to separate the wings of the French army, caused the enemy to abandon his strong position in front of St Jean de Luz, as well as that town, on which occasion he attempted, and partly succeeded in destroying the bridge over the Nivelle at that place; but it being soon after repaired, Sir Thomas Graham's corps took up their quarters in the town.

We encamped for the night in front of the village of Serres, or Sarre, or Zarre. It had rained hard all the day of the 11th, and it continued almost without intermission till our camp was literally swimming. I remember perfectly that the water in my tent was several inches deep; and when I awoke in the morning, I found a Portuguese boy (who had followed us, and had attached himself to our mess as a sort of servant) was sitting holding by the tent-pole, that being the only place where he could find rest for the sole of his foot. In short, we were as wet, clothes and beds and all, as if we had been dragged through a river. The evening before, I well remember, we had been highly amused by my Scotch quartermaster-sergeant and his friends, who had taken up their abode close by, singing, till they rather grew tiresome,

"We are nae fou', we're nae that fou',
But just a drappie in our e'e."

This of course was done to drive away dull care, and to make the best of an uncomfortable situation.

The next day towards afternoon, a considerable firing was heard on our right, which had continued but a short while, till our gallant and unwearied Chief came galloping up, with some few of his staff following, who could with difficulty keep pace with him, and asking most anxiously whereabouts and what the firing was. We could only point out the direction in which we heard it, but could give him no account as to its cause. Away he galloped in the direction we pointed out, and no doubt soon reached the spot.

I forgot to mention, that a man of the Brunswick corps had been hung the day before for plundering by the Provost Marshal, no doubt in compliance with superior orders. It was necessary thus to give the army an example of severity, in order to deter them from committing those acts to which all armies are but too prone. We found indeed very little to plunder, had we been so inclined; for the greater part of the inhabitants had left their houses, taking every thing portable with them. This they had been induced to do from the false statements which Soult had set forth in some proclamations he issued about this time, in which he described the English as savages, nay, even as cannibals, who would not scruple to commit the most monstrous atrocities; so ignorant were the generality of these poor peasants, that many of them implicitly believed his representations. This, no doubt, was done with the view of raising the whole population in arms against us, in order to defend their homes against such a set of wretches as he made it appear we were; but, although many of the natives joined the French army at this time, with which they were incorporated and led to battle, the result of his famous proclamations was not equal to his expectations; for a great part of them declined warlike proceedings, and retired into the interior of the country with their families, leaving only a very small proportion indeed who remained in their houses. As might be expected, the empty houses suffered dreadfully; every piece of furniture almost being destroyed, either for fire-wood, or in seeking for valuables; while the houses of those who remained in general escaped.

General Harispe, being a Basque himself, had the organizing of the new levies now raised; indeed, many of these had taken a part in the irruption into Spain on the 25th July for the relief of Pamplona, and many of them fell on that occasion. We were not so fully aware of the extent of the misrepresentation to which Soult had gone in these proclamations, till some time after we had entered France, and had penetrated considerably into the interior, when some of our officers, either during or after a march, entered the cottage of a peasant who had not left his home, to get a little milk. The poor woman was remarkably civil, offering them any thing the house afforded. They got some milk, for which they offered her money, but which she declined. Her child was running about the house at this time, which, coming near one of the officers, he took it between his knees, and patted it on the head, with which the child seemed very well pleased; but the poor mother, standing at a little distance, and eyeing most intently every motion of the officer, was like to swoon with fear and agitation. But as the mother had declined receiving any thing for the milk, the officer who had the child gave it some small coin, and letting it go, it ran to its mother, who snatched it up into her arms with the utmost joy, and altering her, look, began to say, she thought they had been deceived; for that they had been led to believe from the proclamations of Soult, that we were such barbarians that we would not scruple to kill and eat their children, and which was the cause of her late fear and anxiety, as she expected the officer had taken the child for that purpose; but now she found we were not such people as she had been led to believe. Of course the officer laughed most heartily at having been suspected of a man-eating propensity, and soon convinced the poor woman that the English were not quite such barbarians as that, whatever she might have heard to the contrary.

Chapter Fifteen
Crossing the Nive

We left our wet camp on the 15th, and advanced to the village of Arbonne, where, for the first time during the campaign, we were quartered in houses, except once or twice. During our stay in the camp at Serres, or Zarre, we sent our baggage animals to Passages for corn, on which occasion I lost another horse, the batman pretending it had been stolen, but which, no doubt, he sold, as that trick had often been resorted to by this time, and there was no detecting it.

On the 17th we left Arbonne, and advanced to Arcangues, sending forward picquets to the village of Bassozari, about half a mile in front. My battalion took up into quarters in some straggling houses in front of the church of Arcangues, while our first battalion occupied the chateau and outhouses of Arcangues, about a quarter of a mile to the right and front of the church. The enemy's picquets were close to Bassozari, so that in some places scarcely a quarter of a mile intervened between our quarters and their outposts. They allowed us to take up our outposts very quietly, they being now established in their intrenched camp in front of Bayonne, and which was not far distant from our advance. There were some houses in the line of posts occupied by the French, which, if in our possession, would add greatly both to our security and convenience, and which it was determined to wrest from them if practicable.

Accordingly, on the 23rd the division was put under arms, and our brigade, being in front, had this task assigned to them. The 43rd, not having had so much work during the campaign as our two battalions had, was selected for the purpose of driving in the enemy's picquets, whilst we supported them.–They accordingly attacked and carried the houses without a moment's delay; but unfortunately, Captain Hobkirk of that regiment, advancing with his company beyond the line at which it was intended to halt, got immediately in front of some of their intrenchments, from which he could not extricate himself, in consequence of which our first battalion was ordered to advance to cover his retreat; but he had by this time fallen into the hands of the enemy, with a considerable number of his men: his lieutenant was killed, and altogether the company suffered great loss. The remainder retreated, our first battalion people holding the houses it was intended to occupy. This occurred on the left of the ridge.

On the right, and adjoining a marsh which separated us from some high ground near the river Nive, and which was occupied by another division of our army, were two or three houses also which it was intended to take, as their possession secured us a passage across this marsh by a causeway, which connected two eminences, that on which we stood, and that occupied by the other division, the principal object upon the latter being a large chateau called Garratt's House. One company of the 43rd also took those houses, supported by some more of that regiment and my battalion; but after they were taken, from what cause I know not, an order was sent to evacuate them, on which the 43rd retired. Soon after, they were again ordered to be reoccupied, when a company of ours advanced, and took possession, but had not been there many minutes till another order was sent for them to be evacuated. This order, however, had scarcely reached them, when a charge was made on them by a body of French cavalry, supported by a strong column of infantry. The officer who commanded the company, either from the order he had received, or from want of presence of mind, called to his men to run to the rear when the cavalry charged him, by which he did not suffer much in point of losing men, for only one was wounded by the cavalry; but it had a bad appearance to run away from cavalry, a description of force which we had learnt by this time almost to despise, especially as, from his post, he might have knocked down great numbers of them, and finally have repulsed them, had he allowed his men to fire. The houses were, however, eventually taken possession of by another company of our battalion the next day, which retained them in despite of the enemy. The man who was wounded by the cavalry was shot

211

in the head by a pistol ball: he came to the surgeon, where the main body of the battalion was standing, to be dressed; while this was doing, and the orderly man holding a tin-full of water near, from which the surgeon was sponging and cleaning the wound, a ball came, and, striking the tin, carried it right out from between the hands of the orderly. I was standing close by, and shall not easily forget the blank look which, as might be expected, the poor orderly put on. There was a good deal of firing all day, which, except what the 43rd suffered, as before noticed, did little damage to the brigade.

On the occasion of our company taking these houses the next day, a very young officer, who happened to command it, evinced great fortitude and presence of mind. He advanced on the enemy, who, being then rather inclined to quietness, retreated gradually before him; but after reaching the hedge, just beyond the principal house, told him (for they were quite near enough to speak) that he must not advance any farther, or they would be compelled to fire on him. The young fellow, solicitous about nothing but obeying his orders, told them that he was determined to have the house, and immediately putting his men under the best cover be could, called out that they might begin to fire whenever they pleased, he was ready for them. This young officer (whose name was Cary, and brother to my friend who fell at Badajos) spoke excellent French, so that the enemy understood him perfectly. The enemy did not contend any longer for the post, but planted their sentries within about thirty yards of ours. These sentries, indeed, were still so posted as to prevent a passage across by the causeway, had they been so inclined; but the next day I went with another officer across by this road, on which occasion we actually passed to the rear of the French sentries.

A disposition had for some time been gaining ground with both armies, to mitigate the miseries of warfare, as much as was consistent with each doing their duty to their country; and it had by this time proceeded to such an extent, as to allow us to place that confidence in them that they would not molest us even if we passed their outposts for the purpose I have mentioned. And

212

this mutual confidence in each other was productive of the most comfortable results to both parties. We could move about at any time, and almost in any place, shooting or otherwise amusing ourselves, without the dread of falling in with an enemy's patrol, or of getting among their sentries. They never molested us from this time, except when we either advanced upon them, or they upon us, in hostile array. Our division had two main picquets; all this took place at the right picquet. A few days after I happened to be at the advanced post on the left, commanded by one of my battalion, when the French officers beckoned to us. We, to show we were peaceably inclined, pulled off our swords, and advanced to meet them. A number of inhabitants, who had left their houses on our first entering the country, having heard that we were not what we had been represented, were desirous of returning to their homes, and the officers wished us to admit them, and see them safe through the advanced posts. This of course we gladly promised, and the poor people were quite overjoyed at being permitted to visit their dwelling-places once again; but, poor creatures, I fear they would find little there except the bare walls, if indeed these remained entire, for, from the reasons before assigned, it could scarcely be expected that houses without inhabitants, in the midst of an invading army, would be much respected. Each individual among them, old and young, carried heavy bundles on their heads, no doubt they having removed every thing that was valuable, if portable.

The French officers were extremely polite, and asked us many questions of the news of the day, &c.; but the commander-in-chief, hearing of the familiarity which subsisted between the two armies, issued an order, prohibiting British officers from holding conversations with the enemy; for as all these conversations were necessarily conducted in French, (very few indeed of their officers being able to speak English,) he was apprehensive they might gain such information from our people, from their imperfect knowledge of the French language, as might materially injure our future proceedings. Before this order was issued, the most unbounded confidence subsisted between us, and which it was a pity to put a stop to, except for such weighty reasons. They used to get us such things as we wanted from Bayonne, particularly brandy, which was cheap and plentiful, and we in return gave them occasionally a little tea, of which some of them had learnt to be fond. Some of them also, who had been prisoners of war in England, sent letters through our army-post to their sweethearts in England, our people receiving the letters and forwarding them. They told us also how Hobkirk was situated, and were astonished at the extent and splendour of his equipage, (for he was a great dandy,) and could scarcely be persuaded he was only a captain.

My present commanding-officer, who was the senior captain, and in whose mess I then was, had sent to England, and got out from thence two immense pies, weighing nearly a hundred-weight each, and packed in tin cases. They were composed of every kind of game, and the best description of fowls, such as turkeys, &c, with the bones taken out, and the meat baked till it became like brawn when cut in slices. They were most excellent. One of these he had made a present of to our Major-general, and the other we were eating in the mess. We had also at this time a considerable quantity of good wine, which, by some accident, we had got hold of. We also had bought a pig and killed it, both living quite sumptuously at present, and having a good stock for future use.

But while we ourselves fared so well, our poor horse and mules were literally starving. There was no kind of forage for them, except what they could pick up in the now completely exhausted fields around us. We had nothing else to give them.

In this way we were going on, when, on the 9th of December, Lord Wellington, determining on passing the Nive, preparatory to future operations, ordered our division and all the left, under Sir John Hope, who had now succeeded Sir Thomas Graham, to make a movement in advance, in order that the enemy's attention might be attracted to this point, while he threw over some divisions to the right bank of that river. My battalion had to advance along the ridge by which I had formerly passed in peace, to meet the returning inhabitants, as may be recollected; but now the face of affairs was completely altered;—a heavy fire was kept up by the French picquets from the moment they saw us advance in arms, but we soon drove them from their advanced works, and they were obliged to take shelter in their intrenched camp, which was remarkably strong, and which it was not intended we should attack. We accordingly halted on the brow of the ridge, while they kept up an incessant fire, both from their guns and infantry, but which, considering its extent and duration, was not by any means a destructive fire.

Sir John Hope had a more laborious task to perform, or else his troops went beyond the point intended, for they continued the fight nearly all day, and at one time were considerably in advance, but afterwards recalled.

The passage of the Nive was completely effected, and in the evening we returned to our comfortable houses, a short distance in the rear, and went to bed as usual. Next morning, however, very early, orders were given to turn out immediately, and stand to our arms, for the enemy was advancing; and indeed, when I came to the door, I heard a good deal of firing. The troops turned out at once, but the mules were to get, and the baggage to pack, and send away to the rear, or it might be lost; so I set myself about this with all dispatch; but before any of it was put up, I saw posting by me, with all expedition, a civil officer, who had only a short while joined us, and who, in his hurry, had put up all he could scrape together on his horse, on which he himself was riding. His boots, tied together, were slung over the horse's neck, and in short he looked more like a bagman than an officer, from the number of things he had hanging about him. It was most laughable to see him. I called out and asked him why he was in such a hurry, but he did not stop to give me an answer.

I got up our baggage very well, but what to do with the pie, the pig, and the wine, I knew not, so was constrained to leave them as they were, hoping we might not allow the enemy to penetrate so far. I then moved off the baggage, and, directing the servants who had charge of it to proceed up a lane which carried them towards the rear, I moved on and joined the battalion. Just as I reached the plateau, or high ground in front of the church of Arcangues, I met an officer of ours to whom I had lately lent a fine young mare, for which I had not food sufficient; and he having no horse himself, I thought he would take care of her; but here I met him going into the fight riding on the poor animal, although scarcely able to drag one leg behind the other. I remonstrated with him, but he did not mind me. The result was as might have been anticipated—she soon after dropped down, unable to move farther, and died; thus I lost L.35 more, which she had cost me. By this time the enemy had driven in the regiment which had been on picquet, and one or two of our companies were sent forward to cover their retreat to the church behind us, where they were ordered to take post, it being a high and fine position, and had by this time been partly fortified. My people retired gradually before the enemy, who now advanced in great numbers.

Our 1st battalion were not so fortunate in effecting their retreat. An officer and some men having got into a hollow way, were surrounded by the enemy and taken; another was killed; and another, with his section, had to force their way through a strong body which had got in his rear. My battalion did not fall into any scrape of that nature, but sustained a considerable loss in killed and wounded, from the vast superiority of the enemy in point of numbers, who, no doubt, did not escape with impunity. We held our ground at the bottom of the hill on which the church is built, the French not being able to force us farther back; the 1st battalion, at the same time, holding the fence and ditch in front of the Chateau, as well as that building itself. But a rather unpleasant occurrence took place at this time. When the enemy appeared on the plateau before mentioned, a regiment behind us, without orders, I believe, opened a heavy fire upon them, several shots of which struck among our men. One of them went in at the back of one of our soldiers, and killed him on the spot; another penetrated the back window of a house into which a party of ours had entered for defence, and very near struck an officer, who was in the room at the time. These shots must have been fired either by young soldiers, who scarcely knew how they pointed their muskets, or they must have taken

216

our people for the enemy, from which, indeed, they were not far distant. I am confident it was purely accidental, for no two corps could be on better terms than that regiment and ours always were. The skirmishing continued till dark.

This was one of a series of masterly movements between the two contending generals. Lord Wellington having sent a pretty strong force across the Nive, as before mentioned, Soult imagined he had so weakened his force on the left, as to render it probable he might penetrate it, and thus cause his lordship to withdraw his troops again from the right bank of the Nive; but he was anticipated; for Lord Wellington had no sooner established himself on the other side of the Nive, than he brought one of the supporting divisions of that movement to support us at the church of Arcangues, it being an important post to hold; so that, when we looked behind us, after we retired into position, we saw innumerable bayonets glistening in the sun, and ready to move forward whenever they should be required; but they never were wanted here, the light division being quite sufficient to sustain any attack the enemy had yet made on them. This, however, showed the provident care of his lordship, and how completely he had penetrated Soult's design.

This night two or three battalions of the Nassau and Frankfort regiments came over and left the French. They had heard that the Dutch had declared against Bonaparte, and wished to be transported to Holland, with all their arms and appointments, which they brought with them. We remained in bivouack on the ridge extending between the church and chateau of Arcangues all night, our picquets remaining in possession of the houses and hedges at the bottom of the hill, where we stopped the French in the morning. I visited the picquets at night, in company with my commanding-officer, where we found all well, and alert. The next day, there being no firing between us and those in our front, three French officers, seemingly anxious to prove how far politeness and good breeding could be carried between the two nations, when war did not compel them to be unfriendly, took a table and some chairs out of a house which was immediately in our front, and one which we had lately occupied as a barrack;

and bringing them down into the middle of the field, which separated the advance of the two armies, sat down within 100 yards of our picquet, and drank wine, holding up their glasses, as much as to say your health, every time they drank. Of course we did not molest them, but allowed them to have their frolic out.

During the day, also, we saw soldiers of the three nations, *viz*. English, Portuguese, and French, all plundering at the same time in one unfortunate house, where our pie, our pig, and wine had been left. It stood about 150 or 200 yards below the church, on a sort of neutral ground between the two armies; hence the assemblage at the same moment of such a group of these motley marauders. They plundered in perfect harmony, no one disturbing the other on account of his nation or colour. There were a great number of apples in it at the time we left it, belonging to the owner of the house, but when we returned, two or three days afterwards, the desolation was complete. Our once comfortable quarter contained nothing now but filth and dirt. One poor girl had remained in it all the while, but she could not save one article; indeed, in such a case it would have been a service of danger to attempt it.

At night one of our sergeants played the French a trick. He took with him a few men, and, knowing the ground well, they passed the French sentry unobserved, having reached the house at the top of the field out of which they had brought the table, &c, where their picquet was stationed. He made a rush at their arms, which he found piled in front of the house, and set to work and broke them before the French had time to recover from the consternation into which they were thrown by so unexpected an assault. He and his party then came running off without sustaining any injury. He was a most determined brave soldier this, but afterwards lost an arm at Toulouse, and was of course discharged with a pension.

On the 12th, the enemy made a mighty show of attacking our position, having greatly increased their force in front of us, and had, some way or other, found the means of spreading a report in our lines that 1800 grenadiers had been chosen to lead on the attack. They also traced out batteries, and cut embrasures, apparently with the intention of burning or knocking down the chateau of Arcangues, the owner of which remained in it all this time, and was rather suspected of holding correspondence with his countrymen. It is not unlikely it was by his means the report above alluded to was propagated. Every thing now wore a serious aspect, and of course every thing was done to render their attack abortive. All were animated with the best disposition to defend the post to the last extremity; but while the generality believed all these preparations were serious, there were others who thought it only a *ruse de guerre*; indeed, had our friends, the German hussars, (with whom we had often acted in concert,) been here at this time, it is more than probable they would have been strongly inclined to the latter opinion, for they scarcely ever saw the French make a great bustle and noise, as if about immediately to advance and attack, but they would coolly say, after eyeing them awhile, "Oh, he not come to-day!" "He go away!" and were generally certain of being right. So full of trick and artifice are our French antagonists, that they generally act in quite a contrary manner to what appearances indicate. But they began to be known; hence the scepticism of some of our people on the present occasion. Accordingly, about midnight, when the attack was to have been made, away they went, and retired nearly into their lines, leaving only a few to keep the ground.

At daylight next morning we again moved forward, on which there was a good deal of firing between the Portuguese battalion that had followed them and their rearguard; but when our people advanced to our old post on the ridge, I, happening to be first, took off my cap, and, putting it on the top of my sword, held it up, which the French taking for a signal of peace, as it was intended, the firing on both sides ceased, each party taking up the post they held previous to the late movements. We wondered why the French had retired, but presently heard a tremendously heavy firing in the direction of the Nive. Soult, it seems, had withdrawn nearly all his troops from our flank, and marching rapidly through Bayonne, had attacked General Hill, who commanded on the other side of the Nive, with great impetuosity, thinking Lord Wellington had weakened that force to strengthen us; but here again Soult was outwitted, for he found on that side quite sufficient to give him as sound a drubbing as he ever got; the Portuguese on this occasion, I understand, performing wonders.

These five days' fighting (for on every day there was firing, more or less, in one part or other of the line) were called the Battle of the Nive. We had had three days' work of it—they on our right two—and Sir John Hope's people, on our left, four, I believe, and they not trifling ones. In every thing. Soult undertook, he was completely foiled—all his schemes having been clearly seen through by his more sagacious opponent. Indeed he had inflicted a heavy loss on our left wing, commanded by Sir John Hope, where the fighting had been most severe, but no doubt he suffered equally, if not more severely than they did. I am told that the enemy's light troops were most insolent and annoying to our heavy regiments on the left, on this occasion. What a pity that they could not have been opposed by troops of a similar description!

It may be remembered the civil officer of whom I made mention, as having rode away with the greater part of his wardrobe hanging about his horse; he was more fortunate than we were, for the things which he left, his kind landlady took care of, and hid in some snug corner till the business was over, and on his return restored them all to him. He said the cause of his going off in such a hurry arose from a cannon-shot having struck the lintel of the door or window of his house while he was in the act of shaving, on which he bundled out with whatever he could scrape together, and set off. I verily believe it must have been the effect of imagination, for I remained behind him at least a quarter of an hour, and although our houses were close together, I did not either hear or see a shot fired in that direction till we had reached the hill, nearly an hour after; but he constantly maintained that it was so.

We again took up our old quarters in front of the church; but oh, how changed were they now from what they had formerly been in point of comfort! nevertheless, they still afforded us shelter from the inclemency of the weather. Soon after dark on this evening, a rather unpleasant affair occurred at the left advanced post of our division. An officer and two men coming from the French advance, with what intention is not known, were observed by the corporal who was stationed at our abatis, who immediately took out his rifle and shot the officer through the body, on which his two men lifted him up and carried him into their picquet-house. We were apprehensive this would put an end to that good understanding which had hitherto subsisted between the picquets of the two nations, and much regretted the circumstance. It is more than probable the officer was coming as a sort of patrol, to ascertain whether or not we had left the post, which, being a military undertaking, subjected him to all the chances of war attendant thereon. This is the more probable from his having two soldiers with him armed, as I understand they were; but if it was meant as a friendly visit, as formerly sometimes took place, it was greatly to be lamented; however, they did not, on account of this occurrence, manifest any soreness or ill-will afterwards, and the mutual good understanding continued to subsist between us.

While we remain at rest here a short space, I will endeavour to put the reader in possession of the character of the inhabitants, among whom we have been sojourning for a few months past—I mean the Biscayans. From the time we crossed the Ebro, a wonderful change took place in the appearance of the natives; and I believe the same description of people extend considerably into France, although under another government; they, I understand, still retain their ancient customs, dress, and language; they are denominated Basques, from the name of the province, I apprehend, which is called Biscay. They speak a different language from either the Spaniards, who border them on one side, or the French, on the other; and some of our officers who spoke Welsh, said they could understand a few of their words; it is denominated the Basque language. They generally wear cloth of their own manufacture, which is commonly blue, in some parts red or brown; in the neighbourhood of Pamplona, almost always the latter. The men wear a sort of Scotch bonnet, with a short jacket and trow-sers, and are an amazingly athletic and active people. The women wear a short jacket also, of the same colour with their petticoat; and with their hair, which they encourage to grow to a great length, plaited in one large plait, and tied with a small piece of ribbon; it is allowed to hang down their back, and almost in all cases reaches to, or below their middle. They wear a handkerchief tastefully disposed upon their head. They are a fine, tall, and handsome race of women; but they have a custom of compressing their breasts, so that they appear as flat in the bosom as the men, which, to an English eye, is not becoming. The women do the same kind of work as the men, that is, they plough, and labour at all sorts of husbandry; but what seemed most remarkable to us, was their sole management of the ferry-boats about Passages and St Sebastian; they row as well as any men, being amazingly strong and active; they seem content with their lot, and always appeared cheerful and happy. I believe they are strictly virtuous; and although very handsome in general, they did not seem so fond of admiration as the females of many other countries are; upon the whole, I think they resemble the Welsh more than any other people with whom I am acquainted; their countries are exceedingly similar, being mountainous, and in general not over fruitful, so that constant labour seems to be rendered absolutely necessary to insure to them the means of subsistence; hence they are industrious and frugal, and, upon the whole, an interesting and moral people.

Chapter Sixteen
Into France

On the 3rd of January 1814, we were ordered to quit a part of the country, which, from the various occurances that had taken place since we first arrived in it, had, in some measure, rendered it interesting to us. We moved a little to the right, and crossed the Nive, and again moved in advance about a league or more. This movement was made in support of some operations which Lord Wellington was conducting in the direction of the Adour, which being completed, we returned to the Nive, and took up our cantonments in the villages of Ustaritz and Aurantz. About this time, nearly the whole of the peasantry, who had fled on our entering France, were now returning to their habitations, all fear that we should murder them, and eat their children, having by this time been completely dissipated. Indeed we were often told after this, that they would much prefer having a British army among them, to their own people, for they were always haughty, they said, and overbearing, and never scrupled to take whatever they had a mind for, while we were orderly and quiet, and never took an article without amply repaying the owner for it. Indeed I am well convinced the change the poor people had made in their lodgers was greatly for the better to them.

My battalion was quartered in the village of Aurantz, from which we often took a stroll, to look at the scene of our late operations. The French having, in consequence of Lord Wellington's movements near the Adour, strengthened their army in that direction, which of course rendered it necessary they should contract the limits of their front on the side towards Spain, they had consequently withdrawn their advance considerably within their former lines. We now also had plenty of opportunity for shooting, but were but ill supplied with fowling-pieces, or we might have killed an abundance of woodcocks, every thicket in the neighbourhood being filled with them.

The weather now was extremely bad, and the roads impassable, except by yourself wading up to the knees, or having your horse almost continually nearly up to his belly. In consequence of the difficulty of communicating by dragoons, on account of the roads, telegraphs were established all along from the right of the army, on the banks of the Adour, to St Jean de Luz on our left, the head-quarters of the army. While in these cantonments, an account arrived of our gallant Major-general (Kempt) having been appointed to the colonelcy of the 8th battalion of the 60th regiment, which had just been raised. At the recommendation of my commanding-officer, now Major Balvaird, the general kindly transmitted my name to the War Office for the appointment of paymaster of his battalion; but unfortunately for me, before my name arrived, his late Royal Highness the Duke of York, as Colonel-in-chief of the regiment, had nominated another person to the situation. It had always hitherto been customary for Colonels-commandant, and not the Colonel-in chief, to nominate their own staff, but on this occasion another rule was adopted, which, of course, was a great disappointment to me, as I had, with considerable trouble, got all my sureties, &c. prepared, although they were now not needed.

I had, during our stay here, one or more trips to the paymaster-general for money, for although the paymaster of the battalion had by this time arrived, I had several months' pay still to draw, the army being considerably in arrear in their pay. I had thus an opportunity of visiting St Jean de Luz, and all the enemy's late fortifications and position in that neighbourhood, and amazingly strong they had indeed rendered the ground in front of that town. It was a considerable and well-built town, partaking a good deal of both the Spanish and French character of course, it being the first French town next to the frontier; and, as I said before, there being very little difference between the Basques on either side of the Bidassoa, the change of countries in respect to inhabitants was not very observable except among the better orders.

On the 16th of February we broke up from our cantonments in Aurantz, and commenced the campaign of 1814, crossing the

Nive at Ustaritz, and moving on in the direction of La Bastide de Clarence. We encamped on a wild heath, without any village or town being near us, and again the next morning continued our route to the place above-named, which we reached about noon, and encamped on a hill beyond it.

On the 22nd we advanced to St Palais, having passed other villages, the names of which I have forgot, in the intermediate days. Nothing, however, of any note occurred in that period. On the 23rd we encamped near La Chere and Charrette; on the 24th we crossed two rapid and deep streams of the Bidowse. The first we got over with considerable ease,—it was the Gave de Mauleon, which we crossed at Nabes; but the second, the Gave d'Oleron, was not only both deeper and more rapid than the other, but the passage seemed intended to be disputed with us; some French cavalry having made their appearance on the opposite bank, as we approached the river. The resistance they could offer, however, seemed very trifling, for, on our bringing up some gains to the bank, and a few shots having been fired from them, and from a company of our second battalion, they withdrew.

We now prepared to go over; accordingly, every man was ordered to take off his pouch and buckle it on the top of his knapsack, the ford being so deep as to take the men up to or above the middle. On this occasion I had I know not how many of the poor men hanging about me and my horse. Some were holding by the stirrup, some by the tail, and others by the mane, or wherever they could lay hold, for the stream was so rapid as to nearly sweep them off their legs. Indeed I understand several of those who followed us were actually swept down, and perished.

On reaching the farther bank, we found the French had endeavoured to render it impassable, by throwing harrows, &c, with their spikes upmost, in the only places where you could ascend from the river. I believe a trumpeter of the French was all who fell on this day.

We passed through Ville Neuve, and formed in a field beyond the village, till the whole division had got over. It was in this village where the scene between the mother, the child, and some of our officers, took place. When joined and formed, we moved on to a high and ugly common, not far in rear of the village of Orion, where we bivouacked for the night. It was most uncomfortable.

Before we reached our ground this evening, we observed, at a short distance to our left, a body of about 200 French infantry moving on parallel to us, but apparently making all haste to get away in front of us. Some suggested the idea of attacking and taking them prisoners; but as they were rather before us, it could not have been done without setting one of the battalions at them in double-quick time. and which would not have been an easy operation, after a long and fatiguing march, and fording two rivers. Besides, as our Quartermaster-general said, it was certain they could not be far from their support; consequently it would only bring on an affair, which it was not the General's wish to do at that time, for there was none near to support us should the enemy send a force against us. This day General Picton's division had a sharp affair at Navarreins, where they forced the passage of the Gave we had crossed.

On the 25th, we moved forward early in the morning, and on reaching the village of Orion, we found that Soult had had his head-quarters the night before, with a considerable portion of his army, in and around the village; it was therefore fortunate we did not attack the French detachment before mentioned, for we should certainly have had Soult, with all his people, upon our single division. A French band had remained in this village till our arrival, having deserted in a body from the regiment to which they belonged, or they, seeing they could not make their escape, pretended to desert and join our army.

We bent our course towards Orthes, which was now only a few leagues in front of us. A man brought a cask of excellent wine to the road-side, with the intention of giving every man of the division a drink, but we could not wait, and were consequently obliged to leave the good man's gift. It showed that either good-will or fear had prompted him to this act. I rather think the former was the cause, as he lived some distance from the road. We had not continued long on the march, till we heard a loud and thundering explosion in front of us, which, as it was expected, turned out to be the bridge of Orthes, which the enemy had blown up. A short while after we came in sight of the town, and one of our Portuguese Cacadore regiments being sent forward, a smart skirmish commenced between them and the French, who had been left on and about the bridge to prevent our repairing it. I foolishly went down to see what was going on, and had nigh paid for my curiosity.

We took up our ground behind a height which overlooked the town, through which the enemy were passing in large columns. In consequence of this, we got some guns into a field in front of our hill, and commenced a cannonade upon them, which, we could observe, made them hurry their pace considerably. They also brought some heavy field-guns to bear upon us, and fired some shots, but without doing us much injury. Throughout the whole of the road by which the French had come before us, desolation and misery marked their footsteps; and in the village of Orion, where Soult himself had slept the night before, nothing could exceed the despair and misery of the few remaining inhabitants, who told us they had been literally stripped of their all; indeed, they appeared most forlorn and wretched beings, and, as might be expected, poured out the most heavy and bitter complaints, not unmingled with imprecations, on the heads of their plundering countrymen. I went into a poor weaver's house here, where, if I mistake not greatly, the marauders had actually cut the web he was weaving out of the loom, and carried it off with them.

We remained on this ground all night, and the next morning his lordship was intently occupied for a considerable time in reconnoitring the enemy's position. At length, as if he had fully made up his mind how to act, he ordered our division to fall in, which was promptly obeyed; then, sending his staff with directions, we were ordered to file to the right, and to move down towards the river, apparently with the intention of crossing a little above the bridge, which had been destroyed. On the other side, immediately opposite what appeared to be the ford, were large bodies of infantry, together with a great quantity of artillery.

I recollect my battalion was leading the division, and it appeared at this moment as if we were going to be engaged in a most arduous and hazardous undertaking; for the enemy's artillery would have swept us off the face of the earth before we could possibly have reached the farther bank; however, this was only a *ruse de guerre*, and a most deep-planned and well-executed one it was; for while we were moving down towards the river, a staff-officer came riding, and ordered us all to hide as much as possible from the view of the enemy, by crouching down, &c. as we moved along. It may seem rather paradoxical to be ordered thus to act, at the same time that we wished the enemy to observe our movement; but the fact is, there were probably a thousand eyes fixed on us all the time we lay here, and who watched most closely our every movement; consequently, we could not stir without the enemy being aware of it; and if on this occasion we had made a show and a parade of our movement, it would have been suspected as only a feint at once, as the French themselves, from often practising this stratagem, would have penetrated immediately our object. But our Chief went a step too deep for them, adepts as they are in all the arts of this kind; for he made a pretence of hiding from them his movement, knowing well that we were observed; and this completely deceived them. This threat of crossing here was made in order to favour the construction of a bridge about eight or ten miles down the river, and the crossing there by another division, as they were thus enabled to guess where the principal force for opposition would be required. I believe a better planned or more successful stratagem was never practised. But I own, when we were marching down to the river to cross in front of the immense masses which we saw ready to oppose us, I believed that few would survive to tell the tale hereafter.

The moment when we were just opening from the covered ground to plunge into the river, we were instantly countermarched with all expedition, and moved down the river at a quick pace till we reached the pontoon bridge which had been so successfully constructed and thrown over at the village of Sala. This being now perfectly safe, we encamped at the village for the night.

On the morning of the 27th, we early crossed the river called the Gave de Pau, and moved forward in the direction of the town of Orthes by the great road. On the right bank of that river, when we came within about two miles of the town, we were moved more to our left, ascending the high ridge which runs parallel with the river, and on which the French had taken up a strong position, and were said to be between 30,000 and 40,000 strong. One division had been ordered to move along the summit of this ridge, on which ran the great road to Peyrehourade, and to attack the enemy on that flank, while our division communicated with that and the 3rd division to our right. When the action was commenced, the 2nd division had been directed to ford above the bridge, where our feint had been made the day before, and passing through the town, to attack on the opposite flank, and thus cut off their retreat towards the Pau. The enemy's position proved to be exceedingly strong, and difficult of access by us.

The action commenced by the 4th division attacking on the road leading along the ridge, where an obstinate and bloody conflict took place, without our people being able to make any impression. The attack of the 3rd division, on our right, also commenced immediately after; but such was the nature of the ground on this side, being mostly in long pointed ridges, running out like the rays of a star, and which were exceedingly strong, that no efforts were able to force them from this ground.

General Hill had by this time got over the river, and was approaching the position. My division, having been deprived of two of its regiments, which had been sent, previous to the commencement of our operations this spring, to receive their clothing at St Jean de Luz, being rendered weak in consequence, it was kept in reserve, as I before mentioned. During this unsuccessful attack, our gallant Chief was for a considerable time immediately in front of us, watching with the most anxious care every motion of both armies. He appeared to me to be extremely thoughtful and serious on the occasion, as our troops did not succeed in forcing this stronghold of the enemy. The firing at this time was extremely animated, particularly on the ridge to our left, where great slaughter was made on both sides. And the French having discovered where he and his staff were assembled, opened a smart cannonade on the group, but without doing any mischief, I believe, and without being noticed by him. Their shots generally fell about our division, which was formed immediately behind the hill on which he stood.

At length, whether from the request of Colonel Barnard, who was at this time by his lordship's side, or whether by his own direction, I know not, but the Colonel was ordered to take on the 52nd and 1st Portuguese belonging to the Cacadores, our 2nd brigade, and endeavour to force a passage through the French line, by the gorge of the valley, which lay immediately in his front, and they would thus, if successful, penetrate into the centre of the enemy's position. They accordingly moved up the valley in column of companies, sustaining all the time the most galling and destructive fire, for the enemy were thus on each of their flanks, as well as in front. When they reached within a short distance of the centre height, they formed line, and moving on at a brisk pace and carrying every thing before them, they drove the enemy from the plateau, and thus penetrated into the very heart of their army. This was a most daring and intrepid movement, for although assailed by ten times their force, and nearly surrounded by the enemy, these gallant corps hesitated not to push on, although the very elements seemed as it were to fight against them; for on the brow of the enemy's position the fire had been so heavy and so incessant, that the very furze bushes and herbs of all kinds were in a blaze along the front, through which, with innumerable foes behind it, these gallant men forced a passage at the point of the bayonet.

This movement had the effect of at once deciding the fate of the day, for Soult seeing his very centre and strongest position carried, which separated between his wings, at once ordered a retreat of his whole force. The remainder of our division were now despatched with all speed in pursuit of the flying enemy, but they never attempted after this to make a stand, and nothing was left for us to perform but to give chase to the fugitives. When we reached the enemy's centre position, we found that every thing had been cleared away which could in the least impede his movements; every hedge and ditch had been completely levelled, so that nothing remained but a beautiful plain on the top of the ridge, except where works of defence had been thrown up. We were not successful in capturing any of the enemy, except the wounded, who had necessarily been left on the field, and we did not lay hold of any of his materiel, except a few guns which he had been obliged to abandon in a swamp below the position.

I have related only such things as fell within my own observation, but no doubt many were the heroic and gallant deeds that were performed in this hard contested battle, besides what I have detailed. As might be expected, the gallant 52nd and its supporting corps, the 1st Portuguese Cacadores, suffered dreadfully, leaving probably one-fourth of their numbers on the field.

But I must not omit mentioning one trait of gallantry which attracted the admiration of the whole army. Lord March (now the Duke of Richmond) had for some time been on the personal staff of Lord Wellington where his services had been most efficient. He also was at this time a captain in the 52nd regiment, but from his high civil rank had never served as an infantry officer with his regiment. He was determined to know and practice his duty in every situation, and therefore requested leave from his lordship to be permitted to join his corps as a captain, which was granted of course, and this was his first debut in the character of an officer of foot. It was no doubt a sharp trial; and poor fellow, while bravely leading on the company which his Majesty had intrusted to his command, he fell dangerously (then supposed mortally) wounded. This was a noble example to set our young nobility, and they cannot do better than to follow such a precedent. I understand he has been heard to say, "that the chance of a staff-officer being hit in action, is not near so great as that of an officer of infantry, who must quietly brave all that comes against him, while a staff-officer, being well mounted, can quickly get out of danger; and that if a gentleman wishes truly to learn his profession as an officer, he ought to serve for a time in the infantry whilst engaged in operations in the field.

This was a most decided, but withal an unfruitful victory, and only tended to establish more firmly the superior skill of our commander, and the superior bravery of the British army. We had heard of the proceedings of the allies in the north, and of a number of the French generals having deserted the cause of their once potent, but now fallen master. And I verily believed that Soult had collected his whole force together here for the express purpose of either allowing himself to be surrounded, and thus make a show of being compelled to surrender, or of inducing his whole army to come over at once to the side of the Bourbons, but in all these conjectures I was completely mistaken; for whatever may have been Soult's faults as a man, he has always shown himself a consistent and an able defender of the cause he first espoused, and as such is certainly respectable.

We pursued the flying columns of the enemy for about two leagues beyond the field of action, crossing in our pursuit the river Luy de Bearne, and at night took up our abode in bivouack, near the village of Bonne Garde. The night proved extremely cold and frosty, for in the morning when I intended to arise, I found my cloak frozen to the ground. We had no kind of covering. My commanding-officer had taken up his abode in a cottage close by, where there was no bed but what the people occupied. He therefore got into the kneading-trough, in which he slept very comfortably, but in the morning I remember he turned out like a miller.

We started soon after daybreak, and continued our march, crossing the small river Luy de France. Here I remember our assistant Quartermaster-general told us what great difficulty he found in obtaining information from the inhabitants as to the by-roads which run parallel to the great road from Orthes; for these good people could not conceive why he should be hunting after by-roads of this description, which were generally very bad, while the great road, which was always good, lay so near the line by which he wished to move, not knowing perhaps, or not understanding, that other divisions of the army were moving

232

on the high-road, while we wished to make a corresponding movement on their flank. They would always, however, after directing him how to proceed for a while, bring him again on to the great road, which he wished to avoid for the reason before given.

The comfort and the efficiency of an army in the field depends more, I am persuaded, on the abilities and zeal of officers in the Quartermaster-general's department, than on any other branch of the service; for if they are remiss or unacquainted with their duty, the marches and countermarches, the halts, and the changes of direction, are so numerous and annoying, that the spirits and strength of the troops are soon worn out, and of course dissatisfaction and inefficiency soon follow. But to the credit of the officers of this department at the period of which I am writing, I believe never army possessed more able, more zealous, or more active staff officers, than we did, and that principally owing to the excellent example set them by the head of this department, than whom a more able conductor of an army does not exist. On one of these occasions when our assistant Quartermaster-general had occasion to wait upon the authorities of a village, he jokingly asked them for passports, as is customary in France, to proceed into the country. "*Ma foi*," says the worthy Mayor, "you obtained your passports at Vittoria, you need no others now."

We halted for the night near the village of Duerse. In the morning, we forded the Adour near a small village, the name of which I forget, and making a long and rapid march, we took possession of the city of Mont de Marsan, where we found immense magazines of provisions, which had been collected by the enemy. This was the most valuable capture that had been made by the British army since its arrival in the Peninsula; for although a great deal of treasure was obtained at Vittoria, yet a considerable portion of that fell into the hands of individuals; but this was secured for the benefit of the whole army. The enemy had abandoned the city previous to our arrival, consequently it was a bloodless conquest, which rendered it the more valuable. Mont de Marsan is what may be termed a fine and an extensive city, containing about 3000 inhabitants.

The people received us kindly upon the whole, and showed us great attention. Here we had superb quarters, and the change from what we had lately been accustomed to, produced a rather uncomfortable feeling; for our clothes and all our equipments so little corresponded with the magnificence around us, that we should have preferred less stately mansions, if comfortable, as more congenial with our respective establishments. But we did not long enjoy our splendid lodgings; for, having secured the booty, we left the city, and returned to the banks of the Adour. The march both to and from this city had been along straight flat roads, cut through an immense pine forest, with which this department is almost completely covered. The roads had been for some time much traversed, and having a sandy bottom, were consequently very bad at this season of the year; added to which, a violent storm of snow and sleet assailed us all the march of this day, which made it a rather uncomfortable business. We halted for the night in a village named, I think, St Maurice, and the next day were moved into St Sever, a considerable town on the left bank of the Adour, in which Lord Wellington had taken up his head-quarters. Here we remained some days, doing duty over his lordship, when we crossed to the right bank, and moved up the river, halting at the town of Grenade. We next morning continued our route up that bank till we reached Barcelonne, a considerable town some little distance from the river, and nearly opposite Aire, a large town on the left bank, and near which General the Hon. Wm. Stewart, with the 2nd division, had had a smart brush with the enemy on the day we captured Mont de Marsan.

On the evening of the 10th we halted at the village of Arblade, and, on the 11th, entered Tarsac, where we remained for the night. We were next morning pushed on to a village in front, about a league distant, but were allowed to remain there only for one night, for the enemy now began to appear in our front in considerable force. We were consequently withdrawn, and, passing through Tarsac, the division formed in a wood about halfway between that and Aire. We expected something

234

serious was about to occur, but, from what cause I know not, the enemy again retreated, leaving a body of cavalry on the road about half-a-league beyond Tarsac, to which we again returned and took up our quarters.

On the 16th, as these fellows still continued so near us, although evidently without any infantry to support them, it was determined either to drive them away or take them prisoners. I must observe, our 15th hussars were at this time occupying Tarsac with ourselves, and one squadron of them were selected for this service. The advance of the French consisted only of one squadron, the remainder of their regiment being at some distance in rear as supports; consequently it was but fair that an equal force should attack them. Captain Hancox's squadron (in which was Captain Booth, with his troop) was pitched upon for this affair. The remainder of the 15th were drawn out to support them, if needed, but were not to take any part in the combat. Every one of course went out to see the fight.

Accordingly this squadron moved on to the front, and steadily advanced upon the enemy, who seemed determined to stand the charge, as they put every thing ready to receive our gallant dragoons. When within a proper distance the word "trot" was given, and soon after "gallop," and then "charge," when our fellows dashed in among the French, upsetting them in all directions, and cutting many of them down to the ground. In a few minutes the business was settled, for our people returned, bringing in with them the captain commanding, (and who, I believe, had been personally engaged with Captain Hancox,) with about twenty-five men, prisoners. The rest made their escape. The French captain, and the greater part of the twenty-five men, were wounded, and some were left dead on the road.

I shall not soon forget the little wounded captain. He, I believe, was either a native of Tarsac, or somewhere near, and had been determined to show his valour to the utmost; hence his standing, when he ought to have retired; but all the way, as they were bringing him along into the village, and after he reached the house where he directed them to take him, he kept crying out, "I'm as brave as a lion!—I'm as brave as the devil!" and could scarcely be got to hold his peace while the surgeon was dressing him. Most piteous moaning was made by many of the inhabitants, to whom it seems he was well known.

We understood afterwards that this regiment, the 13th French hussars, had fallen rather under the displeasure of Soult, for some ill conduct on a former occasion, and that they were thus determined to wipe off the stain and retrieve their character; but they would have shown more sense, and have rendered more service to their country, had they retired when they saw it was determined to drive them away.

On the 18th, we again advanced by the road the French had taken, and, crossing the Adour at the bridge and village of La Row or Arros, we pursued our route till we reached the town of St Germain's, where we halted for a short space, and thence to Plaisance, a good town, where we remained for the night. An unfortunate circumstance occurred in or near this town, which might have produced the most disastrous consequences:—A man, who most likely had been resisting the plundering of his house, was basely murdered by some soldier or soldiers of the division; but although every endeavour was made to discover the perpetrators of this vile act, they could not be found out; but a subscription was set on foot among the officers of the division, and 100 guineas were collected and paid to the unfortunate widow, who, though grieved for the loss of her husband, was thankful for the money. I strongly suspect my friends the Portuguese were the culprits on this occasion.

On the 19th we again moved forward, and, passing Obrigort, halted for the night at the village of Aget. Towards the close of this day's march, we both heard and saw smart skirmishing, down on the great road which runs parallel to the ridge on which we were, and from Auch to Tarbes, along the plain on our right, and passes through Vic Bigore. Near this town the firing was very brisk. We understood it was Picton's division driving the French before them.

The next morning we started early, and, continuing our march along the ridge of the height on which our last night's quarters were situated, we reached pretty soon the town of Rabasteins, where we learnt that the enemy had taken up a position in and near the town of Tarbes. We, accordingly, changing our direction, moved to our right, down the road leading from the former to the latter place. We passed on this road the sixth division, which, it seems, was ordered to keep on the flank of the enemy, which, should he make a stand, this division was to turn. When we got within about a mile and a half of Tarbes, we discovered the enemy posted on a strong woody height on the left of the road, with a windmill on its highest and most distant point.

The whole of our 95th people were accordingly ordered forward, to endeavour to drive them from this position. My battalion formed the right, the 2nd battalion the centre, and the 1st battalion the left of our line of skirmishers. We found them covered in front with a great number of light troops, which occupied us some time in driving in, and in which service we suffered considerably, for they occupied the hedges and dikes on the high ground, from which it was necessary we should dislodge them. We bad also a considerably-sized brushwood to pass through before we could get at them. At length, after much smart skirmishing, we gained the height, but found the whole of their heavy infantry drawn up on a steep acclivity, near the windmill, which allowed them to have line behind line, all of which could fire at the same time over each other's heads, like the tiers of guns in a three-decker. We continued, however, to advance upon them, till we got within a hundred paces of this formidable body, the firing from which was the hottest I had ever been in, except perhaps Barossa. At this moment I received a shot through my right shoulder, which compelled me for a moment to retire; but meeting the main support of my battalion advancing with Colonel Ross at its head, and finding my wound had not disabled me, I again advanced with him, until we got close under the enemy's line, and took post behind a hillock, which protected us from their fire.

We here found Colonel Norcott, who then belonged to the 2nd battalion, riding about on his large black mare; but he had not ridden long till he also was wounded through the shoulder, from which he still suffers. While we were in this situation, a shot struck a captain of ours in the side where he had his drinking-horn slung; in fact it struck both the horn and his side; but, from some cause, it did not penetrate the flesh, but bruised it sore, which is generally painful. The captain, and those about him, thought he was shot through the body; they accordingly picked him up, and were carrying him off to the rear, when he cried, "Stop, let me feel," and putting his hand down to the place, and finding no wound, he sprung out of their arms, and, with the most ludicrous appearance possible, returned to his post again. No one present could refrain from laughing at the ridiculousness of this occurrence, although at the moment the men were falling fast around us.

At this time also, a spent shot, one which I imagine had first hit the ground, struck me on the left arm, but did not injure me. I now thought it better to go to the rear to get my shoulder dressed, immediately after which I became quite faint from loss of blood. The firing still continued most animated on both sides; but before an hour had elapsed, the French were driven completely from every position they held on this very strong hill; and as I returned, (after having been dressed, and having swallowed some spirits to remove the faintness,) I found them posting away with all expedition to the plain below, some guns, which had just arrived, giving them an occasional shot, but from which they did not suffer much, they marched with such rapidity. We immediately followed them down to the plain, on reaching which, we perceived a body of French troops coming apparently from the town of Tarbes, pursued by the 3rd division, with whom they had been engaged, and which, with some exertion, we thought we could intercept and cut off; but they, perceiving our intention, inclined considerably to the right, and marching with all speed, they got away before us.

The enemy now having all retired across the plain, began to take up a strong position on a height at its extremity, towards which we continued to advance; but Lord Wellington having expected that the 6th division would by this time have reached their position, and, attacking in flank, have rendered our attack in front more likely to succeed, and they not making their appearance, although it was now nigh dusk, he ordered the divisions here to halt, and bivouack for the night on the plain. I never saw any one more disappointed, or apparently more annoyed by this last order, than our Adjutant-general, the lamented Sir Edward Packenham; he was for attacking them at once; but this could not have been done without a great sacrifice of excellent troops, as all those were who now filled the ranks of the British army, having by this time been completely seasoned, and become almost invaluable. In reviewing the operations of this day, I need say little, as facts speak for themselves. The enemy had on the Windmill hill, as it was vulgarly called, or more properly the hill of Oleac, I believe a whole division, consisting of at least 5000 or 6000 men, while not a shot was fired by any but by the sixteen companies of my regiment, amounting probably to 1000 or 1100 men; it is true the other regiments of the division were drawn up in rear of us, and would have supported us had we been repulsed. But it is not so much to the driving away of this so much stronger force, that I would draw the reader's attention, as to the great loss the enemy sustained, and solely from our fire. I believe I shall not be far from the truth, if I state their loss in killed and wounded as equal to the whole strength of our sixteen companies.

Lord Wellington, in his dispatch, mentions the destruction caused in the enemy's ranks as unusually severe; hence the advantage of rifles over the common musket, or else the superior mode of using our arms beyond what is practised in the line. The Americans tauntingly tell us, our soldiers do not know how to use the weapons that are put into their hands; and, truly, if we are to judge by the awful destruction which they have occasionally inflicted upon our brave soldiers, we should be led to suspect that they understand this science much better than ourselves. It might, however, be easily remedied, if more attention were paid to the instruction of the recruit in this most essential qualification, and more time and ammunition devoted to target practice; but, at the same time, every officer should be made to know, something of projectiles in general, or he will, as at present, be incapable of instructing his men. I will venture to assert, that eight out of ten of the soldiers of our regular regiments will aim in the same manner at an object at the distance of 300 yards, as at one only 50. It must hence be evident that the greater part of those shots are lost or expended in vain; indeed the calculation has been made, that only one shot out of 200 fired from muskets in the field takes effect, while one out of twenty from rifles is the average. My opinion is that our line troops ought to be armed with a better description of musket. If five shillings more were added to the price, it would make a great difference in the article, and be very trifling to the public. Our army has always been too sparingly supplied with flints, which may be had almost for an old song; but if wanted in the field, nothing can supply their place. Many a brave soldier has fallen while hammering at a worn out flint. It is true we can, with the weapons we have, drive any other army out of the field, but not without occasionally sustaining an overwhelming loss, particularly when opposed to the Americans; and could we meet them with the same advantages they possess in point of shooting, our chances of victory would be greater, and at less expense. These are my private opinions only, and are deduced from the experience I have had, both as a heavy infantry soldier and a rifleman. I am now firmly persuaded, that of the near 200 shots I fired on the 2nd of October 1799, in Holland, not one took effect, from my total want of knowledge how to aim. What an useless expenditure this was of both time and ammunition! Much indeed has lately been done by Sir Henry Torrens, to supply the deficiency of which I have been speaking, but still not sufficient, in my opinion, to remedy all the evils attendant thereon.

Our loss on this occasion was very heavy, being about 100 men and eleven officers killed and wounded; the proportion of officers being nearly double what usually takes place. The regiments which supported us also had some casualties, arising from the shots which passed over our heads striking among them; but they were not considerable. My servants having heard I was wounded, went to Tarbes, (where all the wounded were collected,) with my baggage. I should consequently have been very ill off, had not my kind friend and messmate, Major Balvaird, lent me his tent and bed, as he himself had been ordered on picquet. Immediately after nightfall, the enemy had all retired from the position in front of us. We accordingly next morning continued the pursuit, and halted at night at the village of Lannemazen, not far from the borders of the Pyrenees, towards which, in their retreat, they had been inclined.

This day and night, my shoulder had become extremely painful. We started again in the morning; but leaving the Pyrenees, we turned our faces more towards Toulouse, and took up our abode for the night at a considerable-sized town, called Castelnau; here the inhabitants received us very kindly, and we had excellent quarters. However, on the following morning, we were obliged to continue our march, and passing through several villages on the road, halted for the night at L'Isle, in Dodon.

During this day's march, my poor old horse played me a sad trick. He was one which I had been compelled to purchase as soon after I lost my little Portuguese one by the bad shoeing of the blacksmith at Sumbilla, as I could fall in with one for sale. He was a very tall grey horse, rather old, and whose mouth had not been well made in his breaking; he was withal rather stubborn, or more properly speaking stupid, consequently he did not always obey the rein as he ought. The roads were excessively deep and dirty, and as I was riding at the head of the battalion, and had occasion to pull him a little to one side, for some purpose or other, he either would not, or could not, obey the pull of the rein; and as I had but one hand, he took advantage of it, and sat down completely on his haunches, in the very deepest of the mire. Of course I was tumbled right over his rump, and rolled in the mud, and after extricating myself as well as I could, I crawled out, as pretty a figure as may well be imagined. This, as might be expected, raised the laugh of all who saw it, at my expense; but, uncomfortable and ridiculous as my situation was, I was not hurt, the mud being sufficiently deep to protect me from any injury by the fall.

In this village I fell in with a Frenchman who had just come from Toulouse, towards which he understood we were bending our course. He gave me such a flaming account of the *"belle position"* in the neighbourhood of that town, and of the impregnable works which Soult had caused to be thrown up, and of the superb artillery which were stationed there, and which, he said, were those who had served in the famous battle of Austerlitz, and of the utter improbability of any impression ever being made on them by an enemy, that if I had given credit to the half of what he told me, I might have been filled with fear lest all our laurels might here be tarnished. From what motive this rather exaggerated statement was made, I know not, but am inclined to think it was merely an inclination to indulge in a trifling gasconade. On the 25th we reached Mont Ferrand, where we halted for the night.

On the 27th, in the morning, we were moved forward to the village of Tournefoile, where it seems some of our cavalry had been quartered the night before, but who had had their quarters beat up during the night by a body of the enemy, who still held the ground beyond the village. My battalion, and a Portuguese battalion, were sent forward, the remainder of the brigade following. We found the enemy occupying the road leading from the village to a bridge about half a mile distant, together with the hedges and enclosures in the vicinity. My people extended to the left, while the Portuguese battalion kept on the road. A smart skirmish now commenced, during which the enemy gradually retired towards the bridge; but at this time a most remarkable occurrence took place.

One of our men(the servant of a friend of mine) received a shot in the mouth, which struck out several of his teeth. One of these was propelled with such force by the blow that it flew at least twenty yards, and, entering the left arm of one of the Portuguese on the road, inflicted a deep and severe wound. When the surgeon of the 43rd, who was the nearest to this man at the time, came to dress the wounded Portuguese, he, instead of a ball as every one expected, extracted a tooth, at which, no doubt, both he and all about him were quite astonished; and a report was immediately set afloat that the enemy were firing bones instead of balls. This most extraordinary circumstance was not cleared up till they were informed of our man having had his teeth knocked out, when, after comparing the relative

242

situations of the two men, it became quite evident how this most uncommon wound had been inflicted. If any thing like a joke might be permitted on such an occasion, it may with great propriety be said, the Frenchman who fired the shot had killed two birds with one stone. I happened to be near our man at the time, and besides seeing him wounded, I enquired minutely into the circumstances, or I own I should have hesitated before I gave implicit credit to the story; so it may probably be with my reader. Poor fellow, he had afterwards nearly all his intestines torn out by a cannon-shot at the fatal attack near New Orleans, and where I saw him writhing in the agonies of death; his name was Powell, and he was, I believe, a Welshman.

Not long after the commencement of the skirmish, the artillery on both sides was brought into play; but the enemy kept gradually retiring till they crossed the bridge, and as we did not pursue them, they quietly walked off, taking the road towards Toulouse. I cannot conceive for what purpose this body of troops had been sent here, unless it was intended as a reconnoissance, to ascertain whether any, and what description, of troops had arrived at this point, as their waiting, after driving out our cavalry, to see whether any infantry approached, would seem to indicate. Major Balvaird was conspicuously brave on this occasion. The loss on either side was but trifling.

Chapter Seventeen
The Campaign in Southern France

On the 28th or 29th, we were moved forward, and after a short march we reached a beautiful plain, with Toulouse appearing most magnificent in the distance. Here we went into cantonments, in the different villages and chateaux in the neighbourhood, the greater part of which were completely deserted, and many of them most wofully sacked and plundered, which could have been done only by their own troops.

A noble and stately mansion, belonging to a Mr Villeneuve, stood immediately in front of our outposts, which had shared the same fate with all the others, every article of furniture having been entirely destroyed. The cloth had been torn from the billiard-table, the splendid pier-glasses shivered into a thousand atoms, and, in short, every article of luxury or splendour which a man could wish for, might have been found in this princely habitation previous to its desertion by its owner; but now devastation and destruction had laid its unhallowed hands on all in which its possessor had formerly delighted. I, with my messmates, took the liberty of visiting Mr V.'s fish-ponds, where we found some fine-looking carp; and having some hooks by me, we caught a considerable quantity, which we imagined would be a great treat to our messmates; but we found them excessively muddy, and not worth eating. Here also we rejoiced in being able to procure some good provender for our still half-starved horses and mules. The grass and cinque-foil which we found in this beautiful and luxuriant plain, in a few days began to make a wonderful improvement in our poor fellow-travellers. I know not a more gratifying feeling than we experienced in thus being able to feed the hungry; for although they were but of the inferior creation, yet so much did our own comforts, and, indeed, efficiency for service, depend on their being capable of performing the task allotted to them, and so much did the circumstance of our having passed through trials and dangers together attach us to them, that I very frequently would have preferred getting them a meal even at the expense of wanting one myself. Here my little Portuguese horse, which I had originally brought from Lisbon, and who had been my companion in all my wanderings, (except when he was left for a while owing to his bad foot,) began to look quite brisk and lively again; for hitherto his spirits had been very low indeed since he happened by his misfortune, and had been literally starved into the bargain.

A pontoon bridge having been constructed some distance above the town, and which our engineers had been able to accomplish on account of its being thrown over above the junction of the Ariege with the Garonne, on the 31st we moved down towards this point, and crossing it, my battalion was left as its guard in a village on the bank of the river. The remainder of the division moved up the Ariege river with the intention of crossing, and thus approaching Toulouse in that direction; but, from the heavy rains, the river was too much flooded, which, together with the dreadful state of the roads, these troops were unable to effect this operation, and were consequently recalled.

By the 2nd of April the whole had recrossed the Garonne, when we again went into our cantonments on the plain, but now farther down the river than before. We remained here a few days, and I cannot help recording a remarkable circumstance which took place at this time. For want of dwelling-houses we had been obliged to put a certain number of the men of my battalion into a sort of wine-house; it was not a vault, for it was above ground, but had a considerable number of barrels of wine in it, amongst which the men were obliged to sleep. It will scarcely be credited, but not one of these men ever appeared the least intoxicated during the whole time they lay there. Whether they were completely tired of wine, or whether their having been placed in such a situation produced a feeling of honour and pride among them, I know not, but I verily believe less wine was drunk by these men during the time they remained here, than would have been had they had to pay most exorbitantly for it. With soldiers I believe it is as with mankind in general; what is prohibited always appears more valuable or more pleasurable in our eyes, than what we may with freedom enjoy.

On the 6th we moved down the river till within a short distance of Grenade, about twelve miles below Toulouse. We halted near a small village, and encamped. A pontoon bridge had been thrown over the Garonne here, and one division (I believe the 3rd) had crossed; but now, owing to the swollen state of the river, together with several attempts which were now made by the enemy to destroy the bridge, by floating down trees, &c. which might eventually carry it away, it loosened at the farther end, and the anchors being taken up, the whole was allowed to float down to our side of the river, keeping fast the end next our own bank. We remained in this situation for several days, one division only being on the opposite side, with which it was impossible to communicate, or, if attacked, to afford it almost any support. Now was the time for the enemy to bestir himself; for had he marched out of Toulouse with half his force, and been met at this place by the force he had at Montauban, they must have annihilated this division, or taken them prisoners. It is true we might have rendered them some little assistance by our artillery from the bank we occupied, but the distance was so great that a determined enemy would not have held back from the dread of it.

I took a trip from hence to Grenade, where the paymaster-general had established the military chest, as I had not yet quite finished my paymaster's duty. It is a good-sized town, but contains nothing remarkable, only here I remember I got some excellent wine of the Champagne kind, and which my friend poured out of an immense magnum bottle. I understood our Chief was most anxious to have the bridge reestablished by the 9th, which was Easter eve, the weather having now somewhat taken up, and the river of course had fallen; but although the engineer thought he could effect it, and had promised his lordship it should be ready by that time, it was not passable till the morning of the 10th. Early on that morning, my division crossed to the other side, together with the 4th and 6th divisions, and a whole host of Spaniards.

I omitted to mention, that these latter gentry, on their entering France, had behaved most wantonly, and had committed numerous atrocities; on which, his lordship, as Generalissimo, had ordered them back to their own country again; but upon the promise of good behaviour, and an anxious desire to participate in the honourable achievements of the allied troops, he had granted them permission to rejoin the army, and they were to have a post of honour assigned them at the ensuing battle. Such was the current report which prevailed among our army newsmongers: be it as it may, however, they were here in number, I should think, about 6000 or 8000. The whole army now present having crossed, except General Hill with the 2nd division, advanced upon the town of Toulouse. We here found a beautiful country and excellent roads, along which we got on rapidly. The town stands close to the right bank of the river, along which there are numerous quays, and over which there is an excellent bridge, communicating with the suburb on the opposite side, called St Cyprian. From the river on the north side of the town runs the famous canal of Languedoc, with which it communicates by locks, and which, encircling the town on that and on the east sides, with the river on the west, almost entirely encloses it. On the east side of the town, and just beyond the canal, a considerable eminence arises, forming a sort of chain or ridge, on the top of which numerous redoubts and batteries had been constructed, and which, both from the nature of the ground and by the great labour bestowed upon them, had been rendered, as the Frenchman told me, nearly impregnable.

The 6th division, supported by the 4th, had been ordered to move considerably to the left, and, after crossing the Garonne, to attack this formidable position on the outer side, while the Spaniards were to attack it immediately in front. My division was ordered to communicate with the right of the Spaniards, and, extending down to the great Montauban road, was to press upon the town in this direction, in order to aid the attack upon the height before mentioned. The 3rd division joined our right at the Montauban road, and extended from thence down to the river, and were ordered to act similarly to us. The

2nd division, under General Hill, remained on the other side of the river, and was to cooperate by attacking the suburb before mentioned, together with the works for the protec-tion of the bridge, and for the same purpose of our attack, namely, to keep the troops in these parts of the town employed, while the 6th division and Spaniards attacked the height. Immediately in front of our division, we found considerable bodies of troops, at some distance from the town, occupying the houses all along the road, and which it took us a considerable time to drive in. They had also constructed a battery on the bridge over the canal, where the great road passes, and from which they kept up an almost incessant fire. At the hither end of the bridge also there stood a very large convent, which they had fortified in a very strong manner, having loopholed the whole of the surrounding wall, which was twenty feet high, and had also looped the upper part of the convent, which contained a garrison of probably 1000 or 1200 men.

We commenced operations in conjunction with the 3rd division on our right, in driving these people in, and with whom a smart firing was kept up during the whole day. The French had also other troops beyond the canal, and on the Moorish or Roman wall which encircled the town inside the canal, and both of which they had fortified; so that, had it been intended we should force the town on this side, we should have found it a difficult undertaking: we were, however, merely (as said before) to press upon them without committing ourselves; but unfortunately, in the eagerness of some of our people to push forward, they got immediately under the muzzles of the pieces of the men who were defending the convent, and from the loopholes several of our poor fellows were shot without being able to see their antagonists. A good number fell here; for it was not more than thirty yards distant where they had taken up their post, and an unpleasant one it was as well as dangerous; for they were obliged to stand in a drain which ran from a jakes, and which of course emitted no very desirable flavour; or, if they had left it for a moment, they were immediately shot. Our adjutant escaped here as by a miracle, the bole of a very small tree having stopped the ball that would have pierced his body. When, however, we had got them fairly driven in, we had then time to look about us, and the first thing we saw was the Don moving on to the attack of the height with all due ceremony. They gained the first or lower ridge without much opposition, and here getting up some artillery, a pretty heavy fire was opened on the enemy; but the French remained quite passive, not offering to resist the approaching Spaniards till they got within a certain distance of their works on the top of the hill.

The Spaniards, elated by having gained the first ridge so easily, pushed on too rapidly, and without having taken time to reform their columns after the first conquest. They were not aware either that a rather deep ravine separated them from the enemy's works; however, on they pushed, in a very disorderly manner, till they reached the point the French intended they should reach, when a fire was opened out upon them, such as they had never witnessed before. Few troops would have remained unshaken by such a reception, but to the Spaniards it was intolerable; consequently they broke into a thousand parties, and, turning tail, it was who should be first away from such unpleasant doings. I am told that Lord Wellington at this moment could scarcely hold his sides for laughing, and cried out he "wondered whether the Pyrenees would bring them up again, they seemed to have got such a fright." He did not indeed depend on their valour, or he would have made a bad winding up of his Peninsular campaign. The moment they left the height, every man took the way that seemed to him best, and they soon after literally covered the whole plain, and set to work with all expedition to plunder at least, if they would not fight. Some of the villains had the audacity to come and take a poor man's horse out of the stable of the very house which we were then, as it were, defending, and had nigh got off with it; but having been perceived, it was taken from them, and restored again to its owner.

The left of our division was now obliged to be moved up to fill the space vacated by these vagabonds; and in doing which a good deal of hard fighting took place. This also made the people

249

in front of us rally again, and coming out in great numbers hurraing and shouting, we had something to do to drive them back. But by this time we heard, in the distance behind the hill, a dropping and now brisker fire; by and by, approaching the summit, it became quite animated. We could plainly perceive now the different appearance which the French assumed; they no longer lay supine and passive till their enemy approached their works, but fought for every inch of ground, and all was now animation and bustle among them, hurrying to the support of those troops who defended the redoubts, &c. on the point assailed. The battle now raged with great fury, each party with all their might for the mastery, and the French, we could perceive, when compelled by sheer force to yield ground, did it with the utmost reluctance. At length, we saw the British colour waving on the summit of the hill, with the most deadly warfare raging on each side of it; but every move we saw was in favour of the British.

The 42nd regiment had by this time gained possession of the principal redoubt, which they held till their ammunition was all expended, and which the enemy perceiving, or suspecting, again advanced, and gained possession of it. Things did not now wear quite so favourable an aspect; but being promptly supported by other troops behind them, a movement was again made in advance, and again the French were expelled from the redoubt. Great was the slaughter in and about this place, as I saw next day when I visited it.

The enemy were now reluctantly compelled to yield up all those famous works, on which so much time and labour had been expended, and on which they so much relied, and were obliged to abandon (slowly indeed) this long disputed ridge; but they fought till they were fairly forced down into the town, where they still kept up a feeble fire; at length it gradually subsided. This was the principal part of the drama; but it had many subordinate plots. On our right, General Picton, with that ardour which ever characterised him, was scarcely well satisfied to play an under part on this occasion; and, instead of merely keeping his opponents in play, as I before hinted, he was for effecting a forcible entry into the town. He accordingly attacked with his division a strong and well-secured battery, near the canal, in doing which his brave Connaught Rangers, who had scarcely ever hitherto known a reverse, met with a severe and bloody repulse, in which they lost a great number of excellent officers and men. The other corps of his division, who co-operated, also suffered greatly. General Hill strictly obeyed his instructions, and, as he always did, effected every object at which he aimed.

In this action I had another opportunity of witnessing the effect of presentiment. Early in it I was sent forward by my commanding-officer with some orders to a company of ours, which was in front skirmishing, and which had taken possession of a house, which partly screened them from the enemy's battery on the bridge. Behind this house, one of the men was sitting on a heap of stones with the most woe-worn countenance possible. He had separated from the rest of the men, and was sitting here apparently ruminating on his fate, and appeared to be quite absorbed in his meditations. I remarked him most particularly, wondering what could render him so different from the rest of his comrades, who were all life and animation, and from what he had formerly been himself in action. He presently went forward with some of the other men, and soon after fell to rise no more. The poor man's melancholy look made a deep impression upon me at the time, together with his fate soon after.

Thus terminated the battle of Toulouse; our troops maintaining the ground they had gained, while the enemy had retired into the town completely beaten. Soult seemed undetermined how to act, whether to endeavour to hold the town, (which indeed he might have done for a day or two perhaps,) or to leave it by the road towards the south, the only one now open to him. We rested on the field all night, the enemy sending an occasional shot or shell in the direction of our camp. Next morning we still found the enemy retaining possession of the town; and nothing being likely to be done, I rode up with another officer to see the bloody field, with all its redoubts and batteries, and also to see, if I could, in what situation the enemy now appeared. Just as we reached the summit, a cry was given by the 42nd sentry, "Turn out the picquet." There was a good deal of firing going on in the suburbs nearest to the position, which this Highlander thought it right to apprize his people of. We looked a considerable time with our glasses, and observed a good number of troops on a green and open space in that part of the suburbs, and who every now and then would fire their muskets. I thought it must either be a sort of *feu-de-joie,* or a funeral, and it turned out to be the latter. They were burying a general officer, who had fallen the day before, and to whom they were paying the last melancholy honours; but it was conducted in a quite different manner from our military funerals, for they did not fire in volleys like us; but every few minutes apparently a few men only fired, and by and by some others. This had the effect, however, of turning out our whole line in the neighbourhood of the position; and as I was afterwards returning, I met Colonel Barnard and Colonel Colborne (than whom there were not two better officers in the army) riding up to see what was the matter. Colonel Barnard asked me what it was. I told him what I thought it was. He said the whole line had fallen in, thinking it was an attack.

Towards evening we heard that the inhabitants of the city had been most urgent on Soult to withdraw from it; and that he had promised to do so. Indeed, had he not, Lord Wellington might, if he chose, have soon reduced the town to ashes; for the heights we had taken were not 500 yards distant from the city, and completely overlooked it. On the morning of the 12th, therefore, Soult marched out, and was not molested by our troops. He took the road to Villefranche and Carcassonne, up the canal of Languedoc, our cavalry following their track. Now all the loyalists came rushing out of the town to meet and welcome us; every one wearing white scarfs or favours to denote his attachment to the Bourbons. Now all was joy and festivity, and nothing but shaking of hands and embracing was to be seen in all directions. This day also arrived Lord Stewart from Paris with the account of Bonaparte's abdication, and of the Bourbons having been reinstated. It was also rumoured that Soult had received this news previous to the battle; but not being inclined to yield obedience to that dynasty, he had allowed the warfare to proceed. Indeed, what almost puts this beyond a doubt, was his still continuing for many days after this to refuse sending in his submission to the Bourbon government. We also heard afterwards that the courier bringing the official information of Bonaparte's fall, &c. had been detained by the postmaster of Montauban by Soult's direction; for although he had had private intelligence of the fact, he imagined the detention of the official information might screen him hereafter. Such are the surmises of the wise heads respecting this affair, which, as it turned out, is to be regretted; for the sacrifice of so many valuable lives on both sides was a thing of no trifling importance; but I believe Soult felt sore at his having been so often worsted, and hoped here in some measure to retrieve his lost honours; for it cannot be doubted, I believe, that he expected to be able to repel our attack at least, if not to force us to retire from Toulouse.

On the 13th, the divisions marched into the town; my battalion having the fauxbourg adjoining the lately disputed position assigned to it, and in which we found very comfortable quarters. To show that the French people of this place took Lord Wellington either for a very generous person, or a great fool, a man who owned a house on the border of the position, and which the French had fortified by loopholing it, and otherwise rendering it unfit for occupation by its owner, sent in a memorial to his lordship, praying him to order that he might receive out of the military chest a sufficient sum to enable him to put his house in its former state; and this, although it had been done by his own countrymen. I suppose his lordship would laugh at it when he saw it. I should have been inclined to be angry with the fellow. The man showed the memorial to the adjutant and myself before he sent it in—a step which of course we dissuaded him from taking.

Notwithstanding it was notorious that Bonaparte's career was at that time finished, Soult still made a show of holding out for him; in consequence of which the army was again put in motion to compel him either to send in his adhesion to the new government, or to resign his command of troops who had not now a master. He had taken up a position near Villefranche.

Accordingly, we marched, I think, on the 15th or 16th, the which rather alarmed him; and in consequence he despatched Count Gazan with terms to offer to his lordship, the which, after some alterations, were finally agreed upon, and the army returned once more to Toulouse, where we resumed our former quarters.

Thus finished the Peninsular War, the last campaign of which had been the most active probably that is recorded in history. In ten months and a half we had marched from the frontiers of Portugal, had completely traversed Spain, which we had cleared of its long troublesome and insidious invaders; had penetrated far into the interior of that country, which three years before gave law to most of the continental nations; and had worsted, in various actions, those troops, which, except when encountering the British, had been accustomed almost invariably to conquer.

Chapter Eighteen
The End of the War with Napoleon

When I look back on the events of 1813 and 1814, I cannot but deem that the happiest period of my life, for I had been actively, and, as I believed, usefully employed. My mind during this time was tranquil, and I was, with a few exceptions, prosperous in my outward circumstances. All those among whom my lot was cast were now sincerely friendly to me, and I believe I may with confidence affirm that I had not (with the exception of the person before mentioned, and who was now far removed from me) a single enemy in the world. It is true my occupation had not been, strictly speaking, of a Christian character, but I believed I was fulfilling my duty; hence the peace of mind which I enjoyed. I have since learned certainly, that a Christian, to resemble his Master, should be more ready to save than to destroy men's lives; but, at the same time, I cannot see why a Christian soldier should not be as zealous in the defence of his king and country, as those who are actuated by other motives; and it is certain, I believe, although I once doubted whether there was such a precept, that in whatever calling or occupation a man is in when called to become a Christian, that therein he should abide, *1st Cor. vii. 17, 20, and 24.*

But I attribute the peace of mind I then enjoyed as much to the constant employment which the nature of our services entailed upon us, as to any other cause. Be it remembered, I was doing the duties of both paymaster and quartermaster during this period, and my battalion had been as often called into action as any in the army, having been engaged in battles and skirmishes no less than sixteen times in less than ten months. This naturally left little time for reflection. But, above all, I am bound to render thanks to where alone it is due, to that gracious and beneficent Being, who not only watched over me during this period, and protected me from harm, but who poured his choicest blessings upon me, even the blessings of a cheerful and contented heart, together with the means of retrieving my sadly deranged finances; for had I not been appointed acting paymaster, I might have gone to prison on my return to my native country, from the unavoidable losses I had sustained, and which I shall mention by and by. Another cause of comfort and cheerfulness arose from our operations against the enemy having been invariably successful; for we never, from the time of our leaving the frontiers of Portugal, till we took possession of Toulouse, met with any thing like a serious reverse.

Most of my readers no doubt know that the city where we had now taken up our quarters is one of the largest and finest in this part of France; but as it has been so often described, I shall content myself with merely informing my readers, that the people among whom we now resided were truly and veritably French. The character of the inhabitants, since we left our poor friends the Basques, had materially changed; that kind, but rude and simple hospitality, which had on most occasions been displayed by those honest mountaineers, had now given place to all that imposing, but less sincere politeness of the real French character. We were, indeed, treated here with every degree of respect; and perhaps more, or at least an equal degree of attention, was paid to our convenience and comfort, as they would have shown to their own troops. We had every reason, therefore, to be perfectly satisfied.

In this part of the country there are a great number of Protestants, which, of course, permitted us to live on better terms with them than had they been all such stanch and bigoted Catholics as we met with in some parts of the Continent, and where our heretical presence was frequently looked upon as a contamination; for I remember well in the small village of Zalada, where we lay for some time, near Astorga, we never left the village, as they supposed, for a permanency, but the joy bells were rung for our departure. It was our lot, indeed, to be frequently quartered in this village, and such was their invariable custom. It is true the Padre and people of the place only expressed openly the feeling that was covertly, but universally, entertained throughout Spain and Portugal respecting us; for although the monks and priests made great pretences of friendship and good-will towards us, while we were upholding them in their iniquitous dominion over the minds of the people, yet secretly they cordially hated us, and were glad when at last our successes contributed to rid their country of both the invaders and their conquerors. One noble Spanish lady, (I remember well,) when I was quartered at Cadiz, made use of an expression which I am sure would shock and horrify my simple and delicate country-women. She said, "She should rejoice to see all the French then in their country hung up in the intestines (las tripas) of the English, who had come to drive them out." Thus they should get quit of both. This lady, as might be supposed, was a most depraved and abandoned being, yet even she, it seems, looked upon us in the light of a curse or plague sent upon their country, rather than as a generous and gallant people, who had not hesitated to sacrifice much, both of blood and money, in freeing them from their French oppressors.

But such, I fear, is the too general feeling in that country; for while the innumerable religiosos which overrun that nation maintain their cursed dominion over the minds of the other classes, an Englishman will always be looked upon by them as a dangerous and hateful being, uniting in himself both the mortal sins, first, of having totally cast off the Pope's authority, and being the subject of a free and popular government—than either of which, not even Satan himself could be more odious to them.

We were not allowed, however, to remain long in Toulouse, but were distributed over the country in the neighbourhood, lines of demarcation having been pointed out which were to separate the French and British armies. My division was sent down the right bank of the river, and occupied Castel Sarazin, Grissolles, and Castelnau, &c. My battalion was stationed at Grissolles. During our stay here I had two or three opportunities, in company with others, of going to see Montauban, the seat of a Protestant college, and famed in romantic lore. The people were kind and obliging, and showed us every attention; but unfortunately a French garrison was quartered in it, the officers of which took every opportunity of quarrelling with ours. Indeed we had no business there, and were consequently obliged to put up with more than we should have otherwise done, for we were strictly forbid to enter any place within the French lines; but we did not conceive that those fellows, who had shown themselves so friendly and polite near Bayonne, while we were avowedly in arms against each other, would now turn round upon us when peace was made, and endeavour to engage us in quarrels and duelling. But I believe they felt a degree of soreness at our acknowledged superiority as soldiers, (for even the inhabitants of Montauban, where they lay, did not hesitate to express it,) and thus wished to be revenged for the many victories we had gained over them. Indeed there was a sort of recklessness about them which is not easily accounted for, unless they supposed their occupation was gone, and cared not what became of themselves; but they did not succeed, I think, in any instance in obtaining their wishes, for they would not fight with pistols, the only weapon which gives each a fair and equal chance, but insisted upon using the sword,—a mode of fighting to which the English in general were utter strangers. The people uniformly gave us warning as soon as ever they learnt that a plot was laid to insult us, on which we generally came away without subjecting ourselves to it; and when their designs became too evident, we refrained from going there. It was only a short distance from our quarters.

During our stay here, also, the Marquis de Pompignan, a gentleman residing between Grissolles and Castelnau, and where our Major-general had taken up his quarters, gave to the officers of the brigade a splendid fete. I know not exactly how to denominate it, for it was a sort of dramatic medley, part of it being performed in the garden and part in the house, where a private theatre had been fitted up; that in the garden, it was said, was intended to represent some military event,—I think it was the hurning of Moscow, and in which the Marquis's beautiful daughter bore a part.

This young lady was said to be greatly enamoured of an honourable gentleman, aide-de-camp to the General, who was quartered in their house, and between whom it was expected a match would have taken place. She was extremely beautiful and engaging.

We sometimes went a-fishing while we remained here also, but were not successful, there being none other than lake-fish, such as perch, &c., in the neighbourhood, which were scarcely worth taking.

Here, also, for want of better occupation, some of our young gentlemen amused themselves by hunting and lashing the Spanish muleteers as they were returning, after having delivered in their loads at the commissary's stores. They always rode one mule, (sideways, like a woman,) and led one or two more, and were most dexterous in handling the long shank of the halter, with which they sometimes soundly belaboured their pursuers; and had they not been set on by two or three at a time, they would not have liked better fun than to fight one of our gentlemen with his whip, for they saw that it was only for amusement, and generally took it good-naturedly; but our young gentlemen, as they generally do, carried the joke too far, and it was consequently put a stop to. Of course none but the young and idle took any part in this exercise.

We had, while we lay here, also several little balls and hops; and here, for the first time, several of our young-men began to dance quadrilles; in short, there was no want of amusement among this gay and lively people, who are ever intent upon pleasure themselves, and who of course found our wild and thoughtless young fellows ever as ready to second their endeavours to get up something new and enteistaining. Certainly their morality is not the highest in the world, but their vices are most of them divested of that coarse and disgusting appearance which similar vices carry on their front in England; and thus, while they are generally more pleasing, they are the more seducing, and consequently the more dangerous. However, as no person is compelled to enter into these scenes of dissipation and voluptuousness which they rejoice in, I found it, upon the whole, a very comfortable country to live in. The people were kind and civil, and were always good-natured and polite, and, as we now had plenty of the good things of this world at our command, I spent two months here very contentedly. It is true we had none of those excellent privileges with which my native country abounds, and which I have since learnt highly to prize,—I mean the privileges of the gospel,—the food for the nobler and never-dying part; hut I was then ignorant of their value, for although I had been convinced and convicted, I had not been converted. I was still in darkness respecting the way, the truth, and the life, and yet my foolish and carnal mind whispered peace; hence my contentedness in this situation. No! It was not till some years that I discovered that there is but one way to real happiness, but one true foundation on which to build our hope,—even that which is laid in Zion.

But the time had arrived for us to move down towards Bordeaux, preparatory to our quitting France. Accordingly, on the 3rd June, we forded the Garonne, and stopped all night in Grenade, a place I formerly mentioned. We next day reached Cadours, a village near Cologne, where our 2nd battalion was that evening quartered. In the afternoon of that day, a storm collected in the north, which I think had the most frightful appearance I ever witnessed. It was actually as black as night in the direction in which we saw it. It did not reach us, but it alarmed the inhabitants of our village so much, that they set on ringing the church bells with the utmost fury imaginable. We could not account for this strange proceeding till we enquired of them why it was done. They told us the devil was in the storm, and the bells being holy, he durst not, when he heard them, proceed any farther in that direction. Indeed they had ample reason to be in dread of its reaching their village; for the next day, as we passed along the country where it had raged most furiously, the whole face of the country was desolated. It had been a hail-storm such as I never before witnessed. The hailstones were still lying, some of them larger than a bullet; the vines had been all destroyed; the crops of corn completely swept from the face of the earth. Trees knocked down, birds killed; in short, nothing could equal the appearance of misery and woe which this awful hailstorm had inflicted upon the unfortunate inhabitants, many of whom were going about wringing their hands in all the bitterness of heart, which a consciousness of being deprived of every hope of subsistence for the year to come would naturally inspire. Indeed most of them were literally stripped of their all.

On the 6th we marched into Lectoure, a fine town on the river, and famous for having given birth to Marshal Lannes, one of Bonaparte's best generals. It stands on a high ground near the river, and overlooks one of the richest and most beautiful plains I think I ever saw. Here I experienced another misfortune in my steed. My little Portuguese horse (which was now in high condition, and being an entire horse was apt to fight) quarrelled with a large horse belonging to one of our officers, while I was serving out the billets; and although we were both mounted at the time, the quarrelsome animals reared up against each other, and fought most desperately; but his, being the strongest, pulled mine and myself down to the ground. I luckily fell clear of him, and was not hurt; but he by some accident got a kick in his hind leg or foot, which completely lamed him, and I could not ride him any longer.

We passed through Condom, another fine town, and Nerac, also a good town, and nearly full of Protestants. We next day halted at Castel Jaloux, where I was quartered on a house of religeuse. Here my poor little horse was so very ill that I could not drag him any farther. I was consequently obliged to leave him with those good dames, to whom I made him a present, and parted from him in the morning with sincere regret. They promised to take care of him, which I hope they did. We next reached the town of Bazas. Here there was to be another parting scene exhibited. The Portuguese were ordered to leave us here, and proceed towards their own country. The Spanish and Portuguese women who had followed the men were either to be sent home from hence, or their protectors were to consent to marry them. Some adopted the latter alternative, having had children by them, and some others who had not, and the remainder, of course, were compelled to separate. Our division drew up in the morning they marched, and honoured the brave Portuguese (for indeed they had always behaved well in the field) with three cheers, as they turned their faces towards Portugal. Many were the heavy hearts in both armies on this occasion; for it is not easy to conceive how the circumstance of passing through scenes of hardship, trial, and danger together, endeared the soldiers of the two armies to each other. It was perhaps never before felt so fully how much each was attached to the other; but the departure of the poor women caused many heavy hearts, both among themselves, poor creatures, who had a long and dreary journey before them, and among those with whom they had lived, and who had shared in all their good and bad fortune; but among these, several on both sides were not oppressed with too fine feelings. A friend of mine, who was an officer in the Portuguese service, told me afterwards that the women marched down to Spain and Portugal at the same time his regiment did; that they formed a column of 800 or 900 strong; that they were regularly told off into companies; and that the commanding-officer, a major, and all the captains, were married men, who had their families with them—all excellent arrangements; but that they were the most unmanageable set of animals that ever marched across a country. The officers had to draw rations for them all the way; but many of them, he says, left the column and went wherever they pleased. Few reached Portugal in the order in which they started.

We reached Langon on the 12th, and Barsac on the 13th June. This latter place is famed for a fine white-wine, something resembling sauterne. The adjutant (who had now been my chum for some time) and I were here quartered in a fine old baronial castle, the inmates of which showed us great attention. A ball was given in the evening to the officers of the brigade.

On the 14th we halted at Castres, and on the 15th entered Bordeaux. This was the finest town we had seen since we entered the Peninsula, except Lisbon and Madrid. This town had been occupied by the British for some time, a division of the army having been sent by Lord Wellington to take charge of it in the name of Louis XVIII.

We were not, however, destined to be quartered in this southern capital of France, but marched right through it, on the road towards the village of Blancfort. On the road the division was formed, and very minutely inspected by our gallant Chief, who was dressed in all his finery, his orders, and medals, and ribbons, &c., which he wore for the first time that ever I had seen. He looked most splendid indeed, and right proud were we to see him in them. After inspection we moved on to the camp at Blancfort, where we found a great part of the army assembled, waiting for the arrival of shipping to carry them off. Some had sailed a considerable time before our arrival. Besides our tents, the adjutant and I had got a cottage close by, in which our servants and our baggage were put. We had not been here above two or three days, I think, till his two servants, that is, his servant and groom, took it into their heads to desert. This was not the first instance of desertion that had taken place lately; for as we drew near the time of departure great numbers ran off into the interior, mostly bad characters. However, on this occasion, these worthies were determined to have something to carry them on the road, and, without hesitation, broke open their master's panniers, or boxes, and took away all the money he had, which did not indeed amount to any great sum, for it was only 40 dollars, (about L. 10 British,) but it being all he was worth it was a great loss to him.

I have reason to be thankful to Providence for my escape on this occasion. My paymaster's chest was standing close to the adjutant's panniers when they broke them open, and they did not touch it, although it contained about L.400 worth of gold. Had they taken that I might have gone after them. I of course expressed my thankfulness for this lucky escape, and told several people of it. I fancy some person (my groom, I suspect) overheard me telling what a lucky escape I had been favoured with, and determined in his own mind that I should not always come off so well. The sequel will show: A few days after this I had occasion to go into Bordeaux to draw some money from the Commissary-general. The amount was 600 dollars, or about L.150. As I could not conveniently carry them out to the camp, I requested Major Balvairdj who had a quarter in town, to allow me to put them in his portmanteau till I had an opportunity of getting them sent out. His servant had overheard this conversation, and made up his mind at once to desert and take this money with him; but providentially again I escaped. I found the means, before night, of carrying it out to the camp, and the Major gave it me unknown to the servant. That night he broke open the portmanteau, and, taking every thing worth carrying away, (among which was a gold watch of mine,) deserted, and got clear off. This money, also, had it been taken, would have sorely crippled me, although I might perhaps have overcome the loss.

We marched in a few days after, passing through the district of Medoc, famous for Bordeaux or claret wine, and halted for the night at Castelnau de Medoc. The next day we passed through Chateau Margaux, where the best and most expensive of the claret grows, and again encamped at Pauillac, from whence we were to go on board.

Now was the time for the person who had overheard me speaking about my escape with the L.400, to make his grab and start off, or he would be too late. Accordingly, after dark, he or they lifted up a part of the tent where the box was standing, and, pulling it out, set off with it bodily. But, again directed by Providence, I had taken the money out of the box, and given it into the hands of a gentleman, to take care of for me; and there remained in the box my papers and books, public and private, about L.19 in money, an old silver watch, and, among other things, the half doubloon which poor Croudace had given me to take care of for him on the evening previous to his death at Badajos, and which I was preserving as a memorial for his afflicted friends.

As soon as the box was missed I instantly raised the hue and cry, and, reporting the circumstance to my commanding-officer, he ordered the rolls to be called, to see if any man had deserted; but no, they were all present. I then offered a reward of forty dollars to any one who would bring me the box and papers, and did not regard the money. Instantly the whole camp was in a move to find the box, and search was made in all directions. I of course was not idle myself on the occasion; and having a man or two with me, I actually discovered where the box had been opened, for I found the inkstand, that had been in it, lying near a heap of wood close to the bank of the river, into which, after plundering it, no doubt they had thrown it. I now went down to the town and waited on the mayor, offering the same reward

264

to any of his people that would try to find it in the river; but, unfortunately, just as there was the best chance of recovering it, the order came for us instantly to go on board.—Thus was I deprived of every document I possessed, both Paymaster's, Quartermaster's, and private. I had fortunately got my Paymaster's accounts made out up to the very latest period, and transmitted to the War-Office, or I know not what I should have done; but my duplicates were gone, and when afterwards objections were made to some of the items in the charges, (as is always the case,) I, being unable to answer them, was obliged to submit to the loss of them. I had also several private accounts unclosed, on which I lost considerably, so that altogether I calculate this loss fully amounted to L.100, besides the vexation of not having my papers to refer to when wanted.

I had been obliged to part with all my remaining animals for next to nothing, for when the French people found we were obliged to leave them, they offered us the most shameful trifles possible, but which we were compelled to take or give the animals away. One I did actually make a present of, besides my little Portuguese horse before-mentioned. I made a close calculation, and found that my losses in horses and mules, from the beginning of 1812 to June 1814, did not amount to less than L.150, besides sums that I lost by officers who died. By one I lost L.84, and another L.74 odd, so that, as I said before, had I not fortunately been appointed Acting Paymaster, I should have been so much involved, that at this time I durst not have returned to my native country. I do not complain, for most of my losses were sent by Providence, who saw best what was fitting and good for me; but never, till the Peninsular campaigns, were officers obliged generally to provide and keep up their own baggage-animals, and from the loss of which I had suffered so severely; and I cannot but think that rule, always acted upon till these campaigns, ought to be continued, and that subalterns at least ought to have their baggage always carried at the public expense.

Chapter Nineteen
Return to England

We embarked on the 8th July on board his Majesty's ship *Dublin*, of 74 guns, commanded by Captain Elphinstone, which took the five companies of my battalion, with two companies of the 43d. We sailed the next day, I think, and had generally fine weather during our voyage, which lasted till the 18th, when we arrived at Plymouth. She was but a dull sailer, or we ought not to have occupied so many days in so short a passage. During our voyage, as remark-able an instance of heroic fortitude and bodily strength was exhibited by a sailor of this ship as I ever remember to have witnessed. He was doing something on the fore-yard, and by some-accident he was precipitated into the water, but in his fall his shoulder came in contact with the flue of one of the anchors, by which it was deeply and severely cut. The ship was going at about five knots an hour, and it took near half an hour before she could be brought round and a boat sent to his assistance; and notwithstanding the severe cut he had received, from which the blood was fast streaming, he not only contrived to keep himself from sinking by buffeting with a heavy sea, but actually stripped off his jacket in the water, as it seems it had been an encumbrance to him. When the boat reached him, the poor fellow was nigh exhausted, and a few minutes more would have deprived the ship and the service of an excellent sailor, but having been got into the boat, he was brought on board more dead than alive, where every attention being paid to him, he soon afterwards recovered.

We landed at Plymouth on the 18th, and occupied one of the barracks. We did not exactly know what was to become of us. Kent being our regimental station, we expected to be ordered to march and join the left wing in that county, but were still kept at Plymouth, where we met with great kindness and attention from the inhabitants in general, who are upon the whole, I think, an excellent and a moral people. We also fared sumptuously here, every description of food being both cheap and good. Fish in particular is most abundant and excellent. In short, we were here as comfortably and as well quartered as we could desire, and every thing tended to make us perfectly satisfied with our lot. We relaxed by attending the theatre occasionally, which is one of the best provincial ones in the kingdom, and at this time could boast some very good actors. There were a variety of other amusements, such as fishing, &c., which of course we indulged in occasionally. From hence I was called up to London to meet our Colonel, the Hon. Sir W. Stewart, to arrange our battalion concerns, &c. for the few latter years of hurry and confusion, and which was at last got done to the satisfaction of all concerned. Here also we began to replenish our wardrobes, which, it will easily be imagined, were not the most magnificent in the world on our first arrival.

LEONAUR

If you enjoyed 'Surtees of the Rifles' you may also enjoy other books about and by members of the famous 95th (Rifles) published by Leonaur.

These include:

Rifleman Costello
by Edward Costello

Captain of the 95th (Rifles)
by Jonathan Leach

Napoleonic War Stories
by Sir Arthur Quiller-Couch

Bugler & Officer of the Rifles
by William Green & Harry Smith

Ensign Bell of the Cumberland Gentlemen
by George Bell
to be released April 2006

The Compleat Rifleman Harris
by Benjamin Harris
to be released April 2006

Hussar in Winter
by Alexander Gordon
to be released April 2006

An extract from
Rifleman Costello
by Edward Costello
Published by Leonaur

All things arranged, we passed the gates of Brussels, and descended the wood of Soignies, that leads to the little village of Waterloo. It was the 16th -- a beautiful summer morning -- the sun slowly rising above the horizon and peeping through the trees, while our men were as merry as crickets, laughing and joking with each other, and at times pondered in their minds what all this fuss, as they called it, could be about; for even the old soldiers could not believe the enemy were so near.

We halted at the verge of the wood, on the left of the road, behind the village of Waterloo, where we remained for some hours; the recruits lay down to sleep, while the old soldiers commenced cooking. I could not help noticing while we remained here, the birds in full chorus, straining their little throats as if to arouse the spirits of the men to fresh vigour for the bloody conflict they were about to engage in. Alas! How many of our brave companions, ere that sun set, were no more! About nine o'clock, the Duke of Wellington with his staff, came riding from Brussels and passed us to the front; shortly afterwards, orders were given to the Rifles to fall in and form the advanced-guard of our division, and follow. We moved on through the village of Waterloo, and had not proceeded far, when, for the first time, we heard distant cannon; it was, I believe, the Prussians engaged on our extreme left.

About three o'clock in the afternoon we arrived at four roads; at this time there was a smart firing going on in our front; this, I believe, was caused by some Belgians playing at long shot with the enemy. Here I again saw the Duke of Wellington looking through his glass, as we halted a few moments; this was at Quatre Bras, and immediate orders were given by one of the Duke's staff to occupy a clump of trees a little on our left; our company were ordered to take possession of it.

While performing this task I could see the enemy emerging from a wood about a mile on our right, which was rather on a hill, with a clear plain between us. We had scarcely taken possession of the wood, when, for the first time, I beheld a French cuirassier on vidette. He was in an instant fired at by our men and his horse shot under him; he disengaged himself from the stirrups as the horse was falling, waving his sword over his head to put us at defiance, but he was immediately dropped by another rifle shot. I think I can venture to assert that our company was the first of the British army who pulled a trigger at this celebrated battle.

The enemy's light troops, I could soon perceive, in extended order, and in great force coming down to oppose us. This caused a corresponding movement on our part, and we were ordered to take ground to our left, passing close to a pond of water, the main road separating us from the enemy. While executing this, the French commenced a very brisk fire on us, until we gained possession of a few houses on the main road on a rising ground, which two companies of our Rifles instantly occupied. The remainder of our division was now enveloped in one blaze of fire on the plain before mentioned. But we remained very quietly where we were, until the French bringing up some artillery, began riddling the house with round shot. Feeling rather thirsty, I had asked a young woman in the place for a little water, which she was handing to me, when a ball passed through the building, knocking the dust about our ears; strange to say, the girl appeared less alarmed than myself.

Fearing that we might be surrounded, we were at length

obliged to leave the building, in doing which we were fiercely attacked by a number of the French voltigeurs, who forced us to extend along a lane, from whence we as smartly retaliated, and a galling fire was kept up for some time on both sides.

It is remarkable that recruits in action are generally more unfortunate than the old soldiers. We had many fine fellows, who joined us on the eve of our leaving England, who were killed here. The reason of this is, that an old rifleman will seek shelter, if there be any near his post, while the inexperienced recruit appears as if petrified to the spot by the whizzing balls, and unnecessarily exposes himself to the enemy's fire.

An extract from
Captain of the 95th (Rifles)
by Jonathan Leach
Published by Leonaur

Lord Wellington now ordered the infantry to retire in columns, covered by the cavalry and horse artillery. No man who was present can possibly have forgotten that magnificent sight, nor the steadiness and extreme regularity with which the columns fell back over this extensive plain, followed and assailed in flanks and rear by overwhelming numbers of cavalry and artillery.

During this retreat we were exposed to a constant cannonade, and threatened by heavy masses of infantry, ready to close with us if our pace was relaxed for a minute. Nor was the steadiness and gallantry displayed by the cavalry and horse-artillery less worthy of admiration. A halt of two or three minutes would have enabled the French infantry to reach us. Thus we marched some miles over a country as level as a chessboard, in columns of battalions, ready to engage the French infantry if they should overtake us, and equally so to receive their cavalry, in square or close column, if they attempted to charge. The beautiful series of evolutions of the two armies on this day, and on the three following, were such as a man may never witness again if he lives for ages.

The heat was suffocating, and there being no water on this sun-burnt plain, numbers of men dropped on the road, and, of course, fell into the hands of the enemy, as we could not stop to bring them along. Many soldiers, particularly of the Portuguese, died on the road, from the heat and want of water. At length we arrived at the edge of this elevated plain, which looks down on the Guarena, a small river in the hot months; and when we reached it, man and horse made a rush to quench their thirst. I have never quite forgiven our pursuers for pounding us with round shot from the heights above, and not allowing us time to swallow a mouthful of the lukewarm, muddy beverage, without the accompaniment of a nine-pound shot.

Soon after we had got into a position, on some high ground not far from the river, a column of infantry endeavoured to turn our left. The 27th and 40th regiments were posted there, and, by a volley, a cheer, and a resistless charge with the bayonet, instantly drove back the French, taking a general officer and upwards of two hundred men prisoners, killing and wounding many more. During the remainder of the day we were tolerably quiet. A hot wind with a thick suffocating atmosphere set in and lasted a day or two.

It is worthy of remark, that the horse artillery which accompanied our advanced and rear-guards, consisted of light six-pounders only, whereas the artillery attached to the French advanced and rear-guards were usually eight-pounders, equal to British nines. It is obvious, therefore, that our people always laboured under a great disadvantage in this respect, as the French could batter and pound us at such a distance as it was not in the power of our light six-pounders to return with effect. I have heard officers of our artillery complain of this, and have frequently witnessed the fact myself. Surely, if the cats of horses in the French army could drag along, at a pace sufficient to keep up with their cavalry, nine-pounders, the beautiful and powerful English horses belonging to our horse artillery were equally capable of drawing guns of the same weight of metal, and at a much more rapid rate, if required.

It is to be hoped that those who have the direction of affairs at Woolwich, have already considered those matters, and that they will adopt measures accordingly. It is equally desirable that those at the head of the British cavalry should bear in mind, that the French dragoons and chasseurs à cheval were armed during the Peninsular war with a long fusée, which could throw a ball as far as the musket of an infantry soldier, and that our dragoons, on the contrary, both light and heavy, were armed with a little pop-gun of a carbine. The consequence of this was, that when bodies of cavalry met at a distance from their infantry, the French dragoons often dismounted where the country was intersected and woody, and shot at our dragoons at a distance which rendered our short carbines almost useless. I appeal to old Peninsula cavalry men and officers for the accuracy of my statement.

An extract from
Napoleonic War Stories
by Sir Arthur Quiller-Couch
Published by Leonaur

Early next morning Sergeant Wilkes picked his way across
the ruins of the great breach and into the town, keeping well
to windward of the fatigue parties already kindling fires and
collecting the dead bodies that remained unburied.

Within and along the sea-wall San Sebastian was a heap of
burnt-out ruins. Amid the stones and rubble encumbering the
streets, lay broken muskets, wrenched doors, shattered sticks
of furniture -- mirrors, hangings, women's apparel, children's
clothes -- loot dropped by the pillagers as valueless, wreckage
of the flood. He passed a very few inhabitants, and these said
nothing to him; indeed, did not appear to see him, but sat by
the ruins of their houses with faces set in a stupid horror. Even
the crash of a falling house near by would scarcely persuade
them to stir, and hundreds during the last three days had been
overwhelmed thus and buried.

The sergeant had grown callous to these sights. He walked
on, heeding scarcely more than he was heeded, came to the
great square, and climbed a street leading northwards, a little
to the left of the great convent. The street was a narrow
one, for half its length lined on both sides with fire-gutted
houses; but the upper half, though deserted, appeared to be
almost intact. At the very head, and close under the citadel
walls, it took a sharp twist to the right, and another twist,
almost equally sharp, to the left before it ended in a broader
thoroughfare, crossing it at right angles and running parallel
with the ramparts.

At the second twist the sergeant came to a halt; for at his

feet, stretched across the causeway, lay a dead body.

He drew back with a start, and looked about him. Corporal Sam had been missing since nine o'clock last night, and he felt sure that Corporal Sam must be here or hereabouts. But no living soul was in sight.

The body at his feet was that of a rifleman; one of the volunteers whose presence had been so unwelcome to General Leith and the whole Fifth Division. The dead fist clutched its rifle; and the sergeant stooping to disengage this, felt that the body was warm.

"Come back, you silly fool!"

He turned quickly. Another rifleman had thrust his head out of a doorway close by. The sergeant, snatching up the weapon, sprang and joined him in the passage where he sheltered.

"I -- I was looking for a friend hereabouts."

"Fat lot of friend you'll find at the head of this street!" snarled the rifleman, and jerked his thumb towards the corpse. "That makes the third already this morning. These Johnnies ain't no sense of honour left -- firing on outposts as you may call it."

"Where are they firing from?"

"No 'they' about it. You saw that cottage -- or didn't you? -- right above there, under the wall; the place with one window in it? There's a devil behind it somewheres; he fires from the back of the room, and what's more, he never misses his man. You have Nick's own luck -- the pretty target you made, too; that is unless, like some that call themselves Englishmen and ought to know better, he's a special spite on the Rifles."

The sergeant paid no heed to the sneer. He was beginning to think.

"How long has this been going on?" he asked.

"Only since daylight. There was a child up yonder, last night; but it stands to reason a child can't be doing this. He never misses, I tell you. Oh, you had luck, just now!"

"I wonder," said Sergeant Wilkes, musing. "I'll try it again, anyway." And while the rifleman gasped he stepped out boldly into the road.

He knew that his guess might, likely enough, be wrong: that, even were it right, the next two seconds might see him a dead man. Yet he was bound to satisfy himself. With his eyes on the sinister window -- it stood half open and faced straight down the narrow street -- he knelt by the corpse, found its ammunition pouch, unbuckled the strap and drew out a handful of cartridges. Then he straightened himself steadily -- but his heart was beating hard -- and as steadily walked back and rejoined the rifleman in the passage.

"You have a nerve," said the rifleman, his voice shaking a little. "Looks like he don't fire on redcoats; but you have a nerve all the same."

"Or else he may be gone," suggested the sergeant, and on the instant corrected himself; "but I warn you not to reckon upon that. Is there a window facing on him anywhere, round the bend of the street?"

"I dunno."

The rifleman peered forth, turning his head sideways for a cautious reconnoitre. "Maybe he has gone, after all -- "

It was but his head he exposed beyond the angle of the doorway; and yet, on the instant a report cracked out sharply, and he pitched forward into the causeway. His own rifle clattered on the stones beside him, and where he fell he lay, like a stone.

Sergeant Wilkes turned with a set jaw and mounted the stairs of the deserted house behind him. They led him up to the roof, and there he dropped on his belly and crawled. Across three roofs he crawled, and lay down behind a balustrade overlooking the transverse roadway. Between the pillars of the balustrade he looked right across the roadway and into the half-open window of the cottage. The room within was dark save for the glimmer of a mirror on the back wall.

"Kill him I must," growled the sergeant through his teeth, "though I wait the day for it."

And he waited there, crouching for an hour - for two hours.

He was shifting his cramped attitude a little -- a very little-for about the twentieth time, when a smur of colour showed on the mirror, and the next instant passed into a dark shadow. It may be that the marksman within the cottage had spied yet another rifleman in the street. But the sergeant had noted the reflection in the glass, that it was red. Two shots rang out together. But the sergeant, after peering through the parapet, stood upright, walked back across the roofs, and regained the stairway.

An extract from
Bugler & Officer of the Rifles
by William Green & Harry Smith
Published by Leonaur

Bugler William Green:

The forlorn hope was composed of 350 men of the 43rd, 52nd, and Rifle Brigade, all volunteers, and two buglers from each regiment. Our bugle major made us cast lots which two of us should go on this momentous errand; the lot fell on me and another young lad. But one of our buglers who had been on the forlorn hope at Ciudad Rodrigo offered the bugle major two dollars to let him go in my stead. On my being apprised of it, he came to me, and said:

"West will go on the forlorn hope instead of you,"

I said "I shall go where my duty calls me." He threatened to confine me to the guard tent. I went to the adjutant, and reported him; the adjutant sent for him, and said:

"So you are in the habit of taking bribes;" and told him "He would take the stripes off his arm if he did the like again!" He then asked me "If I wished to go?"

I said "Yes, sir."

He said "Very good," and dismissed me.

Those who composed this forlorn hope were free from duty that day, so I went to the river, and had a good bathe; I thought I would have a clean skin whether killed or wounded, for all who go on this errand expect one or the other.

At nine o'clock at night, April 6th, we were paraded; it was then dark, and half-a-pound of bread and a gill of rum were served out to each man on parade. The party was commanded by Colonel M'Cloud of the 43rd regiment, Major O'Hare of the rifles, and Captain Jones of the 52nd regiment. We were told to go as still as possible, and every word of command was given in a whisper. I had been engaged in the field about 26 times, and had never got a wound; we had about a mile to go to the place of attack, so off we went with palpitating hearts. I never feared nor saw danger till this night.

As I walked at the head of the column, the thought struck me very forcibly "You will be in hell before daylight!" Such a feeling of horror I never experienced before! On our way to the wide ditch that surrounded the wall of the town, were laid small bags filled with grass, for each man to take up as he passed along to throw into the ditch to jump on, that we might not hurt or break our legs as the ditch was eight or nine feet deep; a party were in the rear with short ladders to be put into the ditch, and to be carried across for the men to ascend to the surface near the wall.

We had to pass between our batteries and the town; the artillery were firing blank cartridges, while we passed the guns; this we were apprised of, as being designed to keep the enemy from suspecting that we were to storm that night. There was no firing from the enemy until we arrived at the ditch. All had been still so far, but as the bags were thrown and the men descended, the enemy threw up blue lights; we could see their heads, and they poured a volley down upon us.

I was in the act of throwing my bag, when a ball went through the thick part of my thigh, and having my bugle in my left hand, it entered my left wrist and I dropped, so I did not get into the ditch. I scarcely felt the ball go through my thigh, but when it entered my wrist, it was more like a 6-pounder than a musket-ball! It smashed the bone and cut the guides, and the blood was pouring from both wounds, I began to feel very faint.

Our men were in the ditch, while the enemy had shells loaded on the top of the wall about two yards apart. As they were fired they rolled into the ditch, and when they burst, 10 or 12 men were blown up in every direction! However, some of them arrived at the breach, but a great many both killed and wounded lay around me; the balls came very thick about us, and we were not able to move. At length the whole of the light division came past me; my comrade, a sergeant, seeing me (for there was plenty of light!) said:

"Bill, are you wounded?"

I said "Yes, and cannot get up!"

He said "Here is a little rum in my flask, drink it, but I cannot assist to carry you out of the reach of shot."

His name was Robert Fairfoot. Shortly afterwards a musket ball struck him, went through the peak of his cap, and lodged in his forehead; the ball was extracted, he recovered, and through good conduct and his valour as a soldier, he obtained a commission, and was afterwards made adjutant of the regiment.

Harry Smith:

The key of the enemy's position was in our hands, and the great line was our next immediate object. We were speedily reformed, and ready for our attack on the enemy's line-position and strong field fortifications. In descending La Petite Rhune, we were much exposed to the enemy's fire, and when we got to the foot of the hill we were about to attack, we had to cross a road enfiladed very judiciously by the enemy, which caused some loss. We promptly stormed the enemy's works and as promptly carried them.

I never saw our men fight with such lively pluck; they were irresistible; and we saw the other Divisions equally successful, the enemy flying in every direction. Our Riflemen were pressing them in their own style, for the French themselves are terrific in pursuit, when poor dear gallant (Sir Andrew) Barnard was knocked off his horse by a musket-ball through his lungs. When Johnny Kincaid, his adjutant, got up to him, he was nearly choked by blood in his mouth. They washed it out for him, and he recovered so as to give particular orders about a pocket-book and some papers he wished sent to his brother. He did not want assistance; the soldiers loved him; he was borne off to the rear, and, when examined by Assistant-Surgeon Robson, it was found that the ball had not passed through, but was perceptible to the touch.

The surgeon had him held up, so that when he made a bold incision to let the ball out, its own weight would prevent its being repelled into the cavity of the chest. The ball was boldly and judiciously extracted, no fever came on, and in three weeks Barnard was at the head of a Brigade, with one wound still open, and in the passage of the Gave d'Oleron he plunged into the water, and saved the life of a soldier floating down the river.

But to the fight. Everything was carried apparently, and our Division was halted. Some sharp skirmishing was going on, and Colborne and I were standing with the 52nd Regiment, again ready for anything, on a neck of land which conducted to a stronglooking star redoubt, the only work the enemy still held, when Charlie Beckwith, the A.Q.M.G. of our Division, came up with orders from General Alten to move on.

"What, Charlie, to attack that redoubt? Why, if we leave it to our right or left, it must fall, as a matter of course; our whole army will be beyond it in twenty minutes."

"I don't know; your orders are to move on."

"Am I to attack the redoubt?" says Colborne.

"Your orders are to move on," and off he galloped.

Colborne turns to me, and says, "What an evasive order!"

"Oh, sir," says I, "let us take the last of their works; it will be the operation of a few minutes," and on we went in a column of companies.

As we neared the enemy, Colborne's brilliant eye saw they were going to hold it, for it was a closed work, and he says, "Smith, they do not mean to go until fairly driven out; come, let us get off our horses."

I was just mounted on a beautiful thoroughbred mare,

my "Old Chap" horse being somewhat done, and I really believed anything like fighting was all over. I said nothing, but sat still, and on we went with a hurrah which we meant should succeed, but which the garrison intended should do no such thing. My horse was struck within twenty yards of the ditch, and I turned her round so that I might jump off, placing her between me and the fire, which was very hot. As I was jumping off, another shot struck her, and she fell upon me with a crash, which I thought had squeezed me as flat as a thread-paper, her blood, like a fountain, pouring into my face.

The 52nd were not beat back, but swerved from the redoubt into a ravine, for they could not carry it. While lying under my horse, I saw one of the enemy jump on the parapet of the works in an undaunted manner and in defiance of our attack, when suddenly he started straight up into the air, really a considerable height, and fell headlong into the ditch. A ball had struck him in the forehead, I suppose -- the fire of our skirmishers was very heavy on the redoubt. Our whole army was actually passing to the rear of the redoubt. Colborne, in the most gallant manner, jumped on his horse, rode up to the ditch under the fire of the enemy, which, however, slackened as he loudly summoned the garrison to surrender.

The French officer, equally plucky, said, "Retire, sir, or I will shoot you!" Colborne deliberately addressed the men.

"If a shot is fired, now that you are surrounded by our army, we will put every man to the sword."

By this time I succeeded in getting some soldiers, by calling to them, to drag me from under my horse, when they exclaimed, "Well, d— my eyes if our old Brigade-Major is killed, after all."

"Come, pull away," I said; "I am not even wounded, only squeezed."

"Why, you are as bloody as a butcher."

I ran to Colborne just as he had finished his speech.

He took a little bit of paper out, wrote on it, "I surrender unconditionally," and gave it to me to give the French officer, who laughed at the state of blood I was in. He signed it, and Colborne sent me to the Duke.

When I rode up (on a horse just lent me), his Grace says, "Who are you?"

"The Brigade-Major, 2nd Rifle Brigade."

"Hullo, Smith, are you badly wounded?"

"Not at all, sir; it is my horse's blood."

"Well." I gave him the paper. "Tell Colborne I approve."

An extract from
Ensign Bell of the Cumberland Gentlemen
by George Bell
Published by Leonaur

The weather was now mild, but very damp and rainy. The winter had really set in and kept us under cover until the usual time of turning out, one hour before daylight, when all the troops, were on their respective alarm-posts until dismissed and we could see a white horse at a mile distant. This was the most disagreeable part of our war game. On the 8th of December there was a great Stir of cocked hats and orderly dragoons galloping about—a sure indication of a move. The men dived into the secret at once, and began to fix their flints and look to their ammunition. In the middle of the night we received orders to be on our alarm-post earlier than usual in the morning.

The women were all astir in a moment, lighting their fires 'to have a dhrop ov tay for their re spective warriors, jist to warm their hearts before plunging into the river, bad luck to the French.' Well did they know our line of march, and were always in the way; but this intended advance bothered them. How were they to cross the river and follow the troops, against a positive general order? The ladies assembled around a big fire on a dark winter's night to discuss this point. Mother Skiddy, Brigadier-General of the Amazons, so called, addressed the meeting.

'I have the weeest donkey of you all, an' I'll take the wather if I'm to swim for it, and let me see who's to stop me, Bridget Skiddy, who thraveiled from Lisbon here into France. If Dan falls, who's to bury him? God save us! Divil a vulture will ever dig a claw into him while there's life in Biddy, his laful wife. Now, girls, you may go or stay.' and so she began to saddle her ass.

The troops were now assembled in perfect quiet. No drum nor bugle was sounded—not a word was spoken—all as still as death, waiting the signal-gun to make the rush. The outposts on the riverside had their orders not to take any advantage of the enemy when, just at dawn, bang went the first cannon. The French were under arms in a moment. Our pickets on the river-bank gave them the signal to clear off. They took the hint, got out of the way a little, halted, and formed up on the defensive. Bang went another gun, and now the field-day began. Our men had slung their pouches behind their necks, resting on the pack, to keep their powder dry, as the river was swollen. The grand rush was now being made under cover of our guns. We took the stream; some killed and wounded went away with the current, for the French kept up a fire on us now, which was quite lawful. We made good our footing on the right side, fought on all the day, and calling the roll at night, we found there were many widows.

The passage of the Nive being successfully made by our division on the right, there was hard fighting along the left of the entire position, and a desperate attempt made to repulse our whole army. It was known at the time that Soult had written to the Minister of War to expect good news very soon, Wellington's army being divided by the river Nive. Lord Hill's division, being now situated in an angle between the 'Nive and Adour', was cut off from Wellington. It was very unpleasant, to say the least of it, and required great caution and brave hearts, resolute and determined, to keep our ground.

On the 10th Soult attacked Wellington in front of Bayonne with 55,000 men and thirty-seven guns. The ground was very unfavourable for fighting—ugly weather and swampy land, rough and rugged—it was always cheery enough fighting over grass fields and churchyards on a sunny day. The Light Infantry and Rifles liked the tombstones, they said they were such a steady rest for a pot-shot, and a good shield!

The great Marshal Soult got a thrashing today after all his boasting and expectations, but it cost the Duke 1,200 men, 2 Generals hors de combat, and 300 prisoners. However, to balance the account, the French loss was considerably more. Moreover, a whole regiment of Nassau and Frankfort came over to us, their Prince having abandoned the Emperor Napoleon in Germany. But there was no end to this quarrel. We were all fighting again the next day, when there was a trifling loss of some 600 men a side. The 12th was also a bloody day in our army. Death was busy from dawn to dusk, and that was only preparatory to the following day, the 13th December 1813, when Soult tried his grand coup upon General Hill.

An extract from
The Compleat Rifleman Harris
by Benjamin Harris
Published by Leonaur

I remember meeting with General Napier before the
battle of Vimeiro. He was then, I think, a major; and the
meeting made so great an impression on me, that I have
never forgotten him. I was posted in a wood the night before
the battle, in the front of our army, where two roads crossed
each other. The night was gloomy, and I was the very out-
sentry of the British army. As I stood on my post, peering
into the thick wood around me, I was aware of footsteps
approaching and challenged in a low voice. Receiving no
answer, I brought my rifle to the port, and bade the strangers
come forward. They were Major Napier (then of the 50th
foot, I think), and an officer of the Rifles. The major advanced
close up to me, and looked hard in my face.

"Be alert here, sentry," said he," for I expect the enemy
upon us to-night, and I know not how soon."

I was a young soldier then, and the lonely situation I was
in, together with the impressive manner in which Major
Napier delivered his caution, made a great impression on me,
and from that hour I have never forgotten him. Indeed, I
kept careful watch all night, listening to the slightest breeze
amongst the foliage, in expectation of the sudden approach of
the French. They ventured not, however, to molest us. Henry
Jessop, one of my companions in the Rifles, sank and died of
fatigue on this night, and I recollect some of our men burying
him in the wood at daybreak, close to my post.

During the battle, next day, I remarked the gallant style in
which the 50th, Major Napier's regiment, came to the charge.

They dashed upon the enemy like a torrent breaking bounds, and the French, unable even to bear the sight of them, turned and fled. Methinks at this moment I can hear the cheer of the British soldiers in the charge, and the clatter of the Frenchmen's accoutrements, as they turned in an instant, and went off, hard as they could run for it. I remember, too, our feeling towards the enemy on that occasion was the north side of friendly; for they had been firing upon us Rifles very sharply, greatly outnumbering our skirmishers, and appearing inclined to drive us off the face of the earth.

Their lights and grenadiers I for the first time particularly remarked on that day. The grenadiers (the 70th, I think) our men seemed to know well. They were all fine-looking young men, wearing red shoulder-knots and tremendous-looking moustaches. As they came swarming upon us, they rained a perfect shower of balls, which we returned quite as sharply. Whenever one of them was knocked over, our men called out "There goes another of Boney's Invincibles." In the main body immediately in our rear were the second battalion 52nd, the 50th, the second battalion 43rd, and a German corps, whose number I do not remember, besides several other regiments.

The whole line seemed annoyed and angered at seeing the Rifles outnumbered by the Invincibles, and as we fell back, "firing and retiring," galling them handsomely as we did so, the men cried out (as it were with one voice) to charge. "D—n them!" they roared, "charge! charge!" General Fane, however, restrained their impetuosity. He desired them to stand fast, and keep their ground.

"Don't be too eager, men," he said, as coolly as if we were on a drill-parade in Old England; "I don't want you to advance just yet. Well done, 95th!" he called out, as he galloped up and down the line; "well done 43rd, 52nd, and well done all. I'll not forget, if I live, to report your conduct to-day. They shall hear of it in England, my lads!"

A man named Brotherwood, of the 95th, at this moment

rushed up to the general, and presented him with a green feather, which he had torn out of the cap of a French light-infantry soldier he had killed:

"God bless you, general!" he said; "wear this for the sake of the 95th."

I saw the general take the feather, and stick it in his cocked hat. The next minute he gave the word to charge, and down came the whole line, through a tremendous fire of cannon and musketry—and dreadful was the slaughter as they rushed onwards. As they came up with us, we sprang to our feet, gave one hearty cheer, and charged along with them, treading over our own dead and wounded, who lay in the front. The 50th were next us as we went, and I recollect, as I said, the firmness of that regiment in the charge. They appeared like a wall of iron. The enemy turned and fled, the cavalry dashing upon them as they went off.

An extract from
Hussar in Winter
by Alexander Gordon
Published by Leonaur

We had some skirmishing with the enemy's advanced
guard in the early part of the day, but in the afternoon they
pressed us so hard that the regiment was halted, and formed
in column of divisions on a small eminence, masking the guns
of the horse brigade which were brought up to support us.
On observing our position, the enemy retired, and we were
ordered to occupy Cubilos, a small village at no great distance,
where we found a company of the Ninety-fifth. So many
horses had been sent forward, having become unserviceable for
want of shoes, that the regiment at this period could scarcely
muster four hundred in the field, many of which were lame
or quite worn out with fatigue, and the remainder unable
to trot. Considering the jaded state of our horses, and the
fact that almost the whole of the outpost duty ever since the
commencement of the retreat had fallen upon the Fifteenth,
it might reasonably have been expected that one of the other
regiments should have been appointed to this service; but it
seemed to be a settled system of our leaders to save the Tenth
and Seventh as much as possible, out of compliment to the
Prince of Wales and Lord Paget.

It was almost dark when we arrived at Cubilos, and whilst
the quartermasters were making arrangements for getting
the troops under cover, the regiment was drawn up in close
column on an open space of ground in the centre of the
place. We had not remained long in this position, when we
were surprised by a quick and irregular discharge of small
arms; the bullets rattled against the walls and lodged in the

roofs of the houses behind which we were sheltered.

This unexpected attack created a considerable degree of uneasiness, for the horses were so wedged together it was with difficulty they could break into file; and the communication betwixt the village and the highroad was through a narrow hollow-way, where, if a single horse had fallen, it would have occasioned a scene of confusion which must have led to the most disastrous consequences. Having been ordered for duty, I was engaged in telling off the picquet at a little distance from the column when the firing commenced; and strong patrols being immediately despatched to the assistance of the riflemen, who were skirmishing with our visitors, the intruders were soon put to flight. After the regiment was withdrawn from the village, it was determined by the commanding officer to bivouac; it is only extraordinary that under the circumstances he should for a moment have entertained the intention of passing the night in quarters. Three squadrons took up a position near Cubilos; the left squadron was detached half a mile to the rear, where a road struck off to Ponteferrado. Our advanced picquets and patrols were pushed close to the French outposts, and shots were exchanged occasionally when either party encroached too much on the other's ground. The weather was cold and frosty, but we collected fuel enough to supply several large fires; and, as the inhabitants had deserted their dwellings, we were forced to plunder the village in order to procure provisions and forage. But this was a necessary measure, and executed without any breach of discipline. Working parties were sent under the orderly officer and quartermasters to break open the houses, and abundant supplies of bread, meat, wine, corn, and hay, were found, which proved highly acceptable both to men and horses who had been but scantily provided with subsistence since we left San Christoval.

ALSO FROM LEONAUR
AVAILABLE IN SOFT OR HARD COVER WITH DUST JACKET

EW1 EYEWITNESS TO WAR SERIES
RIFLEMAN COSTELLO
by Edward Costello

The Adventures of a Soldier of the 95th (Rifles) in the
Peninsula & Waterloo Campaigns of the Napoleonic Wars.

SOFT COVER : **ISBN 1-84677-000-9**
HARD COVER : **ISBN 1-84677-018-1**

RGW2 RECOLLECTIONS OF THE GREAT WAR 1914-18
WITH THE IMPERIAL CAMEL CORPS
IN THE GREAT WAR
by Geoffrey Inchbald

The Story of a Serving Officer with the British
2nd Battalion Against the Senussi and During
the Palestine Campaign.

SOFT COVER : **ISBN 1-84677-006-7**
HARD COVER : **ISBN 1-84677-012-2**

EW7 EYEWITNESS TO WAR SERIES
A NORFOLK SOLDIER IN THE FIRST
SIKH WAR
by J.W. Baldwin

Experiences of a Private of H. M. 9th Regiment of Foot
in the Battles for the Punjab, India 1845-6.

SOFT COVER : **ISBN 1-84677-023-8**
HARD COVER : **ISBN 1-84677-031-9**

EW8 EYEWITNESS TO WAR SERIES
A CAVALRY OFFICER IN THE SEPOY REVOLT
by A. R. D. Mackenzie

Experiences with the 3rd Bengal Light Cavalry, the Guides
and Sikh Irregular Cavalry from the Outbreak of the
Indian Mutiny to Delhi and Lucknow.

SOFT COVER : **ISBN 1-84677-024-6**
HARD COVER : **ISBN 1-84677-039-4**

AVAILABLE ONLINE AT
www.leonaur.com
AND OTHER GOOD BOOK STORES

ALSO FROM LEONAUR
AVAILABLE IN SOFT OR HARD COVER WITH DUST JACKET

Printed in March 2023
by Rotomail Italia S.p.A., Vignate (MI) - Italy